Mastering Redis

Take your knowledge of Redis to the next level to build enthralling applications with ease

Jeremy Nelson

[PACKT] **open source** ✱
PUBLISHING   community experience distilled

BIRMINGHAM - MUMBAI

Mastering Redis

First published: May 2016

Production reference: 1260516

Published by Packt Publishing Ltd.
Livery Place
35 Livery Street

Birmingham B3 2PB, UK.

ISBN 978-1-78398-818-1

www.packtpub.com

Credits

Author
Jeremy Nelson

Reviewers
Emilien Kenler

Saurabh Minni

Commissioning Editor
Kunal Parikh

Acquisition Editor
Harsha Bharwani

Content Development Editors
Kirti Patil

Mayur Pawanikar

Technical Editors
Utkarsha Kadam

Tanmayee Patil

Copy Editor
Merilyn Pereira

Project Coordinator
Nidhi Joshi

Proofreader
Safis Editing

Indexer
Rekha Nair

Graphics
Abhinash Sahu

Production Coordinator
Aparna Bhagat

Cover Work
Aparna Bhagat

About the Author

Jeremy Nelson is the metadata and systems librarian at Colorado College, a 4-year private liberal arts college in Colorado Springs. In addition to working 8 hours a week on the library's research helpdesk, providing information literacy instructions to undergraduates, and supervising the library's systems and cataloguing departments, Nelson is actively researching and developing various components and open source tools in the Catalog Pull Platform for use by Colorado College, the Colorado Alliance of Research Libraries Consortium, and the Library of Congress. He is also co-founder and CTO of KnowledgeLinks.io, a semantic web startup.

His previous library experience includes jobs at Western State Colorado University and the University of Utah. Prior to becoming a librarian, he worked as programmer and project manager at various software companies and financial services institutions. His first book, *Becoming a Lean Library*, published in 2015, applies lean startup and lean manufacturing ideas to libraries and library operations. Nelson's undergraduate degree is from Knox College and his master's of science in library and information science is from the University of Illinois Urbana-Champaign.

About the Reviewers

Emilien Kenler, after working on small web projects, began focusing on game development in 2008 while he was in high school. Until 2011, he worked for different groups and specialized in system administration.

In 2011, he founded a company that sold Minecraft servers while studying computer science engineering. He created a lightweight IaaS (`https://github.com/HostYourCreeper/`) based on new technologies such as Node.js and RabbitMQ.

Thereafter, he worked at TaDaweb as a system administrator, building its infrastructure and creating tools to manage deployments and monitoring.

In 2014, he began a new adventure at Wizcorp, Tokyo. The same year, Emilien graduated from the University of Technology of Compiègne.

Emilien has written *MariaDB Essentials* for Packt Publishing. He has also contributed as a reviewer on *Learning Nagios 4*, *MariaDB High Performance*, *OpenVZ Essentials*, *Vagrant Virtual Development Environment Cookbook*, and *Getting Started with MariaDB - Second Edition*, all books by Packt Publishing.

Saurabh Minni has an engineering degree with specialization in computer science. A polyglot programmer with over 10 years of experience, he has worked in a variety of technologies, including Assembly, C, C++, Java, Delphi, JavaScript, Android, iOS, PHP, Python, ZMQ, Redis, Mongo, Kyoto Tycoon, Cocoa, Carbon, Apache Kafka, Apache Storm, and ElasticSearch. In short, he is a programmer at heart and loves learning new tech-related things each day.

Currently, he is working as technical architect at Near (an amazing start-up building a location intelligence platform). Apart from handling several projects, he was also responsible for deploying an Apache Kafka cluster. This was instrumental in streamlining the consumption of data in big data processing systems such as Apache Storm, Hadoop, and so on at Near.

Saurabh is also the author of a book on Apache Kafka, *Apache Kafka Cookbook, Packt Publishing*.

He has also been a reviewer on the book *Learning Apache Kafka, Packt Publishing*.

He is reachable on Twitter at @the100rabh and on GitHub at https://github.com/the100rabh/.

This book would not have been possible without the continuous support of my parents, Suresh and Sarla, and my wife, Puja. Thank you for always being there.

www.PacktPub.com

eBooks, discount offers, and more

Did you know that Packt offers eBook versions of every book published, with PDF and ePub files available? You can upgrade to the eBook version at `www.PacktPub.com` and as a print book customer, you are entitled to a discount on the eBook copy. Get in touch with us at `customercare@packtpub.com` for more details.

At `www.PacktPub.com`, you can also read a collection of free technical articles, sign up for a range of free newsletters and receive exclusive discounts and offers on Packt books and eBooks.

`https://www2.packtpub.com/books/subscription/packtlib`

Do you need instant solutions to your IT questions? PacktLib is Packt's online digital book library. Here, you can search, access, and read Packt's entire library of books.

Why subscribe?

- Fully searchable across every book published by Packt
- Copy and paste, print, and bookmark content
- On demand and accessible via a web browser

Table of Contents

Preface

The intention of *Mastering Redis* is to build upon your basic knowledge of Redis through two ways; provide the deeper meaning of the context and theory behind Redis and its technologies, and increase your practical day-to-day skills with Redis. The *Mastering* in this book's title implies an ongoing process and not an end destination. What is exciting about Redis is its ongoing and public evolution into the powerful data manipulation and storage technology of today.

The philosophy behind Redis

Salvatore Sanfilippo has, over the lifespan of the project, articulated a distinct view and opinion about the direction and functionality of Redis. In a January 2015 blog post about benchmarking Redis against other databases, Sanfilippo states "I don't want to convince developers to adopt Redis. We just do our best in order to provide a suitable product, and we are happy if people can get work done with it. That's where my marketing wishes end." Sanfilippo and a small core group of Redis developers follow the successful open source governance model of the "benevolent dictator for life" (BDL), where a single person is the ultimate arbitrator of what is committed into the Redis code base. The success of the BDL model, evidenced by open source projects such as Linux kernel development and the Python programming language, is replicated in Redis with Sanfilippo as its primary developer and maintainer.

The BDL model failure modes can be catastrophic if the dictator abandons the project, or worse, is incapacitated through illness or death. Another significant problem that has emerged particularly with Redis is when potential contributors submit pull requests and action on their pull requests is delayed, or more often, ignored. To be fair, the volume of changes that must be examined, tested, and merged into the main code base can be substantial and requires a passionate and dedicated gatekeeper. Linus Torvalds, the initial creator and current BDL for the Linux kernel project, has seen his role evolve more into merging code contributed by others and providing vision and leadership for Linux than writing code himself. Sanfilippo, while acknowledging this problem in a thread on the main Redis e-mail distribution, gives two main reasons for continuing with the current BDL model for Redis:

- A consistent vision for the project's development and future directions
- Accountability for any new or merged changes

Sanfilippo's vision of Redis, as an easy-to-configure, small-memory-footprint (for itself and NOT for its datasets!) and reliable key-value data store has been crucial to the continued rise in Redis's popularity among developers and organizations. His vision does cause tension, especially when new features for Redis are proposed, such as expiring specific sub-values in a hash or offering loadable modules for optional functionality, and these features are rejected for inclusion into Redis. Sanfilippo's desire to keep Redis small and focused on being a memory-only database drives his decisions and development practice.

In 2011 blog post, he elucidated his vision for Redis in a seven-point manifesto for Redis and the Redis development process. Briefly, here are the seven points:

1. **A DSL for Abstract Data Types**: Redis is a Domain-Specific Language (DSL) for representing and using abstract data structures. These data structures include both the operations (Redis commands) as well as the memory efficiency and time complexity of storing and manipulating those data structures with the associated Redis commands.

2. **Memory storage is the #1**: By storing all of the data in a computer's RAM, Redis's performance across different systems is more consistent, the various algorithms used to implement these data structures run in a more predictable fashion, and more complex data types such as sorted sets are easier to implement in an in-memory database.

3. **Fundamental data structures for a fundamental API**: Redis implements a fundamental API for its fundamental data structures. This API, made up of Redis commands and corresponding data structures, tries to intelligibly resemble the data structures the API reads and writes to the computer's memory. Following this design, the Redis API builds more complex operations into the API by building from simpler operations on data structures in the API.

4. **Code is like a poem**: The most elusive of the seven points in this manifesto. Sanfilippo gives his aesthetic preference for code that fits into a larger narrative of the entire Redis project. His point is that Redis's coding style and approach are geared for humans to construct a narrative. So, inclusion of third-party code depends in part on how well the code fits into the large narrative of Redis and Redis's source code.

5. **We're against complexity**: Complexity in code is to be avoided. Given a choice to build a small feature with a lot of implementing of code or to forgo the functionality, Redis will take the latter route and forgo the extra complexity and overhead of adding complexity to the code base.

6. **Two levels of API**: Redis starts with a subset of its API to run in a distributed manner and a larger, more functionality-rich API to support multikey operations. This separation allows significant features such as the Redis master-slave and Redis cluster modes of operation.

7. **We optimize for joy**: An emotional appeal and very intelligent statement, for developers and operators of technology in general, the thrill of tuning technology to solve difficult and complex problems does elicit feelings of happiness and excitement about the future possibilities of Redis.

What this book covers

As you read *Mastering Redis*, two themes will emerge that parallel the development/ operations dualism of the popular and trendy operations and processes, commonly known as DevOps. To help guide your approach to the material contained in the chapters, each chapter's topics will be identified as either software development or system operations focused. Due to the increasingly blurred line between the two, getting a topical understanding of the topics in each trend increases your and your team's abilities to quickly and efficiently develop and deploy Redis solutions for your project or as a piece of your technological infrastructure requirements.

In the following diagram, each chapter's horizontal position visually represents whether the topics weigh towards software development or systems operations:

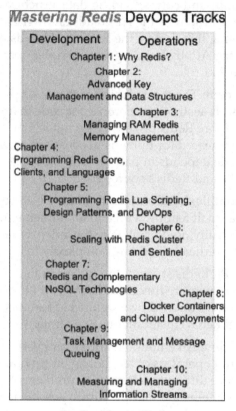

DevOps Chapter Tracks

Chapter 1, Why Redis?, introduces the Redis development philosophy as articulated by Salvatore Sanfilippo, the founder and primary maintainer of Redis.

Chapter 2, Advanced Key Management and Data Structures, builds upon your basic knowledge of Redis by expanding and explaining Redis data structures and key management, including the important topic of constructing meaningful and expressive key schemas for your applications.

Chapter 3, Managing RAM – Tips and Techniques for Redis Memory Management, looks at the various options Redis provides to optimize the memory usage in your applications including Redis support for various caching and key eviction strategies based on Less Recently Used (LRU) implementations in Redis.

Chapter 4, Programming Redis Part One – Redis Core, Clients, and Languages, is an advanced topic on programming applications. This chapter starts with an overview of Redis's core C programming language implementation and includes an in-depth examination of selected C code snippets to deepen your knowledge of Redis. It continues with how to use three different Redis clients, with short programming exercises in Python, Node.js, and Haskell.

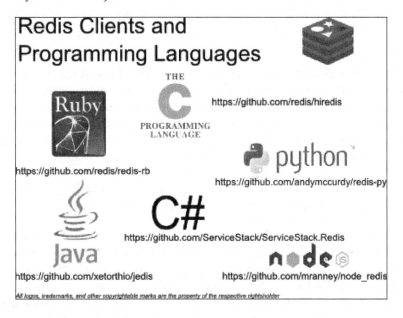

Chapter 5, Programming Redis Part Two – Lua Scripting, Administration, and DevOps, is an advanced topic on programming applications. It starts with an overview of Redis server-side Lua scripting and how to use Lua more effectively with Redis. The chapter next expands on a few popular programming design patterns with Redis, with specific examples of how different people and companies have used these patterns in their operations. This chapter ends with how Redis is used in typical DevOps scenarios from the perspective of a software developer.

Chapter 6, Scaling with Redis Cluster and Sentinel, explores two relatively recent additions to Redis—Redis Cluster and Redis Sentinel. Redis Sentinel is a special high-availability mode for monitoring the health of masters and slaves, along with the ability to switch if a failure occurs in any master or slave Redis instance. Redis Cluster, mentioned previously, is now a production-ready way to store large amounts of data that may be too big to fit into the memory of a single machine, by running multiple Redis instances through key sharding. While these topics have more of an operational focus, engineering solutions with Redis should, at the minimum, know the benefits and limitations of how to use Redis Cluster.

Chapter 7, Redis and Complementary NoSQL Technologies, starts with the recognition that for most organizations, their information technology stack includes a heterogeneous mixture of different types of data and processing solutions. Redis is an ideal way to extend the functionality of other NoSQL data storages options, and in this chapter, we'll see how Redis can be used with MongoDB, ElasticSearch, and Fedora Digital Repository. This chapter should be of interest to both developers and system administrators who may need to develop and support complex business requirements with multiple solutions.

Chapter 8, Docker Containers and Cloud Deployments, shows how using Redis as in Docker containers and images can simplify management and improve security and reliability of your Redis solutions. Docker is an open source container technology for applications that is rapidly being adopted by many enterprises. Building upon Docker with Redis, we'll then examine specific challenges of using Redis on the most popular computing cloud providers starting the largest and most established, Amazon Web Services, followed by Google's Compute Engine and Microsoft Azure, with special attention to other cloud service providers such as Rackspace and Digital Ocean. We'll finish the chapter by examining Redis's offerings of specialized cloud services that focus on hosting and managing your Redis instances.

Chapter 9, Task Management and Messaging Queuing, begins with an in-depth exploration of Redis Pub/Sub commands. This involves first looking at various examples of how publishers and consumers can communicate between different processes, programs, Redis clients, operating systems, and remote computers. Further in the chapter, we'll expand upon Redis Pub/Sub and look more generally at using Redis as a messaging queue between different layers in an enterprise computing ecosystem. This chapter ends by wrapping up all the concepts through a detailed example of using Redis with Celery as task management and a messaging queue with Pub/Sub support.

Chapter 10, Measuring and Managing Information Streams, builds upon the previous chapter's concepts to show how Redis is be used as a real-time data aggregator for disparate data streams of various technology systems used within an organization. We'll then examine the Redis security model and new security features with the latest version Redis. A web-based, operational dashboard will visualize the incoming data flows into Redis using our knowledge of Redis clients. Next, we'll show how to apply machine learning algorithms, such as Naive Bayes, to these Redis-based information flows to provide a richer snapshot and deepen your understanding of the operations occurring within an organization or department.

Appendix, Sources, acknowledges the source of extracts used in the chapters and presents links chapter-wise for further reading.

Earn your Mastering Redis Open Badge

The Mozilla Foundation—the same open source organization that sponsors the development of the Firefox web browser—started a project called Open Badges that allows organizations to create and then issue portable and non-proprietary badges to individuals to signal accomplishments:

At the *Mastering Redis* website, you have the opportunity to signal to your current and potential employers your increased knowledge and skills with Redis by taking a series of online quizzes and earning your *Mastering Redis* Open Badge. Your Open Badge can be shared through popular social networking sites such as Facebook, Twitter, or LinkedIn.

The *Mastering Redis* Open Badge is free to readers who have purchased the book. However, for readers who don't own a copy, you can still earn your Open Badge at the book's website for a nominal fee. The opportunity to connect with other badge earners, learning from their experiences with Redis while sharing your own stories and knowledge and thus encourages learning long after you have finished reading *Mastering Redis*. Our hope is that this book can immediately help your understanding of Redis and that by earning your Open Badge, you can document this professional achievement.

What you need for this book

Redis is intended to be run under a POSIX-based environment such as Linux or Mac OX with a modern C++ compiler. Microsoft Windows versions of Redis are available but not officially supported. Please see the Windows section at `http://redis.io/download` for more information. Examples in this book also use Python 3.5 with the Redis Python client (`https://github.com/andymccurdy/redis-py`), Lua, and Node.js with the Redis Node.js client (`https://github.com/NodeRedis/node_redis`).

Who this book is for

If you are a web developer with a basic understanding of the MEAN stack, experience in developing applications with JavaScript, and basic experience with NoSQL databases, then this book is for you.

Conventions

In this book, you will find a number of text styles that distinguish between different kinds of information. Here are some examples of these styles and an explanation of their meaning.

Code words in text, database table names, folder names, filenames, file extensions, pathnames, dummy URLs, user input, and Twitter handles are shown as follows: "First, when you call a timeout with the EXPIRE command on a key, the timeout can only be cleared if you delete the key or replace the key."

A block of code is set as follows:

```
defcreate_tea(datastore, name, time, size):
  # Increment and save global counter
  tea_counter = datastore.incr("global/teas")
  tea_key = "tea/{}".format(tea_counter)
  datastore.hmset(tea_key,
      {"name": name,
      "brew-time": time,
      "box-size": size})
  return tea_key
```

Any command-line input or output is written as follows:

```
127.0.0.1:6379> LATENCY HISTORY command
1) 1) (integer) 1433877379
   2) (integer) 1000
2) 1) (integer) 1433877394
   2) (integer) 250
```

 Warnings or important notes appear in a box like this.

 Tips and tricks appear like this.

Reader feedback

Feedback from our readers is always welcome. Let us know what you think about this book—what you liked or disliked. Reader feedback is important for us as it helps us develop titles that you will really get the most out of.

To send us general feedback, simply e-mail feedback@packtpub.com, and mention the book's title in the subject of your message.

If there is a topic that you have expertise in and you are interested in either writing or contributing to a book, see our author guide at www.packtpub.com/authors.

Customer support

Now that you are the proud owner of a Packt book, we have a number of things to help you to get the most from your purchase.

Downloading the example code

You can download the example code files for this book from your account at http://www.packtpub.com. If you purchased this book elsewhere, you can visit http://www.packtpub.com/support and register to have the files e-mailed directly to you.

You can download the code files by following these steps:

1. Log in or register to our website using your e-mail address and password.
2. Hover the mouse pointer on the **SUPPORT** tab at the top.
3. Click on **Code Downloads & Errata**.
4. Enter the name of the book in the **Search** box.
5. Select the book for which you're looking to download the code files.
6. Choose from the drop-down menu where you purchased this book from.
7. Click on **Code Download**.

Once the file is downloaded, please make sure that you unzip or extract the folder using the latest version of:

- WinRAR / 7-Zip for Windows
- Zipeg / iZip / UnRarX for Mac
- 7-Zip / PeaZip for Linux

The code bundle for the book is also hosted on GitHub at https://github.com/PacktPublishing/Mastering-Redis. We also have other code bundles from our rich catalog of books and videos available at https://github.com/PacktPublishing/. Check them out!

Downloading the color images of this book

We also provide you with a PDF file that has color images of the screenshots/ diagrams used in this book. The color images will help you better understand the changes in the output. You can download this file from `https://www.packtpub. com/sites/default/files/downloads/MasteringRedis_ColorImages.pdf`.

Errata

Although we have taken every care to ensure the accuracy of our content, mistakes do happen. If you find a mistake in one of our books—maybe a mistake in the text or the code—we would be grateful if you could report this to us. By doing so, you can save other readers from frustration and help us improve subsequent versions of this book. If you find any errata, please report them by visiting `http://www.packtpub. com/submit-errata`, selecting your book, clicking on the **Errata Submission Form** link, and entering the details of your errata. Once your errata are verified, your submission will be accepted and the errata will be uploaded to our website or added to any list of existing errata under the Errata section of that title.

To view the previously submitted errata, go to `https://www.packtpub.com/books/ content/support` and enter the name of the book in the search field. The required information will appear under the **Errata** section.

Piracy

Piracy of copyrighted material on the Internet is an ongoing problem across all media. At Packt, we take the protection of our copyright and licenses very seriously. If you come across any illegal copies of our works in any form on the Internet, please provide us with the location address or website name immediately so that we can pursue a remedy.

Please contact us at `copyright@packtpub.com` with a link to the suspected pirated material.

We appreciate your help in protecting our authors and our ability to bring you valuable content.

Questions

If you have a problem with any aspect of this book, you can contact us at `questions@packtpub.com`, and we will do our best to address the problem.

1
Why Redis?

Why Redis? Or, why any technology? Such questions are often mumbled under the breath or asked by the more brave, cynical, or knowledgeable when encountering any new technology or service. Sometimes, the answer is obvious, the technology or service offers features and functionalities that meet an immediate need or solves a vexing problem. In most situations, the reasons for adopting a technology may not be as clear-cut or as apparent or are cloaked in sometimes hyperbolic or indecipherable marketing jargon. Depending on your needs, Redis falls somewhere closer to the obvious end of the spectrum instead of a marketing sales pitch. You may already know and have used Redis for some uses, such as meeting a data storage need or service requirement for an application, but you may not be aware of all that Redis can do or how other people are using Redis in their own organizations. Redis, best known for its speed, is not only fast in its execution but also fast in the sense that solutions built with Redis have fast iterations because of the ease in configuring, setting up, running, and using Redis.

The growing popularity of Redis, an open source key-value NoSQL technology, is a result of Redis's stability, power, and flexibility in executing a wide range of data operations and tasks in the enterprise, **REmote DIctionary Server (Redis)**, is used by a diverse set of companies from start-ups to the largest technology companies such as Twitter and Uber, as well as by individuals and teams in government, schools, and organizations. We'll start this chapter with a short survey of a few popular design patterns for Redis and then, provide practical advice on determining whether Redis is the right choice for you.

We'll then go through a detailed example of how Redis a legacy metadata format used by public and academic libraries – including some museums – to illustrate Redis's flexibility and power with just three data structures and an intentional key design. Finishing this chapter off, we'll touch upon recently added functionalities and commands to Redis.

Is Redis right for me?

A relatively common question posted to the general Redis e-mail mailing list, asks whether Redis is a good choice for a variety of uses, such as running reviews on a website, caching results from MySQL databases queries, or meeting other specific requirements that the poster might have for his/her project, product, website, or system. In general, Redis excels as a tool for a fast read/write of data and has been used with great success by small and large organizations alike for a wide range of uses. Salivator Sanfilippo makes a strong case that Redis does not need to replace the existing databases but is an excellent addition to an enterprise for new functionalities or to solve sometimes intractable problems1.

Being a single-threaded application with a small memory footprint, Redis achieves durability and scalability through running multiple instances on the current multicore processors available in data centers and cloud providers. With Redis-rich master-slave replication and now with Redis clusters are released in production, creating multiple Redis instances are relatively cheap operation in terms of memory and CPU requirements, allowing you to both scale and increase the durability of your larger applications.

Redis allows you to conceptualize and approach challenging data analysis and data manipulation problems in a very different manner as compared to a typical relational data model. In an SQL-based relational database, the developer or database administration creates a database schema that organizes the solution domain through normalizing the data into columns, rows, and tables with connecting joins through foreign-key relationships.

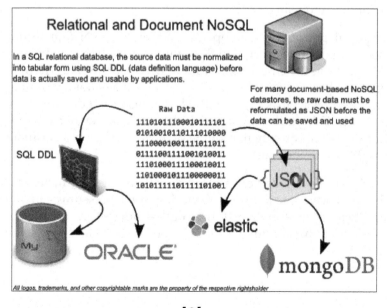

Even other NoSQL data storage technologies such as MongoDB or Elasticsearch require the data to be modeled as JSON document data structures first before being loaded into the actual storage. Redis skips this intermediate but necessary step in these other technologies, by just providing sets of commands for specific data structures such as strings, lists, hashes, sets, and sorted sets. In this approach, you are algorithmically interacting with your data, constructing solutions directly with how the data is stored in Redis and the available commands, and enabling a more direct tuning and monitoring of the underlying operating system's memory and hard disk space.

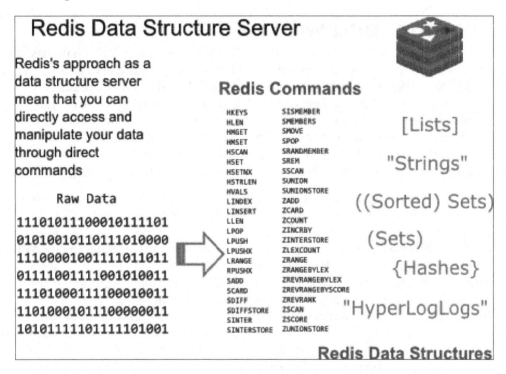

Thinking how data is represented and managed as basic computing data structures such as lists, hashes, and sets, allows you to grasp both positive and negative characteristics of the data and its structures in a more fundamental, mathematical fashion. Going through the intermediate structuring process such as normalizing your data for a relational database or converting it into a JSON document for MongoDB or Elasticsearch, while valuable, imposes a structure that Redis does not. As you architect your solutions, you may discover that your data and your problem need more of the persistence and structure of a technology other than Redis, but in the meantime, your exploration of the properties and the structure of data in Redis will be a useful exercise because of this algorithmic approach to your information and problem.

Redis may not be the best technology to use when you have a large amount of infrequently used data that does not require immediate access. An SQL-based relational database or a document-store NoSQL technology such as CouchDB or MongoDB may be a better choice than Redis. However, with Redis Cluster now fully supported as of version 3, large datasets can be sharded and used in Redis as a distributed key-value data store. As more organizations and individuals gain experience with the use of Redis Cluster, expect that this reason to not choose Redis for a project will fade away.

Experimenting with Redis

Redis's rich set of data types allows for easy and fast experimentation of data-based algorithms and approaches on information. In my own experience with Redis, this ability to quickly model and use solutions is based on the characteristics of the different data structures of Redis and the flexibility in defining the structure and syntax of the keys. I was impressed and excited to be able to name a chunk of malleable data and to relate this name with other keys through the naming semantics of the key. This is a great feature of Redis that is sometimes underappreciated as to how powerful and useful a tool it can be in developing and understanding your data.

I first started experimenting with Redis in 2011 as a metadata and systems librarian at Colorado College at the base of the Pikes Peak Mountain in Colorado. Most libraries around the world store and structure their bibliographic data in a somewhat surprisingly durable binary format called, **MAachine-Readable Cataloging (MARC)**, substantially developed in the late 1960s by Henriette Avram of the United States Library of Congress. The current version, MARC 21, is officially supported by the Library of Congress (however, it is in the process of replacing MARC with a new RDF-based linked data vocabulary called BIBFRAME). MARC21 initially encoded information about the books on the library's shelves and has been extended to support e-books available for checkout; video, music, and audio formats; physical formats such as CDs, Blu-ray discs, and online streaming formats; and academic libraries. In fact, an increasingly large percentage of its budget is devoted to the purchase of journal articles through online publishers and electronic-content vendors.

The MARC format is made up of both fixed length and variable-length fields numbered in the three-digit range of 001–999, which in turn can have either character data or subfields with data. In addition, each field can have up to two indicators that modify the meaning of the field. Two of the most common and important MARC fields are the 100 Main Entry – Personal Name field and the 245 Title Statement field. Here is an example from David Foster Wallace's book Infinite Jest:

```
=100  1\$aWallace, David Foster

=245  10$aInfinite jest :$ba novel$cDavid Foster Wallace
```

To use this MARC data in Redis, each MARC record was a hash key modeled as marc:{counter} with the counter being a global incremental counter. Each MARC field is a hash with the key modeled as marc:{counter}:{field}. As some MARC fields are repeatable with different information, the hash key would include a global counter such as marc:{counter}:{field}:{field-counter}. Simply storing these two fields would result in the following six Redis commands:

```
127.0.0.1> INCR marc
(integer 1)
127.0.0.1:6379> INCR marc:1:100
(integer 1)
127.0.0.1> HSET marc:1:100:1 a "Wallace, David Foster"
OK
127.0.0.1:6379> INCR marc:1:245
(integer) 1
127.0.0.1:6379> HMSET marc:1:245:1 a "Infinite jest :" b "a novel"
c "David Foster Wallace"
OK
127.0.0.1:6379> HGETALL marc:1:245:1
1) "a"
2) "Infinite jest :"
3) "b"
4) "a novel"
5) "c"
6) "David Foster Wallace"
```

This key structure in Redis looks like the following:

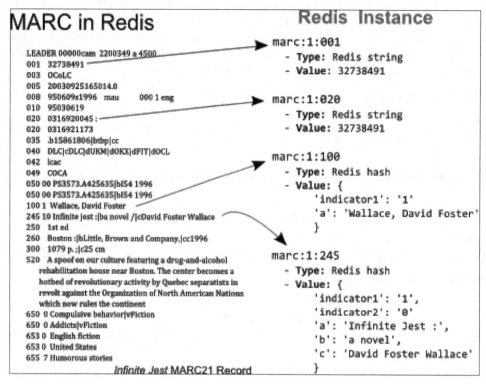

MARC in Redis

The storage of MARC data in Redis can be accomplished with just a single Redis data type, a hash, along with a consistent key syntax structure. To improve the usability of this bibliographic data in Redis and to realize a very common use case of retrieving library data as a list of records sorted alphanumerically by title and author name (in library parlance two access points) is also accomplishable with other Redis data types such as lists or sorted sets.

Representing MARC fields and subfields in Redis by using hashes and lists was informative. Further, I wanted to see if Redis could handle other types of book and material metadata models that were being put forward as replacements for MARC. The Functionality Requirements for Bibliographic Record, or FRBR, was a document that put forward an alternative to MARC and was based on **entity-relationship (ER)** models. The FRBR ER model contained groups of properties that were categorized according to abstraction. The most abstract is the Work class, which represents the most general properties to uniquely identify a creative artifact with such information as titles, authors, and subjects.

The `Expression` class is made of properties such as edition and translations with a defined relationship to the parent Work. Manifestations and Items are the final two FRBR classes, capturing more specific data where Item is a physical object that is a specific instance of a more general Manifestation.

With few actual systems or technologies that implement an FRBR model for library data, Redis offers a way to test such a model with actual data. Using existing mappings of MARC data to FRBR's Work, Expression, Manifestation, and Item, the MARC 100 and 245 fields from the above would be mapped to an FRBR Work in Redis as shown by these examples of using the Redis command-line tool, redis-cli, to connect to a Redis instance:

```
127.0.0.1:6379> HMSET frbr:work:1 title "Infinite Jest" "created by"
"David Foster Wallace"
```

OK

This new work, frbr:work:1 can be associated with the remaining classes with the following Redis keys and hashes:

```
127.0.0.1:6379> HMSET frbr:expression:1 date 1996 "realization of"
frbr:work:1
```

OK

```
127.0.0.1:6379> HMSET frbr:manifestation:1 publisher "Little, Brown and
Company" "physical embodiment of" frbr:expression:1
```

OK

```
127.0.0.1:6379> HMSET frbr:item:1 'exemplar of' frbr:manifestation:1
identifier 33027005910579
```

OK

In the previous example for Expression, a specific date is captured along with a relationship back to `frbr:work:1` through the realization of a property. Similarly, the `frbr:manifestation:1` hash has two fields; a publisher, and the physical embodiment of. The physical embodiment of field's value is the `frbr:expression:1` key that links the Manifestation back to the Expression. Finally the `frbr:item:1` hash has a barcode identifier property and a relationship key back to the `frbr:manifestation:1` hash.

In both the MARC and FRBR experiments, the Redis hash data structure provided the base representation for the entity. This strategy starts to fail when there can be more than one value for a specific property, such as when representing multiple authors of a work. The first attempt to solve this problem for those properties with multiple values is by creating a counter for each MARC field as outlined above. For example, the MARC 856 field – Electronic Location and Access – stores the URL for e-books or other material that has a network-resolvable URL. If we want to add two URLs to the preceding MARC example, such as a link to the book in Google Books and a wiki on the book, the Redis commands would be as follows:

```
127.0.0.1:6379> INCR global:marc:1:856

(integer) 1

127.0.0.1:6379> HMSET marc:1:856:1 ind1 4 ind2 1 u https://books.google.
com/books?id=Nhe2yvx6hP8C

OK

127.0.0.1:6379> HMSET marc:1:856:2 ind1 4 ind2 2 u http://infinitejest.
wallacewiki.com/

OK
```

This naming approach for the MARC keys meets the requirement for repeating MARC fields, but how can we support the edge case wherein a single MARC field has multiple, repeating subfields? The first pass to solve this problem may be to store a string with some delimiter between each subfield as the value for a particular filed in the MARC. This would require additional parsing on the client side to extract all the different subfields, and we would lose any additional advantages that Redis may provide if these multiple subfields were stored directly in Redis. The second approach to solving the MARC field with multiple subfields in a MARC field would be to further expand the Redis key syntax and use a list or some other data structure as value for each subfield key. Expanding the MARC 856 example, if we wanted to add a second e-book URL, maybe a URL to the Amazon Kindle version, it would look like the following in Redis:

```
127.0.0.1:6379> LPUSH marc:1:856:1:u https://books.google.com/
books?id=Nhe2yvx6hP8C http://www.amazon.com/Infinite-Jest-David-Foster-
Wallace/

(integer) 2

127.0.0.1:6379> HSET marc:1:856:1 u marc:1:856:1:u

(integer) 0
```

Storing multiple subfields in a Redis list works well, but what if I don't want any duplicate values in a MARC field's subfields? This can be easily solved by the use of Redis's set data type, which, by definition, only contains unique values. The use of sets for the subfield values seems like a good solution, but it fails, if we need to keep the ordering of the values in the subfield.

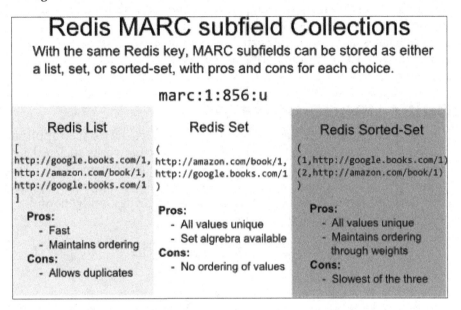

Fortunately, Redis's sorted set data type fits our use case admirably by ensuring a collection of unique subfield values with no duplications, and finally maintaining, the subfield ordering. The resulting Redis commands for storing the URLs of a book in the MARC 856 field would look the following:

```
127.0.0.1:6379> DEL marc:1:856:1:u
(integer) 1
127.0.0.1:6379> ZADD marc:1:856:1:u 1
https://books.google.com/books?id=Nhe2yvx6hP8C 2
http://www.amazon.com/Infinite-Jest-David-Foster-Wallace/
(integer) 2
127.0.0.1:6379> ZRANGE marc:1:856:1:u 0 -1 WITHSCORES
1) "https://books.google.com/books?id=Nhe2yvx6hP8C"
2) "1"
3) "http://www.amazon.com/Infinite-Jest-David-Foster-Wallace/"
4) "2"
```

In this example, we examined how to represent a legacy format for library data called MARC, and how MARC's fields and subfields data can be stored in Redis by using hashes, and how the storing of subfields changes as more requirements are met, moving from storing subfields first as Redis lists, followed by sets, and finally finishing by using the sorted set data type. This iterative experimentation hopefully illustrates an important reason for using Redis, namely the ability to quickly test out different methods of storing data and how the characteristics of different Redis data types such as hashes, lists, sets, and sorted sets can be used to represent both the data and some of the requirements for storing and accessing this data.

Popular usage patterns

A very popular use pattern for Redis is as an in-memory cache for web applications. Redis is available as a caching option for popular web frameworks such as Django, Ruby-on-Rails, Node.js, and Flask. As a popular caching technology Redis excels in web applications for storing new data while evicting stale data. For web applications, the cached data can range from single HTML character strings, widgets, and elements to entire web pages and websites.

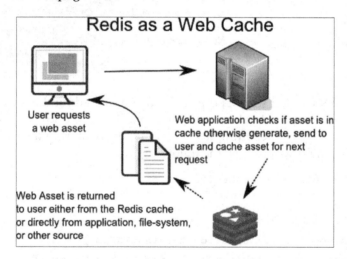

By utilizing Redis's ability to set an expiration time on a key, one of Redis' popular caching strategies called **Less Recently Used** (**LRU**) is robust enough to handle even the largest web properties, with the most popular content remaining in cache but stale and little-used data being evicted from the data store. This caching use case doesn't assume that the original web element or page is generated from the data in Redis; most likely, the web content was dynamically generated from other sources of data with Redis, in this use pattern, and operates as an excellent web caching layer in this setup.

The second popular use pattern for Redis is for the metric storage of such quantitative data such as web page usage and user behavior on gamer leaderboards. Using bit operations on strings, Redis very efficiently stores binary information on a particular characteristic. Usage for a website could be stored with a key constructed from a date such as page-usage:2016-11-01, which has a string attached with a bit flipped to 1 the first time a web page is accessed by a user.

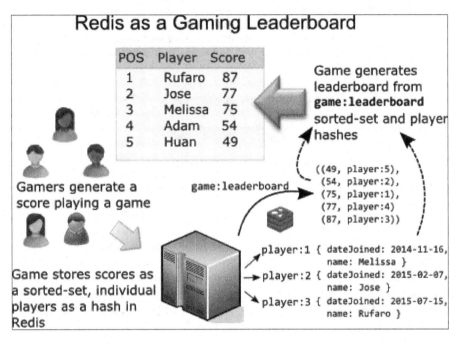

The daily usage for the website for November 1 can be obtained through a simple BITCOUNT Redis command on the page-usage:2016-11-01 key. In a 2011 blog post, individuals at a start-up named Spool explain in detail how they use bitmaps and Redis bit operations to store the user activity on their website with this design pattern.

The third popular Redis use pattern is as communication layer between different systems through a publish/subscribe (pub/sub for short) model, where one can post messages to one or more channels that can be acted upon by other systems that have subscribed to or are listening to that channel for incoming messages.

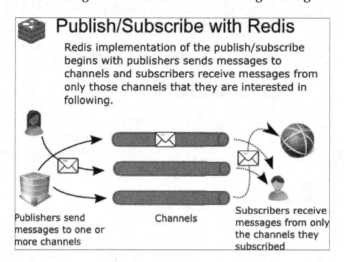

Typically, publishers do not need to know the specific subscribers to send messages to them (say in a point-to-point messaging model); only the message contents and what channel to send the message should be known. Similarly, a subscriber does not need to know individual publishers, only the channel to receive messages. The pub/sub pattern is nice because it scales easily, and the publishers and subscribers can be very different programs and systems.

Redis isn't right because …try again soon!

As an active open-source project, Redis adds new functionality and improvements that may solve a problem that you or someone in your organization decided it wasn't suited for in the past. Optimizing the use of such a valuable and functional tool as Redis means understanding its recent history and keeping current with new functionality being developed and tested for inclusion in the latest stable version of Redis. Redis follows a common semantic versioning pattern of `major.minor.patchlevel` with a minor even number denoting a stable version and an odd minor number an unstable branch.

For example, the Redis 2.8.9 release introduced two of the more significant improvements, namely the HyperLogLog, a highly efficient data structure for a population estimate and of unique elements, and the new ZRANGEBYLEX, ZLEXCOUNT, and ZREMRANGEBYLEX commands for sorted sets. Both these are improvements that will be discussed at length in *Chapter 2, Advanced Key Management and Data Structures*. Redis Cluster – released for production use in early 2015 with Redis version 3.0 – is one of most important additions to the Redis ecosystem, which we will go over in much more detail in *Chapter 6, Scaling with Redis Cluster and Sentinel*.

For the next major release Redis added **Geographic Information Systems (GIS)** commands and modified sorted sets along with new Lua scripting support for Redis Cluster and a new Lua debugger in Redis version 3.2. To visualize the rate of change to the Redis code base, the following graphic shows the rate of change in the Redis code base during the Redis 2.x series to Redis version 3.0.

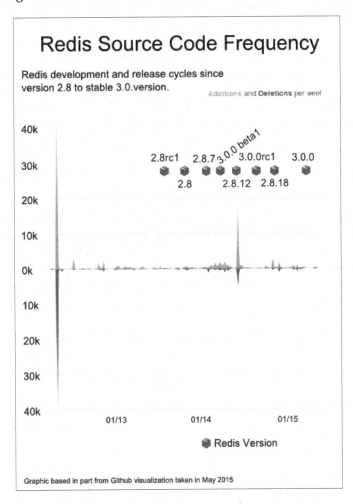

Be aware of the dynamic nature of Redis development when asking yourself, why Redis? The limitations that you thought Redis had might no longer be the case and as you continue to grow your knowledge and improve your skills in mastering Redis, keeping up with Redis changes should a critical priority as you improve your existing technology and build new and exciting opportunities for the future.

Summary

The decision as to whether Redis is the correct choice for a new project or to solve a data problem you might be experiencing really depends on the nature of your data and what you're trying to accomplish with your project. Redis, unlike relational databases or NoSQL document stores, does not require you to structure your data first before using it. Redis provides a direct, more algorithmic manipulation of your data through the use of a variety of data structures such as lists, hashes, sets, and sorted sets. Even if Redis is not your final choice, the exercise of breaking down your data into these data structures will help deepen the context and the analysis of the issue that you're trying to solve. A detailed example of such experimentation was given while representing a legacy library standard called MARC in the basic Redis hashes, lists, sets, and sorted sets. We then briefly reviewed three popular design patterns for using Redis as a web cache, Redis as the backend for a gamer leaderboard, and Redis used as a publish/subscribe messaging system. We finish this chapter by illustrating some recent changes to Redis that expand the types of problems that Redis can be the primary data solution that in the past traditional SQL database or other NoSQL technologies may have been adopted instead.

In the next chapter, we are going to first examine Redis keys and the importance of organizing these keys with a Redis key schema generated either through a Redis object mapper or through manual documentation. Chapter 2 then introduces the Big O notation, followed by a systematic review of the basic Redis data structures and commands based on time complexity measures, Chapter 2 finishes with an introduction to some of the newer data structures and commands, including `bitstrings` and `HyperLogLog`.

2
Advanced Key Management and Data Structures

Using Redis as data storage in your application starts by considering two sides of the solution: the keys and the data structures used as the key values in Redis. Coming up with a good Redis key schema, syntax, and naming convention can mean the difference between an effective and sustainable solution and a technological mess. Because of the flexibility that Redis gives you by allowing most string serialization as keys, much more intentional thought and design should be given to this important step in designing a Redis-based project. Likewise, using an appropriate data structure for any particular key also directly impacts the usability and functionality of any application built with Redis. This chapter covers the following:

- Designing and managing a Redis key schema and the associated data structures

- Using Redis client object mappers that use different strategies that hide the specific key schemas and data structures

- Creating a simple application using a Javascript Redis object mapper and analyzing how the object mapper uses Redis commands and data structures as an example of a Redis key schema

- Introducing the Big O notation and how this measure of worst-case algorithmic effectiveness at scale is used in evaluating the performance of Redis's commands and how this performance directly relates to Redis's underlying data structures

This focus on the Big O notation in Redis's official documentation provides a method of estimating the time complexity of an application's use of Redis and helps in evaluating your Redis-based application's performance. Together, the Redis key and values should complement and reinforce the solution, while balancing the memory efficiencies of smaller-length keys with enough verbosity for explaining the purpose of the keys to the application designer, developer, or end user.

Redis keys

Effectively, using Redis in your application involves understanding how Redis stores keys and the operations to manipulate the key space within a Redis instance. Running a 32-bit or 64-bit version of Redis dictates the practical limits to the size of your Redis keys. For the 32-bit Redis variant, any key name larger than 32 bits requires the key to span multiple bytes, thereby increasing the Redis memory usage. Using 64-bit Redis allows for larger key lengths but has the downside that keys with small lengths will be allocated the full 64 bits, wasting the extra bits that are not allocated to the key name.

The flexibility of Redis allows for a wide diversity in how keys are structured and stored. The performance and maintainability of Redis can be either positively or negatively impacted by the choices made in designing and constructing the Redis keys used in your database. A good general practice when designing your Redis keys is to construct at least a rough outline of what information you are trying to store in Redis and an initial idea of how the data will be stored in one of the many different Redis data structures. Finally, you'll want to diagram how your data structures relate to the other information stored in different keys in your Redis database. This process is generally lumped under the rubric of "Redis Key Schema" construction, but your Redis key schema doesn't need to be code-based, just a simple text file documenting your syntax, how your keys relate to each other, and what data structures are stored in your various keys, should be sufficient for small projects or use cases.

Redis key schema

Although the official Redis tutorial on `data types`1 recommends using a consistent schema when naming keys, Redis itself does not have any schema checking or validation functions although some basic validation can be done through the use of the `EXISTS` and `TYPE` Redis commands. If your application requires that a Redis key with a certain type exists in the instance, checking for the key's existence is easily accomplished with the `EXISTS` command followed by the subsequent `TYPE` command to confirm that the key is the expected Redis data structure stored in that key location. Beyond these two commands, validating the Redis key syntax and structure requires client-side code.

Adding this additional validation logic layer to your application may be useful if your Redis application is to be shared across different systems and organizations. An accurate and detailed Redis key schema can greatly assist you and the application developers and operators in troubleshooting or debugging problems. Another avenue to validate your Redis Key schema would be to include specific unit tests in your Redis application that test for boundary conditions, schema key syntax, and structure, along with the expected data structures for each validated key. The third option for validating your Redis key schema is to use a DTD or another XML-based validation of your key structure or to use a new schema validation technology such as JSON Schema available at `http://json-schema.org/`.

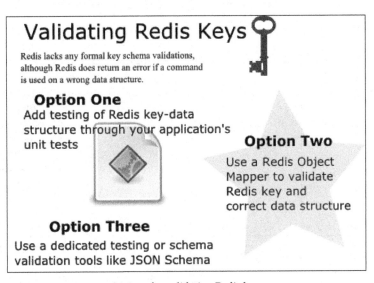

Validating Redis Keys

Redis lacks any formal key schema validations, although Redis does return an error if a command is used on a wrong data structure.

Option One
Add testing of Redis key-data structure through your application's unit tests

Option Two
Use a Redis Object Mapper to validate Redis key and correct data structure

Option Three
Use a dedicated testing or schema validation tools like JSON Schema

Options for validating Redis keys

A good key schema should also provide guidance for adding new Redis keys to an existing Redis-based application. There should not be any mysteries about what the name of a new Redis key should be if the schema is descriptive and consistent. Know and use both singular and plural forms of nouns to identify what and how many of an entity is being saved to Redis. For example, `book:1` could be a Redis hash storing field related to a single book, while the Redis key `books:sci-fiction` could be a set of all books that are classified as part of the science fiction genre. A sorted set could be used for book sales ranking with the `books:sales-rank` key name with the number of books sold as the weight or the sorted set score and the book key as the value.

An example of a text-based Redis schema for a simple book application could look like the following:

Name	Redis data type	Description	Relationships
`book:{counter}`	Hash	Stores title, author, ISBN, format, copyright date, page number, and price metadata for a book	Key is stored in different genre sets and sales ranking sorted sets
`books:{genre}`	Set	A set of Redis keys for books classified as a genre, such as popular fiction, mysteries, science fiction, and technical books	Stores all book keys that have been classified as a single genre. Used with other genre sets for calculating books in multiple genres with `SINTERSTORE` and books that are only in a single genre with `SDIFFSTORE`
`books:sales-rank`	Sorted set	Stores the sales ranking of each book with the total number of titles sold as the score in the sorted set	Stores the ranking of all Redis book keys

Adding key schema documentation as part of your project's source code repository is a good practice to follow, even with simple, one-off Redis projects.

Key delimiters and naming conventions

You'll notice that in the last example that colon ':' is being used as a key delimiter. The colon is one of the suggested delimiters for compound Redis keys. This is just a convention, and you should feel free to use any other delimiter in your own application. For a web application, using a forward slash '/' may make better sense (although of course, you should never pass public URL requests directly to Redis without some preprocessing to sanitize the user's request).

Another delimiter for Redis keys is the period '.' making it easier to map to a common object-oriented syntax favored by many of the most popular programming languages such as C++, Object C, Python, Swift, and Ruby. There is nothing precluding or preventing you from mixing delimiters in your Redis key schema as long as the delimiter use is consistent and properly documented. The goal in choosing which delimiters to use should be intelligibility and consistency both to you and the eventual users of your application.

Where an effective Redis key schema excels is in establishing naming conventions relating keys together. These relationships loosely couple Redis keys together onto which application and business logic can be applied through client code. A Redis key schema weaves a narrative relating your data in a way that is intelligible to you and that meets your users' needs. Take, for example, the earlier book key schema and expanding the requirements to include other media types in your Redis databases, running a KEYS command from the Redis command-line tool, and doing some formatting. These display a pattern and implicit relationships through the Redis key schema:

```
all:sales-rank
global:book
book:1
book:2
book:3
books:genre:popular-fiction
books:genre:sci-fiction
books:format:ebook
books:format:paperback
books:sales-rank
global:film
film:1
film:2
films:genre:comedy
films:genre:drama
films:format:bluray
films:format:dvd
films:sales-rank
```

In this Redis application, both book and film provide the base prefix from which supporting data structures are associated with either a singular book or film key or a collection that contains additional entity hashes.

Each work is a hash with the Redis key being the prefix along with a global counter. Other supporting data structures, in this case, a book's or film's genre and format, are Redis sets that store all the book or film keys that are classified as belonging to a particular genre or format. For example, properties of Isaac Asimov's Foundation would be stored in the `book:2` hash, and `book:2` would also be a member of the `books:genre:sci-fiction` and `books:format:paperback` sets with entries in both the `books:sales-rank` and `all:sales-rank` sorted sets. Likewise, Orson Well's Citizen Kane, would be stored in the `film:1` hash, with membership in the `films:genre:drama` and `films:format:dvd` sets and entries in the `films:sales-rank` and `all:sales-rank` sorted sets.

A common requirement in an application is the need to retrieve a collection of values on the basis of common characteristics. In the book example, we may be tempted to retrieve all the book genres with the KEYS command and a `books:genre:*` pattern. The use of the Redis KEYS command is highly discouraged for applications running in production as Redis needs to iterate through every single key in the datastore. With a consistent naming convention and appropriate data structures such as set, hash, or sorted sets, your application should not need to use the KEYS command for retrieving values. The SCAN command, with an option for retrieving values from Redis should not be thought of as a replacement for the KEYS command. The SCAN command extracts a random slice of key and then, applies any existing pattern provided with the MATCH option to the random slice. Going back to the previous example, the following use of SCAN in a running `Redis-cli` program only works if you have a small datastore:

```
127.0.0.1:6379> SCAN 0 MATCH books:genre*
1) "0"
2) 1) "books:genre:popular-fiction"
   2) "books:genre:mystery"
   3) "books:genre:teen"
   4) "books:genre:sci-fiction"
   5) "books:genre:fantasy"
   6) "books:genre:romance"
```

If your datastore is larger, using the same SCAN command may not return any matches or only a small subset of the total number of matches. Much better would be to store all the genre keys in a `books:genres` set that your application uses as an index to quickly retrieve all of the book genre keys with an SMEMBERS command:

```
127.0.0.1:6379> SMEMBERS books:genres
1) "books:format:ebook"
2) "books:genre:popular-fiction"
3) "books:format:paperback"
4) "books:genre:sci-fiction"
5) "books:sales-rank"
```

Testing your relationships and how they relate to each other through your Redis key naming conventions will depend on a number of factors, including if your application interacts directly with an active Redis instance. Adding unit tests that specifically check your key delimiters as well as the naming conventions in your Redis application ensures that the assumptions and requirements that your application depends upon are accurately represented in the data being stored in your Redis database. Here is an example of a unit test in Python that tests for a colon delimiter for the Redis key schema book example (the full example is available for download at `http://mastering-redis.com`).

```
def  test_delimiter(self):
    """Method tests for a colon in  Redis keys in the datastore."""
    first_key = self.test_db.scan(0, "book*", 1)[1][0].decode()
    self.assertTrue(first_key.startswith("book:"))
```

The first line uses the Python Redis client to run a `book:*` pattern with the scan starting with an initial cursor of 0 and a count of one command returning the first instance and decoding the string to unicode while saving it to the `first_key` variable. The second line asserts that `first_key` starts with the prefix and delimiter that we expected in our Redis schema. We'll next take a different scenario and start by first outlining the major types of data that we want to capture in our Redis application and then, discussing how we can use our business requirements and nomenclature to create the corresponding Redis keys and data structures.

Manually creating a Redis schema

This graphic outlines our basic scenario of a simple two-product online storefront from which we will construct our Redis schema.

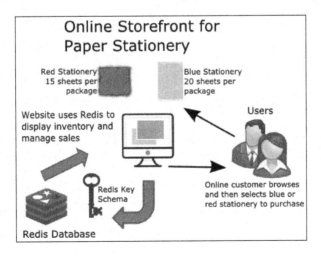

Imagine that you have an online storefront selling paper products and you want to manage different stationary products that are offered for sale. Embedded within this seemingly simple business need, the following narrative starts with these separate steps:

1. An online customer comes to our website looking to buy paper stationery.

2. We offer two choices of paper stationery: a blue rectangle package of 20 sheets printed on rice paper and a red square, and a 15-sheet stationery package also printed on rice paper.

3. The basic entity in our example is a package of stationery that has three basic properties: color, height, width, and number of sheets. (Until we start selling paper stationery made out of non-rice paper, we will ignore material as a property. Another future enhancement would be to add a more friendly, human name for each stationery package).

4. Managing a small inventory of these two types of stationery, we record a sale when a customer purchases a paper package from our website, noting the time and the amount received, as well as decreasing the inventory by the number of packages sold.

The first step in manually creating a Redis schema is establishing a global stationery counter appended to a stationery prefix for the type and brand of stationery that we are offering for sale. We'll store the color and dimension properties as fields in a `stationery:{id-counter}` hash and store the number of sheets in a separate string value in the `stationery:{id-counter}:sheets` key. These data structures can be demonstrated with the following commands by using the Redis CLI program connecting to an instance of Redis running on a local host:

```
127.0.0.1:6379> INCR global:stationery1
```

The returned integer 1 will be used as the id counter for the first stationery:

```
127.0.0.1:6379> HMSET stationery:1 color blue width '30 cm' height
'40 cm'OK
```

To associate the number of sheets for the `stationery:1:sheets` set, we use the INCREBY command:

```
127.0.0.1:6379> INCRBY stationery:1:sheets 20(integer) 20
```

Now, we call the INCR command again to generate the second id counter for our second stationery type, populate the hash, and increment by 15 the number of sheets:

```
127.0.0.1:6379> INCR global:stationery
(integer 2)
127.0.0.1:6379> HMSET stationery:2 color red width '45 cm' height '45 cm'
15
127.0.0.1:6379> INCRBY stationery:2:sheets 15
(integer) 15
```

Next, the inventory of stationery packages for a particular type is stored using the following key pattern, stationery:<stationery id>:inventory, with the value in that key being a simple integer representing all of the available packages for that type of stationery. This can be illustrated through the following Redis-CLI commands where an initial inventory of 250 packages is set as an integer:

```
127.0.0.1:6379> SET stationery:1:inventory 250
```

When one or more packages are sold, the integer value stored in stationery:1:inventory is decremented by the number of packages. Likewise, when new packages of the stationery arrive from the distributor, the key is incremented by the number of new stationery packages.

```
127.0.0.1:6379> DECR stationery:1:inventory
127.0.0.1:6379> INCRBY stationery:1:inventory 10
```

Sales information for each package is stored as a sorted set by using a Unix timestamp (an integer that represents the time since the epoch) as the score and the amount of sale as the value in a sorted set row. Using the Redis key of stationery:1:sales for the sorted set, the Redis command for documenting a twenty-dollar sale from the Redis CLI would be as follows:

```
127.0.0.1:6379> ZADD stationery:1:sales 1430861194 20.00
```

Even with this simplistic example, having a common pattern for the Redis keys gives the Redis application a method of relating information between our data in an online store for stationery.

The following diagram shows how the information for each stationery type is clustered and how sales and other information can quickly be extracted from the datastore by using Redis.

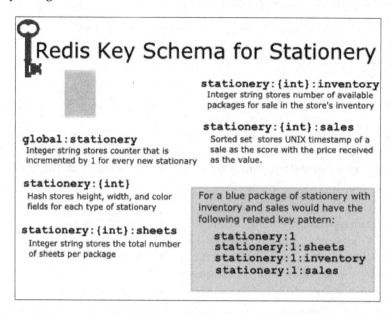

Deconstructing a Redis object mapper

Redis's rich ecosystem offers a number of object mappers for Redis that hide the key naming management from the designer and the user while offering, through client-side code, a functionality that may be present in other data storage technologies. Examining how a Redis object mapper implements this functionality with a particular pattern of keys and data structures can help you learn about existing patterns and allow you to extend and improve your own Redis-based applications. Using a Redis object mapper can also be helpful if you do not want to re-implement a functionality that may already exist and run it in production environments in your code base. A few of the more popular programming languages have these object mapper projects that all provide ways to persist object semantics and data in Redis while offering more object-oriented methodologies and techniques for the developer who may be more familiar with these techniques and ideas in their preferred programing language. These object mappers manipulate Redis keys and values by using the nomenclature and conventions of the programming language that the object mapper has developed while hopefully reducing the maintenance and the training overhead for Redis-based solutions in the organization.

For the node.js Redis object mapper called **Nohm** (available at `https://github.com/maritz/nohm/`), the Redis schema is created through a JavaScript object model. Returning to the previous paper-product web storefront example, modeling a stationery entity with Nohm first requires defining a stationary JavaScript model with color, height, and width properties by using the following code:

```
nohm.model('Stationary', {
  properties: {
    color: {
      type: 'string',
      unique: false,
      validations: [
      'notEmpty'
     ]
    },
    height: {
     type: 'string',
     unique: false
    },
    sheets: {
     type: 'integer',
     defaultValue: 20
    },
    width: {
     type: 'string',
     unique: false
    }
   }
});
```

Creating an equivalent stationary object in the `stationery:1` hash from the previous section generates the following Redis commands and values on a running Redis database for a new stationary Javascript object with color, width, and height being set to the same values as in `stationery:1`. Running the MONITOR command from the `redis-cli` program provides the following output:

```
1431204654.386408 [0 127.0.0.1:61217] "info"
1431204654.404005 [0 127.0.0.1:61217] "get"
"paper:meta:version:Stationary"
1431204654.405394 [0 127.0.0.1:61217] "sismember"
"paper:idsets:Stationary" "-1431204204839"
1431204654.406943 [0 127.0.0.1:61217] "set"
"paper:meta:version:Stationary"
"1bf8ca04e698cd589baa17c661498b1109f8d65c"
1431204654.407516 [0 127.0.0.1:61217] "set"
```

```
"paper:meta:idGenerator:Stationary" "default"
1431204654.407547 [0 127.0.0.1:61217] "set"
"paper:meta:properties:Stationary"
"{\"color\":{\"type\":\"string\",\"unique\":false,\"validations\":[\"n
otEmpty\"]},\"height\":{\"type\":\"string\",\"unique\":false},\"sheets
\":{\"type\":\"integer\",\"defaultValue\":20},\"width\":{\"type\":\"st
ring\",\"unique\":false}}"
1431204654.411575 [0 127.0.0.1:61217] "sadd"
"paper:idsets:Stationary" "i9hiar0q75vit5d9rgc5"
1431204654.418524 [0 127.0.0.1:61217] "MULTI"
1431204654.419119 [0 127.0.0.1:61217] "hmset"
"paper:hash:Stationary:i9hiar0q75vit5d9rgc5" "color" "blue"
"height" "40 cm" "sheets" "20" "width" "30 cm" "__meta_version"
"1bf8ca04e698cd589baa17c661498b1109f8d65c"
```

Unpacking this Redis database activity when a Nohm stationary object is saved to Redis, we will examine each Redis key from and what the object mapper is doing with the Redis key and the corresponding data structure in the Redis database. From this analysis, the Redis key schema being used by Nohm becomes more intelligible. We start building the Redis schema as a Nohm's Redis schema by following a very common Redis design pattern of using a paper namespace for all the object mapper's Redis keys and note that Nohm uses a colon as a key delimiter in its underlying schema.

- `paper:meta:version:Stationary`: This Redis metadata key stores a string version used for stationary stores the version. A random metadata version string of `1bf8ca04e698cd589baa17c661498b1109f8d65c` is then set as the current value of this key. Nohm tracks each change that we make to the stationary model and then stores version information of our model.

- `paper:idsets:Stationary`: This Redis set stores all stationary IDs. This set is first checked with a negative UNIX timestamp, and then, an ID string of `i9hiar0q75vit5d9rgc5` is generated and added to this set. This set is used to track stationary objects, and a random value should minimize problems related to duplicate keys.

- `paper:meta:idGenerator:Stationary`: This Redis string is used by Nohm to determine the method for generating an ID. The default option generates a random string, while the increment option uses an integer counter.

- `paper:meta:properties:Stationary`: A Redis string stores the serialized JSON metadata for the stationary object.

- `paper:hash:Stationary:i9hiar0q75vit5d9rgc5`: Wrapped in a Redis transaction, the stationary Javascript object instance stores its property values in a Redis hash by using `i9hiar0q75vit5d9rgc5` as the last part of its Redis key.

Next, add a second stationary package, say a red square, 45-cm high × 45-cm wide, with an initial sheet count of 15 results to the following Redis keys in our database:

`paper:meta:properties:Stationary`

`paper:meta:idGenerator:Stationary`

`paper:idsets:Stationary`

`paper:hash:Stationary:i9hjsdjv4o9csf8eeonj`

`paper:meta:version:Stationary`

`paper:hash:Stationary:i9hiar0q75vit5d9rgc5`

We'll see how a more complicated Redis key schema comes into play using Nohm to model the sales of a stationery item by using two supporting classes from the `schema.org` metadata vocabulary, namely an offer (`http://schema.org/Offer`) class and an order (`http://schema.org/Order`) class. The `schema.org` vocabulary is cosponsored by Google, Microsoft, Yahoo, and Yandax for representing structured data on the web. The `Offer` class contains the price and the available inventory along with a `priceCurrency` property to support offers in other currencies. For now, our default currency for `priceCurrency` will be the United States dollar. Our `Order` class contains the `acceptedOffer` and `orderDate` properties, with the `acceptedOffer` property linking to the specific order that we created for our stationery. So far, we have only replicated the initial storage of each stationery package with Nohm. Adding two new models to represent our sales, namely offer and order, we'll want to be able to use the relationship modeling available in Nohm to link the stationery objects. Unlike other object mappers for SQL-based databases that require the relationship to be predefined before use, Nohm allows any model to be associated with another model through a link method.

```
nohm.model('Offer', {
  properties: {
    inventoryLevel: {
      type: 'integer',
      unique: false
    },
    price: {
      type: 'float',
      unique: false
    },
    priceCurrency: {
      type: 'string',
      unique: false,
      defaultValue: 'USD'
    }
  }
});
```

The order class contains two properties, namely orderDate and orderedItem, although the order class could be expanded to include other order properties from the schema.org vocabulary such as customer and discount as the requirements change for the paper stationery web storefront. You'll notice that we didn't add orderedItem as a formal property for the order class because we will be creating orderedItem through a Nohm link to the item stationery.

```
nohm.model('Order', {
  properties: {
    orderDate: {
      type: 'datetime'
    },
  }
});
```

When a sale occurs, the Nohm approach is to create a linkage between the offer, the order, and the stationery objects. After creating a new order instance with a timestamp of when a sales transaction occurred, Nohm uses a couple of supporting Redis sets to model the relationships between the three different classes. Nohm stores the relationship information in a few different sets as seen from these snippets from the Redis cli program:

First, paper:hashOffer: ia4ev8iu8cns7w6p968h is a hash key that sets its inventory level property as 50 and the price as 15 for the red stationery.

```
1432589868.318914 [0 10.0.2.2:55200] "hmset"
"paper:hash:Offer:ia4ev8iu8cns7w6p9
68h" "inventoryLevel" "50" "price" "15" "priceCurrency" "USD"
"__meta_version" "
229e1d3b89b02804b4bdad9909fa75aa442197d5"
```

Next, the paper:relationKeys:Offer:ia4ev8iu8c ns7w6p968h and paper:r elations:Offer:itemOffered:S tationery:ia4ev8iu8cns7w6p968h sets are created; the first set stores all the keys to the sets that create the linkages between offer and stationery with the itemOffered property. The second set stores all the individual stationery IDs by creating a specific link between this specific offer and the stationery.

```
1432589868.323265 [0 10.0.2.2:55200] "sadd" "paper:relationKeys:Offer:
ia4ev8iu8cns7w6p968h"
"paper:relations:Offer:itemOffered:Stationery:ia4ev8iu8cns7w6p968h"
1432589868.323281 [0 10.0.2.2:55200] "sadd"
"paper:relations:Offer:itemOffered:Stationary:ia4ev8iu8cns7w6p968h"
ia4ev8itec2wq9gc0qnt"
```

When an order is received and thereby a sale is recognized, first, a Redis `paper:hash:Order:1` hash is created with the order date field, and with all Nohm, a metadata version id is also stored with the hash as a field.

```
1432589868.325604 [0 10.0.2.2:55200] "hmset" "paper:hash:Order:1"
"orderDate"
"Mon May 25 2015 15:33:33 GMT-0600 (Mountain Daylight Time)"
"__meta_version" "a881a941cb6ff674a79c7f652f8d8153b7b47b"
```

Two additional sets, namely `paper:relationKeys:Order:1` and `paper:relations:Order:offer:Offer:1`, create the linkage between our `order` and `offer` with the first set storing all the relationship links for `order` and the second set storing the specific `Offer` for the `order` that was added in the previous command:

```
1432589868.327808 [0 10.0.2.2:55200] "sadd"
"paper:relationKeys:Order:1" "paper:
relations:Order:offer:Offer:1"
1432589868.327829 [0 10.0.2.2:55200] "sadd"
"paper:relations:Order:offer:Offer:1"  "ia4ev8iu8cns7w6p968h"
```

The following graphic illustrates the JavaScript code flow that creates this linkage between `stationery`, `offer`, and `order` for our online paper store.

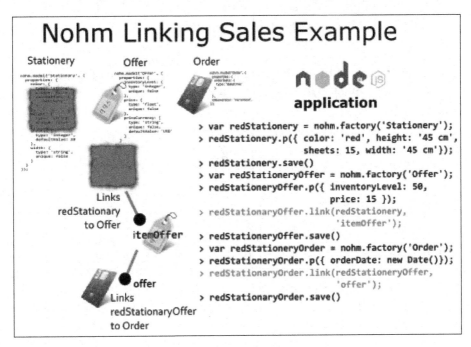

Key expiration

A significant feature of Redis is the ability to set the expiration time for a key. By being able to automatically delete expired keys, a Redis application can better manage both the size and the memory usage of the datastore as well as reduce the amount of client code for keeping track of every key in the datastore.

In the next chapter on optimizing and managing RAM for your Redis instance, the topic of key expiration will be examined in more detail. Key expiration is most often discussed in the context of keeping the memory usage of a Redis instance within acceptable performance limits by ejecting the expired keys from the database. Redis offers a number of different modes for setting the automatic ejection of expired keys depending on your application's needs and performance limits, which can be set either by setting an option in the your Redis configuration file or by run-time commands sent to your Redis database.

Key cautions

Over the years, certain best practices have emerged that are briefly articulated in Redis `tutorial1`. The practices revolve around the legibility and performance trade-offs in your running Redis database and supporting client code. The size of the Redis keys should be limited not only because of memory issues that may arise if the key size is greater than 1024 bytes long but also because larger-size keys can be confusing to the developer and the user of the Redis instance. Another problem of larger key names is that as the size of the Redis instance increases, each one of these larger key names begins to consume larger amounts of memory, thereby reducing the amount of available memory for the data.

Likewise, if the key name is too small, the extra memory saved may not be worth the problems that can occur later when trying to troubleshoot Redis or adding a functionality through new Redis keys. For example, a key name of u11:2 may be short but does not convey the meaning of what value is being managed while a key name of the same data, `user:11:clicks`, is a better descriptor for the value stored in this Redis key and the application context of this key. This can be a challenge for applications that develop and evolve over time but can be mitigated by adopting a consistent Redis key schema that allows room for further growth in the future. Even a small amount of time devoted to thinking of possible future uses when developing a Redis key schema can alleviate massive refactoring of the client code and data migration in Redis to handle emerging needs from the use of your application by individuals and other programs.

The Redis KEYS command should be used as a last resort as its use creates a long-running blocking call on the Redis instance and can even result in Redis running out of memory. SCAN provides an iterator over all of the keys in the Redis instance that can be incrementally called upon all of the keys. The Redis SCAN, and the equivalent HSCAN, SSCAN, and ZSCAN commands for hashes, sets, and sorted sets, respectively, are relatively newer commands that meet a real requirement for Redis applications. A note of caution when using SCAN and its related iterator commands is that SCAN cannot guarantee that an element will be returned if that element was not consistently present from the start to the end of the iteration.

Big O notation

As you may already know and fully appreciate, Salvatore Sanfilippo intentionally documents the worst-case algorithmic performance of each Redis command on Redis's website at http://redis.io/commands/. This focus on an algorithmic measure of performance as a core actionable metric differentiates Redis from the other data storage technologies. A mathematical definition of Big O is that it "symbolically expresses the asymptotic behavior of a given function.2. Within computer science and more pertinent to our understanding of the big O notation within Redis, with this notation and understanding, we can classify the performance of a Redis command by how the commands perform with increasing inputs to the command over time.

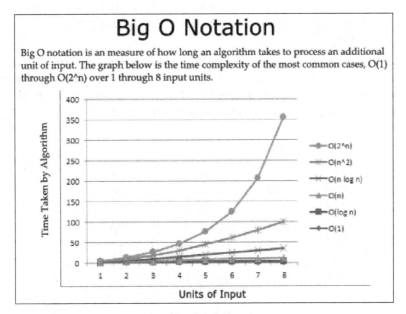

Graphing Big O Notation

In the Redis documentation for each command, the time complexity of each Redis command is given in these big O cases:

- The **O(1)** case in the big O notation is shorthand for increasing the number of inputs that do not change the time or processing. In **O(1)** algorithms, the upper bound of performance is in linear time, meaning that increasing the number of inputs does not degrade performance but is bound by the algorithm's complexity processing.

- The next best big O case is **O(log n)** or logarithmic time where for each input, an operation is applied and the result returned is greater than **N(1)**, but the performance is equivalent to applying a logarithm to n.

- An intuitive grasp of the term **O(n)** in the big O notation follows the common sense idea that adding an extra unit increases the amount of time by a constant, proportional amount.

- In **O(n log n)** or log linear time, for each input, **O(log n)** is applied to the input. For practical purposes, each time input is more than doubled in an O(n log n) algorithm.

- For **O(n^2)** or quadratic time, as the size of n increases, the amount of time doubles. For each doubling of n, the time processed is four times as long. The performance of **O(n^2)** algorithms may be acceptable at smaller values for n but becomes quickly unrealistic for most uses as n increases in size.

- In the case of problems that are solvable in **O(2^n)** or exponential time, for every additional input, the time doubles, making **O(2^n)** unusable for most larger inputs of n.

- The most time-complex algorithms are noted in **O(n!)** factorial time where processing becomes quickly prohibitive as n increases slightly. For example, the difference for an **O(n!)** algorithm at 5 units vs. 6 units is significant (120 units of elapsed time vs. 720 units of elapsed time).

	O(1)	O(log n)	O(n)	O(n log n)	O(n^2)	O(2^n)	O(n!)
1	1	0	1	0	1	2	1
2	1	1	2	2	4	4	2
3	1	1.58496	3	4.75488	9	8	6
4	1	2	4	8	16	16	24
5	1	2.32192	5	11.60964	25	32	120
6	1	2.58496	6	15.50977	36	64	720
7	1	2.80735	7	19.65148	49	128	5040
8	1	3	8	24	64	256	40320
9	1	3.16992	9	28.52932	81	512	362880
10	1	3.321928	10	33.21928	100	1024	3628800

Computing big O notation for custom code

With Redis documentation providing the big O notation for each command, we can calculate a rough efficiency estimate of any proposed Redis-based solution. A simplistic approach is to take the sum of all of the Redis commands' big O notations for a certain level of n and then, estimate the big O notation for the implementing code to reach a rough estimate of time efficiency for your entire solution. For example, a simple cache in Redis may just be a single Redis SET and GET call, leading to $O(1)$ + $O(1)$ ≈ 2 units of time for the solution. More complicated use cases require more commands with higher big O notations.

Evaluating the time complexity of your data structures involves not just the data structure itself but also the optimization of the total number of Redis commands, both ingestion and extraction. Depending on your use case, it may be perfectly acceptable to have poor time execution of your ingesting data into say, a sorted set, with an equal to or lower than big O case for the access commands. The opposite use case of low latency in ingesting large amounts of data, you need faster (low-complexity big O cases) ingestion, while accessing the data may not need to be as fast. For these situations, say when storing logging information that expires after a certain amount of elapsed time, optimizing writes is more important than access, although access is still important for the application.

So, returning to the stationery example from before, let us compare our first custom Redis solution with the second Nohm-based solution focusing just on the Redis commands since we do not have the client code yet for the first. We'll start by examining the total time complexity of adding the blue and red stationery packages to our Redis database.

Redis command	O(n)	Total
INCR	+1	1
HMSET	+3	4
INCRBY	+1	5
HMSET	+3	8

The total complexity for adding one stationery object to our custom Redis solution is four, so adding an additional red stationery package brings our total to eight.

Now, we will analyze the Nohm Redis Monitor command and summarize the result of setting up and saving both the blue and the red stationery:

Redis Command	O(n)	Running total
INFO	+1	1
GET	+1	2
SISMEMBER	+1	3
SET	+1	4
SET	+1	5
SET	+1	6
SADD	+1	7
HMSET	+3	10
SADD	+1	11
HMSET	+3	14

The total complexity of adding one stationery object, including various setup commands, to the Nohm solution is 10, and similar to our custom Redis solution, that of adding an additional red stationery package is 14. Depending on your application models, using a Redis object mapper in the programming language of your choice may only have a relatively minor overhead as you scale your application. Ideally, we keep the time complexity of our client code at the most, $O(n \log n)$, with the goal being $O(1)$ or $O(\log n)$. This grows increasingly difficult as your application matures over time and lets you discover and work through edge cases and from end-user feedback.

Although the differences between the summary time complexity of the two Redis solutions is relatively small, the Nohm Redis object mapper provides a lot of essential functionalities that we need to replicate if we want to build a full node.js application by using Redis as our database. Again, there are tradeoffs between an extremely fast but with limited support for object tracking and validation in our custom Redis solution, or the additional functionality of object metadata and field validations that Nohm provides to our application.

Reviewing the time complexity of Redis data structures

With this understanding of the computing big notation, we'll next briefly review Redis's basic data structures, paying attention to the time complexity implications of using the data structure with the current commands supported by Redis.

Strings

The most basic data structure for Redis values is a string, the same data type as a Redis key. Using Redis at its simplest is as a string-to-string key-value storage. Note that Redis has similar performance characteristics to other key-value data storage solutions such as Memecached3.

In Redis, a string does not merely contain alphanumeric characters as strings are normally understood to be in higher-level programming languages, but contain serialized characters in C, the principal programming language used in Redis. The most basic GET and SET commands for Redis strings are O(1) operations, making Redis extremely fast as a simple key-value store. The speed and ease of using GET and SET should not be overlooked when thinking through your Redis solution. In my own experience with Redis, I'll often jump prematurely to using one of Redis's more complex data structures such as a sorted set, when a simple Redis string may be a faster and less complicated approach to solving the problem in front of me.

For most Redis string operations, both access and ingestion commands are either O(1) or O(n) in time complexity with the O(n) string commands being mostly bulk commands such as GETRANGE, MSET, and MGET. The GETRANGE command is an O(n) operation with n being the length of the return string. This makes intuitive sense if we think of the operation as a series of small GET commands (although GET does not return a subrange of a string value stored in the key). We can illustrate this with Redis CLI, SET, and GETRANGE:

```
127.0.0.1:6379> SET organization:1 "The British Library"
127.0.0.1:6379> GETRANGE organization:1 4 10 "British"
```

Therefore, in this example, the big O notation for SET is +1 and the GETRANGE is +6, the equivalent of retrieving six characters by issuing individual pseudo GET commands.

Because Redis stores all data as strings, the type information for particular strings is also maintained to support the INCR/DECR and bitstring commands. For the INCR and DECR commands, the value stored is a base-10 64-bit signed integer string, which if modified by the other Redis string commands such as APPEND, may corrupt the value; therefore, further integer-related Redis commands will fail if applied to the same key. We can easily replicate this situation from Redis CLI with the following INCR, GET, and DUMP commands on the new:counter key:

```
127.0.0.1:6379> INCR new:counter(integer) 1
127.0.0.1:6379> GET new:counter
"1"
127.0.0.1:6379> DUMP new:counter
"\x00\xc0\x01\x06\x00\xb0\x95\x8f6$T-o"
127.0.0.1:6379> APPEND new:counter "a"
```

```
(integer) 2
127.0.0.1:6379> INCR new:counter
(error) ERR value is not an integer or out of range
127.0.0.1:6379> GET new:counter
"1a"
127.0.0.1:6379> DUMP new:counter
"\x00\x021a\x06\x00\x8br\x9a\x98-9\x9a\xa6"
```

Hashes

Hashes, otherwise known as dictionaries or associative arrays in other programming languages, are data structures that map one or more fields to the corresponding value pairs. In Redis, all hash values must be Redis strings with unique field names. The field's values are simple Redis strings that are returned by calling the Redis HGET or HMGET commands with the appropriate Redis key and one or more field parameters. For many uses, Redis hashes provide excellent O(1) performance for the HSET and HGET commands. Similar to the string bulk commands, the hash HGETALL, HMSET, HMGET, HKEYS, and HVALS commands are all O(n) cases. If your hashes are small, there may not be any appreciable difference between returning all of the hash's keys and values with the HGETALL and HMGET commands. As your hash size increases in terms of the number of fields and values, the difference between the two can make a difference in your application. Take a hash with 1000 fields; if your application only regularly uses 300, the time complexity of a call to Redis with the HGETALL or HVALS command is O(1000), while with HMGET, the time complexity is only O(300) because although both HGETALL and HMGET are both O(n) cases, the HMGET upper bound is only the total number of fields being requested and not the entire hash. Finding and replacing the HGETALL commands with HMGET is one way to increase your application's Redis performance if the overall size of the hash is small. For large hash sizes, an HMGET command returning a large number of values can significantly impact the overall performance of Redis for other clients who are blocked from receiving any values until the HMGET command finishes execution within the Redis server. In this case, targeted HGET would be a better choice.

While Redis hash values cannot contain hashes, lists, or other data collection structures, Redis does offer the HINCRBY and HINCRBYFLOAT commands, which allow you to treat the string value stored in a field as an integer or a float, respectively. Redis returns an error if you try to update a field's value with the wrong data type as seen in the following example from the Redis command line:

```
127.0.0.1:6379> HMSET weather:2 temperature 46 moisture .001
127.0.0.1:6379> HINCRBY weather:2 temperature -1
127.0.0.1:6379> HGET weather:2 temperature
"45"
127.0.0.1:6379> HINCRBY weather:2 moisture 1
(error) ERR hash value is not an integer
```

```
127.0.0.1:6379> HINCRBYFLOAT weather:2 moisture 1
127.0.0.1:6379> HGET weather:2 moisture
"1.001"
```

You'll notice that Redis treats the setting of the value of 1 as either an integer or a float depending on the command.

Lists

Lists in Redis are ordered collections of strings that allow for duplicate string values. A list in Redis is more accurately labeled and implemented as a linked list. Because Redis lists are implemented as linked lists, adding an item to the front of a list with LPUSH or to the end of a list with RPUSH is a relatively inexpensive operation performed at a constant time complexity of $O(1)$. For the LINSERT and LSET commands, the time complexity is linear, $O(n)$, but with some significant differences. For the LSET command, where you can set a list value as an index value, the time complexity for the n variable is the length of the list while setting either the first or the last value in the list with LSET is $O(1)$ because the lists are linked lists. For the LINSERT command, which allows you to insert a value before or after a reference value, the abovementioned time complexity is $O(n)$, with n being the number of list elements that the command must go through before reaching the reference value, with the worst case inserting a value at the end of the list. Remember that with the big O notation, we're interested in the worst case scenario, so the time complexity of the LINSERT command is considered to be $O(n)$, even if the reference value is the first list element making the time complexity of the LINSERT command $O(1)$ in this special case.

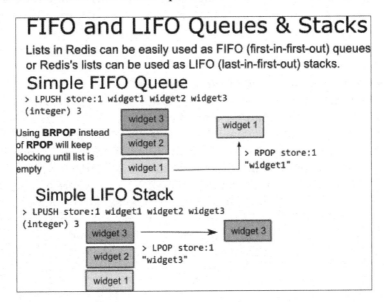

For the LRANGE command, the official Redis documentation gives the complexity class for this command as O(s+n), with s being the number of elements to offset either from the head of the list or from the end of the list depending on the size of the list. The n variable for LRANGE is the total number of elements to be returned. If you want to return the entire list, the common list LRANGE pattern is LRANGE mylist 0-1, which results in a time complexity of O(10+10) for a list of length 10. LTRIM typically has a big O notation of O(n), where n is the number of elements to be returned to the calling client. As mentioned in the official documentation for the LTRIM command 4, using LTRIM with either RPUSH or LPUSH is a common way to only store a fixed-length collection of elements. For example, if you only want to keep the last seven days' worth of average temperature data, use the following Redis commands:

```
127.0.0.1:6379> LPUSH temp:last-seven-days 30 45 50 52 49 55 51
127.0.0.1:6379> LPUSH temp:last-seven-days 56
127.0.0.1:6379> LTRIM temp:last-seven-days 0 6
127.0.0.1:6379> LRANGE temp:last-seven-days 0 -1
1) "56"
2) "51"
3) "55"
4) "49"
5) "52"
6) "50"
7) "45"
```

As we see, this pattern allows us to store the last seven days' average temperature and when used in this way, the time complexity of our LTRIM command now approaches O(1) as long as only one value is pushed on to the list at a time.

Sets

Sets in Redis are a type of collection primitive where the uniqueness of string values is guaranteed but the ordering of these values is not. Redis sets also implement union, intersection, and difference set semantics along with the ability to store the results of these set operations as a new Redis set in the Redis instance. With the current implementation of the Redis cluster, the union, intersection, and difference set semantics are more limited and can only be used in a limited fashion. The SADD command, which adds one or more values to a set, is O(n), where n is the number of members to be added to the set. The important SISMEMBER command evaluates whether a value is a member of the set or not and is an O(1) operation, while the SMEMBERS command that returns all of the elements in the list is an O(N) operation. Sets may have a similar performance to that of the other data structures in Redis or in certain cases have much better memory usage when storing integers over hashes.

Where sets are extremely useful in Redis is its support for the union, intersection, and difference set operations, all of which have different time complexities but again are of much limited use with a Redis cluster.

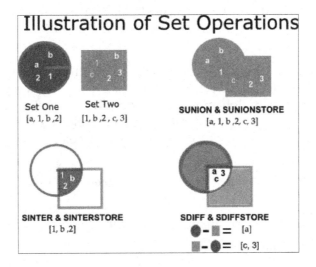

The SUNION and SUNIONSTORE commands allow you to return all the members of one or more sets to either the call client or a new set stored in Redis. Both these commands are O(n), where n is the total number of members in all the sets. The SINTER and SINTERSTORE commands returns the intersection or stores the set when using the SINTERSTORE command. in Redis, the common members of one or more sets result in a time complexity of O(n*m), where n is the size of the smallest set and m is the total number of sets. Finally, the SDIFF and SDIFFSTORE commands either return or store in Redis the difference between the first set and zero or more subsequent sets. As for the SUNION command, the time complexity of SDIFF and SDIFFSTORE is O(n), where n is the total number of members of all the sets. The utility of the Redis sets is in these set operations that allow interaction at a very basic Boolean logic level with your data. However, as your set size increases, the amount of processing time increases at a minimum of O(n) time.

Sorted sets

In Redis, the sorted-set data type combines the characteristics of both Redis lists and sets. Similarly to those of a Redis list, a sorted set's values are ordered, and like a set, each value is assured to be unique. Of all the various data structures in Redis, the sorted set is the closest to a killer feature. The flexibility of a sorted set allows for multiple types of access patterns depending on the needs of the application. Using a single sorted set for a player's scores in a game both the top and the bottom players are easily fetched for a leaderboard by either the ZRANGE or ZREVRANGE Redis commands.

For sorted sets, the ZADD command adds a member with a score to the sorted set. The time complexity of ZADD is $O(\log(n))$, meaning that as the size of the sorted set increases, the rate of increase in the processing time is a constant. Therefore, the difference between adding a new member to a large sorted set is trivial; the difference between $\log(10000) \sim 9.21034037$ and $\log(10001) \sim 9.21044036$ is .000099.

Another, very nice feature of Redis's sorted sets is that if the score is the same for all or part of the elements in a sorted set, then the values in the sorted set are ordered lexicographically, that is, by alphanumeric ordering. This characteristic can be easily exploited as an easy way to order text strings in alphabetical order. We can demonstrate this feature as follows: first we'll add seven colors to a sorted set called colors:

```
127.0.0.1:6379> ZADD colors 0 red 0 blue 0 green 0 orange 0 yellow 0
purple 0 pink
```

Now, we can use the ZRANGE command to extract the colors in alphabetical order:

```
127.0.0.1:6379> ZRANGE colors 0 -1
1) "blue"
2) "green"
3) "orange"
4) "pink"
5) "purple"
6) "red"
7) "yellow"
```

With the ZREVRANGE command, we reverse retrieve our values in a reverse alphabetical order:

```
127.0.0.1:6379> ZREVRANGE colors 0 -1
1) "yellow"
2) "red"
3) "purple"
4) "pink"
5) "orange"
6) "green"
7) "blue"
```

In either case, in the colors sorted set, all scores are set to the same value as demonstrated with a ZREVRANGE command with the keyword WITHSCORES as follows:

```
127.0.0.1:6379> ZREVRANGE colors 0 -1 WITHSCORES
1)  "yellow"
2)  "0"
3)  "red"
4)  "0"
5)  "purple"
6)  "0"
7)  "pink"
8)  "0"
9)  "orange"
10) "0"
11) "green"
12) "0"
13) "blue"
14) "0"
```

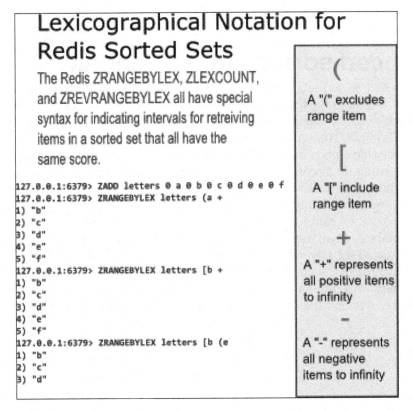

Lexicographical Notation for Redis Sorted Sets

The Redis ZRANGEBYLEX, ZLEXCOUNT, and ZREVRANGEBYLEX all have special syntax for indicating intervals for retreiving items in a sorted set that all have the same score.

```
127.0.0.1:6379> ZADD letters 0 a 0 b 0 c 0 d 0 e 0 f
127.0.0.1:6379> ZRANGEBYLEX letters (a +
1) "b"
2) "c"
3) "d"
4) "e"
5) "f"
127.0.0.1:6379> ZRANGEBYLEX letters [b +
1) "b"
2) "c"
3) "d"
4) "e"
5) "f"
127.0.0.1:6379> ZRANGEBYLEX letters [b (e
1) "b"
2) "c"
3) "d"
```

(
A "(" excludes range item

[
A "[" include range item

+
A "+" represents all positive items to infinity

—
A "-" represents all negative items to infinity

Redis also provides specific commands to retrieve elements in a lexicographical order through the LRANGEBYLEX and LREVRANGEBYLEX commands introduced in Redis 2.8. These commands allow us to specify the start and the end of a sorted set through a special syntax. The (character before a character string will exclude that value, while the [will include it. Also, using a + is shorthand for all positive strings and - for all negative strings. The following commands using the previous colors sorted set can help illustrate these differences:

```
127.0.0.1:6379> ZRANGEBYLEX colors (b [p
1) "blue"
2) "green"
3) "orange"
127.0.0.1:6379> ZRANGEBYLEX colors - +
1) "blue"
2) "green"
3) "orange"
4) "pink"
5) "purple"
6) "red"
7) "yellow"
```

Advanced sorted set operations

Similarly to sets, sorted sets in Redis support the set operations of union and intersection, although the time complexity of these operations for sorted sets is worse than for sets. Another problem with the sorted set operations is that when using a Redis cluster, union and intersection operations can only be used when the sorted set keys have been sharded to the same hash slot and run on the same node. The ZINTERSTORE Redis command has a time complexity of $O(nk)+O(mlog(m))$, where n is the size of the smallest sorted set; k, the total number of sorted sets being intersected, and m, the number of elements in the resulting final sorted set. Likewise, for the ZUNIONSTORE command, the time complexity is $O(n)+O(M log(M))$ with n being the total size of all the sorted sets and m being the total number of elements in the final sorted set. Given the characteristics of sorted sets, the additional time required for these two set operations may be an acceptable trade-off. It is good to keep in mind this difference in performance between large sets and sorted sets irrespective of whether the data and your requirements require ordering or not.

Bitstrings and bit operations

Specialized uses of Redis strings with the corresponding commands allow for the use of memory-efficient data structures in Redis for a comparatively small number of bits, and depending on your use case and data, using sets or hashes would offer better performance. In `bitstrings`, 8 bits are stored per byte, with the first bit at position 0 being the significant one that is set to either 0 or 1. The maximum size for Redis bitstrings is 512 MB, the same limitation for all Redis keys and values.

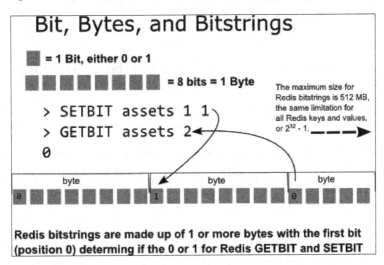

One reason that makes a bitstring so efficient and fast is that most of its commands are the O(1) or O(n) operations. With `SETBIT` and `GETBIT`, bits are either set to 0 or 1 or the value retrieved by both O(1) operations and the use of a bitstring to store the binary information across a range of sequential values is extremely fast. For the `BITOP`, `BITPOS`, and `BITCOUNT` commands, the time complexity is O(n) but offers power semantics for using `bitstrings`.

A common use case for bitstrings is storing data that can be represented as a Boolean yes/no, as a zero or one, across a range of sequential keys. As first explained in a blog post about creating an operational dashboard using Redis 4, storing usage information by month, day, or even hour can be accomplished in a very efficient manner by using a general usage Redis key. For example, if you wanted to track the daily usage on a website, you could start with a simple customer: pattern that stores a username, hashed password, and e-mail address for each customer, as follows:

```
127.0.0.1:6379> INCR global:customer
2445
127.0.0.1:6379> HMSET customer:2445 username mmaxwell password
'49fdb34f64be0a29af77ae77370a77232c3d6c37' email
mmaxwell@gmail.com
```

Assuming that the customer: counter starts at zero, customer mmaxwell is the 2445th consecutive customer. Now, to record when mmaxwell visits our website on February 11, 2016, we would set the 2445 byte in the 2016/02/11:usage bitstring as one as follows:

```
127.0.0.1:6379> SETBIT 2016/02/11:usage 2445 1
```

If we wanted to see whether customer mmaxwell visited our website on that day, we can retrieve the bit stored at 2445 with the GETBIT command as follows:

```
127.0.0.1:6379> GETBIT 2016/02/11:usage 2445
(integer) 1
```

Finding the daily customer count on the website for February 11 is easily accomplished through the BITCOUNT command as follows:

```
127.0.0.1:6379> BITCOUNT 2016/02/11:usage
(integer) 365
```

On that date in February, we had 365 unique customer visits. Assuming that we are tracking customer usage on a daily basis, we can use the BITOP command with the OR operations to generate the usage across multiple bitstrings, which is then stored in a new key as follows:

```
127.0.0.1:6379> BITOP OR 2016/02/week2:usage 2016/02/07:usage
2016/02/08:usage 2016/02/09:usage 2016/02/10:usage 2016/02/11:usage
2016/02/12:usage 2016/02/13:usage
127.0.0.1:6379> BITCOUNT 2016/02/week2:usage
(integer) 1834
```

To calculate a monthly total that is stored in a new key of 2016/02:usage, you can then execute a second BITOP on all four weekly usage keys:

```
127.0.0.1:6379> BITOP OR 2016/02:usage 2016/02/week1:usage 2016/02/
week2:usage 2016/02/week3:usage 2016/02/week4:usage
(integer) 306
127.0.0.1:6379> BITCOUNT 2016/02:usage
(integer) 6893
```

Finally, a yearly count for the entire website can be accomplished with another BITOP OR operation on all 12 monthly bitstrings:

```
127.0.0.1:6379> BITOP OR 2016:usage 2016/01:usage 2016/02:usage
2016/03:usage 2016/04:usage 2016/05:usage 2016/06:usage 2016/07:usage
2016/08:usage 2016/09:usage 2016/10:usage 2016/11:usage 2016/12:usage
(integer) 306
127.0.0.1:6379> BITCOUNT 2016:usage
(integer) 73190
```

HyperLogLogs

The newest Redis data type is a probabilistic data structure that provides an estimated count of unique items in a collection. Under typical or normal situations, to get a unique count of a collection's items requires an amount of memory that is equal to the number of items or at least a time complexity of $O(n)$. Why? To ensure that no items are double-counted if they are duplicated in the collection, the algorithm must keep a record of each item for comparison with any new items. This amount of overhead becomes quite large and expensive to calculate as the size of the collections increases in the order of millions of items. In contrast, storing unique elements in a HyperLogLog structure computes and stores an estimate of the size of the set as a probability instead of the actual value with a relatively small error rate of less than 1%. Adding one or more elements to a HyperLogLog with the PFADD command is an $O(1)$ operation, while retrieving the count of unique items with a PFCOUNT command on a single HyperLogLog is also an $O(1)$ operation. With the PFCOUNT command, you can also calculate the count for multiple HyperLogLogs, but the performance of PFCOUNT is $O(n)$ with n being the total number of keys.

To see the difference in performance between a set and a HyperLogLog, consider an example where you have over 50,000 unique customers that are constantly being added to and subtracted from by your enterprise CRM system. Storing the keys for each of the 50,000 customers in a set can be easily accomplished through the following commands:

```
127.0.0.1:6379> SADD customers-set customer:1 customer:2 customer:3 ...
customer:52111
127.0.0.1:6379> SCARD customers-set
 (integer) 52411
```

Execute the same operations using a HyperLogLog as follows:

```
127.0.0.1:6379> PFADD customers-hll customer:1 customer:2 customer:3
... customer:52111
127.0.0.1:6379> PFCOUNT customers-hll
(integer) 52213
```

We can see from this example that the HyperLogLog estimate of 52213 differs from the actual count in the Redis set of 52411 by 198, a percentage difference of .004% well under the worst-case HyperLogLog count estimate of .01%. Your results will vary depending on the size of your data, but if you do not need an exact count of unique items and a good enough estimate will work for your application, the HyperLogLog is a new tool in your Redis solution.

Summary

Any Redis application has two critical parts, namely the keys and the values that are stored in these keys. For most Redis solutions, the design of your key names is important whether you manually design a schema or use a Redis object mapper that hides the details behind a client layer of abstraction. The performance of all Redis's data structures and the corresponding write and access commands is evaluated using the big O notation, a method used in computer science to calculate the worst-case performance for an algorithm when this algorithm is given an increasing number of inputs. Using the big O notation, we can estimate the effectiveness of our Redis-based solutions by summarizing the performance of all our Redis commands in a function, method, or class in our client code. Next, we carry out a basic complexity analysis of Redis's strings, hashes, lists, and sets, while expanding on some advanced usage of Redis's sorted sets, `bitstrings`, and `HyperLogLogs` data structures.

The next chapter will focus on a critical aspect of any Redis project, the need to optimize, improve, and manage your available memory for your Redis database. We'll expand upon how constructing your Redis key schema can impact your memory usage both positively and negatively, and we'll also expand on the various key expiration options that are available in Redis and how Redis's various caching approaches including **Least Recently Used** (**LRU**) can help keep the size of your Redis database within the constraints of your environment.

3
Managing RAM – Tips and Techniques for Redis Memory Management

More than most data storage technologies, the effective usage of Redis requires an understanding of the computer's random access memory or RAM, as well as the network and disk latency to track down performance bottlenecks, resource planning, and allocation. With Redis loading all of your data into RAM, your application's writes and reads are constrained by the technical limits of your hardware and network connections then on slower hard disk read/writes operations used by more traditional relational databases like Oracle or MySQL. As we saw in the last chapter, the time complexity of your software and how it interacts with Redis becomes more important as a target for suitable optimization. This chapter starts with a review of a few of the memory-related directives that can be set in the `redis.conf` file for configuring Redis.

Next in this chapter on optimizing memory, is a section on memory considerations that are to be made when using Redis's master-slave replication followed by the counter-intuitive topic of using a 32-bit version of Redis server for memory maximization. After examining the options for expiring keys in Redis, we'll then look at the related topic of the different policies for evicting keys that Redis can use to handle the critical use case when it runs out of memory. A popular approach is the **Less Recently Used** (**LRU**) caching algorithm used to evict keys. After using the LRU approach, we'll experiment with the special, memory-efficient data structures that Redis uses for smaller hashes, lists, sets, and sorted sets. This lends itself well to a discussion of a Redis memory-saving key-value usage pattern for using hashes in your Redis-based application. We'll finish the chapter with a short discussion about the hardware and network latency issues and how Redis can partially compensate for these latencies by adjusting memory usage.

Configuring Redis

Running a memory-efficient Redis database starts with understanding all of the memory related directives that can be set in the `redis.conf` configuration file. The `redis.conf` file provides a rich, inline documentation for most directives, making the sometimes complex options for memory optimization easier to understand, change, and test. Most of the Redis configuration directives can also be set at runtime using the `CONFIG SET` command.

For LRU related configuration directives are part of the LRU key evictions topic in this chapter.

The first configuration directive that we'll examine that has memory trade-offs is the `rdbchecksumdirective`, with the default value of yes places a cyclic redundancy check 65-bit (CRC64) checksum at the end of an RDB snapshot file as an anti-corruption measure. Performing an RDB snapshot with this CRC64 checksum imposes a 10% increase in memory usage when Redis spawns a child process that saves the snapshot in the disk.

The second configuration directive we'll examine is `activerehashing`. In `activerehashing`, the main Redis hash table, which links the main keys to values, is rehashed once per 100 milliseconds if this directive is set to yes. This rehashing process releases the deleted keys' memory for use by the operating system, with minimal impact on client connections as the `activehashing` occurs during downtime. As recommended in the `redis.conf` comments, `activerehashing` should be set to no if you have hard latency requirements, or if the Redis server needs to support a high level of concurrent clients that could be delayed during active rehashing.

Master-slave

An excellent feature of Redis is the ability to scale and offer a high degree of reliability through the use of master-slave replication. In this setup, a Redis instance can be switched to a slave through the slave-of directive, which then allows the slave instance to duplicate the data of another running Redis instance designated as the master instance. Memory and latency — both hardware and network — directly impact the performance of both the master and any attached slaves. Improving Redis redundancy when used in the master-slave mode is about trade-offs that you can make between the memory, hardware, and network traffic depending on your circumstances.

The `repl-disable-tcp-nodelay` directive is one option for a better handling of the network traffic congestion between the master and slave Redis instances. By making the trade-off between denser data sync between the Master and instances and less network traffic, this replication can improve the network performance in high traffic situations.

32-bit Redis

In the official documentation on Redis.io's website on Memory Optimization3, one suggestion is to compile Redis in 32-bit mode instead of using the default 64 bit instance.

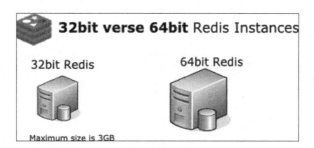

Using a 32-bit Redis instances for datasets under 3 GB is smaller than the same dataset in the 64-bit version of Redis. This can be illustrated in the following tests. We'll launch two Redis instances, `INSTANCE64` and `INSTANCE32`. We'll create a quick Python function, `test_redis_32k_65k`, in a Python command line to create 100,000 keys using a UUID as a string value:

```
>>>def test_redis_32k_64k():
  for i in range(100000):
    key = "uuid:{}".format(i)
    value = uuid.uuid4()
    INSTANCE32.set(key, value)
    INSTANCE64.set(key, value)
>>> test_redis_32k_64k()
```

To see what happens to the memory usage of 32-bit verses 64-bit type of Redis instances, we'll compare the output of two Redis-cli sessions by connecting to each instance.

For the Redis 32-bit instance:

```
127.0.0.1:6378> INFO memory
# Memory
used_memory:12447072
used_memory_human:11.87M
used_memory_rss:13733888
used_memory_peak:12447072
used_memory_peak_human:11.87M
For the Redis 64-bit instance:
127.0.0.1:6379> INFO memory
# Memory
used_memory:14871888
used_memory_human:14.18M
used_memory_rss:16805888
used_memory_peak:14871888
used_memory_peak_human:14.18M
```

About the INFO memory

Each value of the INFO memory means the following:

- `used_memory`: Number of bytes allocated by libc, jemalloc, or other allocated used by Redis

- `used_memory_human`: Previous value formatted for human consumption in megabytes

- `used_memory_rss`: **Resident set size (rss)** is the memory allocated as seen by the OS and reported by UNIX tools like `top`

- `used_memory_peak`: Maximum memory in bytes used by Redis

- `used_memory_peak_human`: Previous value formatted for humans in megabytes

- `used_memory_lua`: Bytes used by Redis's Lua subsystem

- `mem_fragmentation_ratio`: Ratio between `used_memory_rss` and `used_memory`

- `mem_allocator`: The allocator that was used for Redis during compilation

As we can see, for this simple test using identical data, the 32-bit Redis instance uses 11.87 megabytes of RAM, while the 64-bit Redis instance uses 14.18 megabytes, which is a relatively small difference attributable to the small sample of 100,000 keys and the use of the Redis string data structure. To help illustrate the trade-offs and possible issues between using 32-bit versus 64-bit Redis versions, we will compare the results of storing 1 million integers, floats, and strings using the Redis string, list, hash, and set data structures in the following table:

	32-bit Peak Memory	**64-bit Peak Memory**	**Difference**
SET command sets 1,000,000 keys with an integer of 1	35.19 megabytes	54.79 megabytes	19.6 megabytes or 36% more for 64-bit
SET command 1,000,000 keys with a float of 3.142	65.71 megabytes	85.26 megabytes	19.55 megabytes or 22% more for 64-bit
SET command 1,000,000 keys with a value of 385e7bc8-0075-4922-9dfa-a0b2592d5c78	96.23 megabytes	115.77 megabytes	19.54 megabytes or 16% more for 64-bit

If your application uses integer sets, the 32-bit memory savings can be significant as long as your overall memory requirements do not exceed the 4GB maximum size limit. As the sizes and types of the values are stored, the memory savings decrease significantly as a percentage difference between the 32-bit and 64-bit Redis variations. For string-heavy applications that use sets, 64-bit Redis may be a better choice because of the additional space per bit (32 vs. 64) along with more efficient encoding of strings that is available with the 64-bit version.

For the hash data structure the differences between the 32-bit and 64-bit Redis instances are not as great, as can be seen by the following table:

	32-bit Peak Memory	**64-bit Peak Memory**	**Difference**
Add 1,000,000 fields to a Redis hash with the field values set to 1	50.15 megabytes	69.69 megabytes	19.54 megabytes or 28% more for 64-bit
Add 1,000,000 fields to a Redis hash with all field values set to 3.142	80.68 megabytes	100.24 megabytes	19.56 megabytes or 19% more for 64-bit

	32-bit Peak Memory	64-bit Peak Memory	Difference
Add 1,000,000 fields to a Redis hash with all field values set to `385e7bc8-0075-4922-9dfa-a0b2592d5c78`	111.18 megabytes	130.74 megabytes	19.56 megabytes or 14.9% more for 64-bit

For Redis hashes, the overhead between 32-bit and 64-bit is roughly consistent at 19.56 regardless of what type of value is stored as the field values.

Running this same test with a Redis list has the following peak memory results:

	32-bit Peak Memory	64-bit Peak Memory	Difference
Add 1,000,000 consecutive integers as values to a Redis list	46.15 megabytes	61.69 megabytes	15.54 megabytes or 25% more for 64-bit
Add 1,000,000 consecutive floats to a Redis list	46.45 megabytes	77.24 megabytes	30.78 megabytes or 39.8% more for 64-bit
Adds the string 385e7bc8-0075-4922-9dfa-a0b2592d5c78 1,000,000 times to a Redis list	76.97 megabytes	92.51 megabytes	15.54 megabytes or 16.8% more for 64-bit

For Redis lists in the 32-bit variant, storing integers and floats is significantly better for lists that can be stored within the overall 32-bit limitations. Strings show the least amount of improvement between 32 and 64-bit when stored in lists.

We'll now run our three tests using a Redis set to compare performance with a 32-bit and 64-bit instance:

	32-bit Peak Memory	64-bit Peak Memory	Difference
Add 1,000,000 integers to a Redis set	50.15megabytes	69.71 megabytes	19.56 megabytes or 28% more for 64-bit
Add 1,000,000 floats to a Redis set	50.45 megabytes	85.24 megabytes	34.79 megabytes or 40.8% more for 64-bit
Add 1,000,000 unique UUID strings to a Redis set	80.97 megabytes	108.53 megabytes	27.56 megabytes or 25.39% more for 64-bit

There are some considerations and cautions about using 32-bit instances.The use of 32-bit Redis has not been as widely deployed and tested among the Redis user base and therefore may have undiscovered bugs compared to the 64-bit version. Another caution is that bit-operations such as BITOP and BITCOUNT have been optimized for Redis 64-bit versions and therefore are less efficient. Finally, setting the maxmemory parameter—we will go into much more in-depth later in this chapter on caching—can be more difficult with 32-bit version of Redis because communication, master/slave replication, I/O buffers all can contribute to Redis randomly crashing if the maxmemory is set too close to the 4 GB maximum for the 32-bit variant.

Key expiration

A simple and robust method to keep your Redis database from exceeding it's available memory is to set timeouts on keys that will be automatically evicted after the key's timeout expires. If your application does not need to retain stale or old data, having an effective expiration strategy for your key-space will keep the memory demands for your Redis application more manageable. A popular Redis design pattern using key expiration is to save expired or evicted data into another relational SQL database or other more disk-based NoSQL platform like MongoDB.

There are some aspects of key expiration that you should be aware of when implementing this feature in your application. First, when you call a timeout with the EXPIRE command on a key, the timeout can only be cleared if you delete the key or replace the key. Any subsequent commands that alter the value do not change or clear out any timeouts you set. Let's create a scenario where you are programming an application that brews three types of teas. Each tea has a different brew time. Our Redis key schema will use a forward slash delimiter instead of a colon as a convenient shorthand if we want to add a REST service later, and we will use an incremental unique counter. Each box will be an integer set for the total number of tea bags. Finally, when the application brews a tea bag, we will pop a random integer from the box, use that for the key counter, and then set an expiration timeout of the length of the recommended time. When the tea bag key is evicted, the application stops the brewing. We can now model and test this use case with the following Python function that takes an instance of the Python client, a name, brew time, and box size, and returns the newly created tea_key for further use in our application:

```
def create_tea(datastore, name, time, size):
    # Increment and save global counter
    tea_counter = datastore.incr("global/teas")
    tea_key = "tea/{}".format(tea_counter)
    datastore.hmset(tea_key,
        {"name": name,
```

```
            "brew-time": time,
            "box-size": size})
        return tea_key
```

Now, we'll import the Redis module for Python, instantiate a `StrictRedis` class, and create three teas as hashes from a Python shell with this function:

```
>>> import redis
>>>tea_datastore = redis.StrictRedis()
>>>earl_grey = create_tea(tea_datastore, "Earl Grey", 5, 15)
>>>earl_grey
'tea/1'
>>>tea_datastore.hgetall(earl_grey)
{b'box-size': b'15', b'name': b'Earl Grey', b'brew-time': b'5'}
>>>lavender_mint = create_tea(tea_datastore, "Lavender Mint", 2,
20)
>>>peppermint_punch = create_tea(tea_datastore, "Peppermint Punch",
4, 10)"""""
```

To add individual tea bags to the first box of tea for each of the tea types, we'll create a second function:

```
    def add_box_of_tea(datastore, tea_key, number):
      box_counter = datastore.incr("global/{}/boxes".format(tea_key))
      tea_box_key = "{}/box/{}".format(tea_key, box_counter)
      datastore.sadd(tea_box_key, *range(1,number+1))
      return tea_box_key
```

We'll add the first box for each type of tea from our Python shell, as shown here:

```
>>>earl_grey_box_1 = add_box_of_tea(tea_datastore, earl_grey, 15)
>>> earl_grey_box_1
'tea/1/box/1'
>>>tea_datastore.smembers(earl_grey_box_1)
{b'2', b'1', b'3', b'5', b'4', b'13', b'10', b'11', b'14', b'7',
b'12', b'15', b'6', b'8', b'9'}
>>>lavender_mint_box_1 = add_box_of_tea(tea_datastore,
lavender_mint, 15)
>>>tea_datastore.scard(lavender_mint_box_1)
15
>>>peppermint_punch_box_1 =  add_box_of_tea(tea_datastore,
```

```
peppermint_punch, 10)
>>>tea_datastore.scard(peppermint_punch_box_1)
10
```

Now, we will add a third function that takes the Redis instance and tea box key, brews a random tea bag from each box by setting an expiration time equal to the number of seconds of brew time for that type of tea, adds the tea bag key to a brewing set, and finally returns the `tea_bag_key`:

```
defstart_brew(datastore, tea_box_key):
  tea_box = tea_box_key.split("/box")[0]
  # Brew time is in minutes, we multiple by 60 for expire in
    seconds
  expire_time = int(datastore.hget(tea_box, "brew-time"))*60
  tea_bag_number = datastore.spop(tea_box_key)
  tea_bag_key = "{}/bag/{}".format(tea_box_key,
    tea_bag_number.decode())
  datastore.set(tea_bag_key, "brew")
  datastore.expire(tea_bag_key, expire_time)
  datastore.sadd("brewing", tea_bag_key)
  return tea_bag_key""""""
```

Calling the `start_brew` function three times, once for each type of tea, creates three tea bag keys and sets the expiration time depending on the type of tea:

Our final Python function iterates through all of the tea bags in the brewing set, polls the remaining time for each tea bag with the TTL command, and then either prints a message with the remaining time until the tea is finished brewing or a message that the tea is ready to drink depending on whether there is any remaining time before the tea bag key expires in our tea datastore:

```
def poll_brewing(datastore):
  active_tea_bags = datastore.smembers("brewing")
  for tea_bag in active_tea_bags:
    time_left = datastore.ttl(tea_bag)
    if time_left> 0:
      print("{} seconds left for {}".format(time_left,
          tea_bag))
    else:
      print("{} Ready to Drink!".format(tea_bag))
      # Remove expired tea bag from brewing set
      datastore.srem("brewing", tea_bag)
```

We will call the `poll_brewing` Python function three times, once near the beginning:

```
>>>poll_brewing(tea_datastore)
80 seconds left for b'tea/2/box/1/bag/5'
215 seconds left for b'tea/3/box/1/bag/3'
243 seconds left for b'tea/1/box/1/bag/5'
```

Again in approximately 60 seconds:

```
>>>poll_brewing(tea_datastore)
22 seconds left for b'tea/2/box/1/bag/5'
157 seconds left for b'tea/3/box/1/bag/3'
185 seconds left for b'tea/1/box/1/bag/5'
```

And finally at around 90 seconds:

```
>>>poll_brewing(tea_datastore)
b'tea/2/box/1/bag/5' Ready to Drink!
124 seconds left for b'tea/3/box/1/bag/3'
152 seconds left for b'tea/1/box/1/bag/5'
```

If the value is altered for a key that has a timeout, for example, using the APPEND command for a Redis string, the timeout still continues. From a Redis-cli session, we can replicate setting a string value to a tea bag with a timeout of 300 seconds:

```
127.0.0.1:6379> SET tea/1/box1/bag/8 brew
OK
127.0.0.1:6379> EXPIRE tea/1/box1/bag/8 300
(integer) 1
```

First we'll check to see what is the remaining TTL for `tea/1/box/1/bag/8`, and then we will add an additional text to the value held at the key, and check the TTL again, as shown here:

```
127.0.0.1:6379> TTL tea/1/box1/bag/8
(integer) 288
127.0.0.1:6379> APPEND tea/1/box1/bag/8 ing
(integer) 7
127.0.0.1:6379> GET tea/1/box1/bag/8
"brewing"
127.0.0.1:6379> TTL tea/1/box1/bag/8
(integer) 259
```

If SET or GETSET is called on a key with a set timeout, the timeout will be cleared and then the key won't be evicted from the database. So, if SET is called on the tea/3/ box/1/bag/3 key before it has expired, when the TTL is called on the tea/3/box/1/ bag/3 key, Redis responds back with -1. This is a default message for the keys that do not have a timeout.

```
127.0.0.1:6379> TTL tea/3/box1/bag/3
(integer) 225
127.0.0.1:6379> SET tea/3/box1/bag/3 brew
OK
127.0.0.1:6379> TTL tea/3/box1/bag/3
(integer) -1
```

So far, we have used the TTL as a polling mechanism to retrieve the value of any remaining timeouts that have been set on the keys we are interested in. Using client-side polling does have disadvantages, one of which is that if a delay occurs between the client-code and the server, our tea could become over-brewed. Redis offers a notification mechanism based on Pub/Sub that can be set up to send a message when a key expires, functionality that we'll explore in a later chapter on Redis messaging.

You can also use the PERSIST command to clear out a timeout that has been set on an existing key. Finally, calling EXPIRE on a key that has had a previous timeout set will clear out and set a new timeout.

```
127.0.0.1:6379> TTL tea/1/box1/bag/8
(integer) 118
127.0.0.1:6379> EXPIRE tea/1/box1/bag/8 300
(integer) 1
127.0.0.1:6379> TTL tea/1/box1/bag/8
(integer) 295
```

Even though this example is contrived, it should illustrate the basic operations of Redis key expiration. Redis sets the TTL with EXPIRE using an absolute UNIX timestamp from the underlying operating system. If you set a timeout on a key but then shut down the Redis database with the data saved into a snapshot, restarting the Redis database after the timeout has expired will evict the key automatically. Redis uses two methods for doing the actual expiration in the key-space, the first is if the key is actively requested by a client, and the second method is a probabilistic algorithm that randomly tests 20 keys with an associated expiration time stamp and deletes all of the keys in the sample that have expired.

In this chapter's next topic, we will take this knowledge about key expiration and see how Redis can modify it's behavior when it reaches its maximum allowed memory and keys within the key-space have timeouts set.

LRU key evictions

To demonstrate the various options for key evictions in Redis, we'll start with a simple example by setting a small memory Redis instance that the maxmemory directive sets to 1 megabyte. The maxmemory directive allows you set a hard upper bound on the amount of memory that is available to a running Redis instance. Echoing the warnings in the default redis.conf file, setting the maxmemory has ramifications that we'll now see. To start with, we'll just create a very simple Redis key schema, that of generating and storing a unique id for a web application. After connecting to a Redis instance through Redis-cli, we'll run the following commands to clear out our datastore and then set the maxmemory directive to 1 megabyte:

```
127.0.0.1:6379> FLUSHALL
OK
127.0.0.1:6379>CONFIG SET maxmemory1mb
OK
```

Next, we'll implement a function that takes a Redis instance, increments a global uuid, and then generates a random UUID from the standard uuid Python module. The add_id function code in Python is presented as follows in this code snippet:

```
>>> import uuid
>>>def add_id(redis_instance):
redis_key = "uuid:{}".format(redis_instance.incr("global:uuid"))
redis_instance.set(redis_key, uuid.uuid4())
```

When Redis runs out of memory, the default behavior - the noeviction policy - is illustrated in the following image:

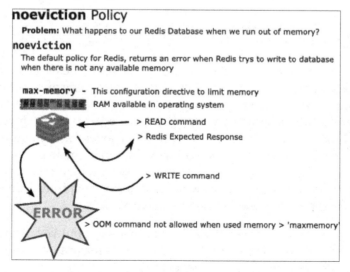

The default `maxmemory-policy` policy is noeviction. In noeviction, no keys are set to expire and any write commands will cause a Redis error if there is no available memory to Redis. To confirm that our directives are set for experiment, we will first check whether the `maxmemory` and `maxmemory-policy` are set to 1 megabyte and a noeviction policy respectivelythat is confirmed by checking the values of this directives by running the following CONFIG GET commands in our Redis-cli session:

```
127.0.0.1:6379>CONFIG GET maxmemory

1) "maxmemory"

2) "1048576"

127.0.0.1:6379>CONFIG GET maxmemory-policy

1) "maxmemory-policy"

2) "noeviction"
```

To test the `noeviction` policy, we will run a loop in Python until we receive an error, as shown here:

```
>>> while 1:

add_id(local_redis)
```

Quickly, we receive an exception from the Redis client, as follows: `redis.exceptions.ResponseError`, OOM command not allowed when used memory > 'maxmemory'.

Our `while` loop cycles through 181 times before we hit the 1 megabyte memory limit, with our counter value set at `181`. Now to check the state of our datastore by running the `INFO memory` command from the our Redis-cli and looking at the `used_memory_peak_human`:

```
127.0.0.1:6379> INFO memory

# Memory

used_memory:1048608

used_memory_human:1.00M

used_memory_rss:1769472

used_memory_peak:1048608

used_memory_peak_human:1.00M

used_memory_lua:35840

mem_fragmentation_ratio:1.69

mem_allocator:libc
```

Now, if we retrieve the global `uuid` counter key we set in the `add_id` function, we can see that we have 181 UUID stored in our 1 megabyte datastore which is the same value as our counter variable we incrementally increase by one in our loop:

```
127.0.0.1:6379> GET global:uuid"181"
127.0.0.1:6379> GET uuid:181
"1930a94e-38ff-4dbd-8885-eb44aed96122"
```

From the Redis-cli, we'll test the `noeviction` policy by trying to increment a second variable, like `tmp:1`, this is the error we receive:

```
127.0.0.1:6379> INCR tmp:1
(error) OOM command not allowed when used memory > 'maxmemory'.
```

When Redis tries to execute any write (`SET`, `INCR`, `SADD`, `HSET`, and so on) or other commands that increase memory usage under no available memory conditions, you will receive an error similar to the one seen in the preceding snippet. The next policy we'll examine is how Redis handles LRU when one or more keys have a timeout set. The first expiration LRU policy named `volatile-lru` evicts the less recently used keys but only if those keys have an expiration timeout set with `EXPIRE SET`. If there are not any keys that are eligible for eviction, Redis will return the same exception when trying to write as in the `noeviction` policy.

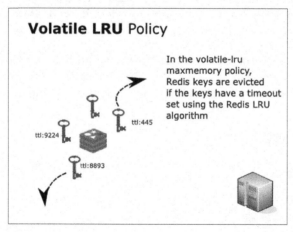

Volatile LRU Policy

In the volatile-lru maxmemory policy, Redis keys are evicted if the keys have a timeout set using the Redis LRU algorithm

ttl:445
ttl:9224
ttl:8893

An important note when using this policy is that when Redis runs out of memory it will start deleting keys that have an expiration timeout even if there is time remaining for the key. To test the `volatile-lru` policy, we'll flush our Redis instance. Running the same loop without setting an eviction time on any of the keys results in the same behavior as the `noeviction` policy:

```
127.0.0.1:6379>FLUSHDB
127.0.0.1:6379>CONFIG SET maxmemory-policy volatile-lru
```

```
127.0.0.1:6379> GET global:uuid
"181"
127.0.0.1:6379> INFO memory
# Memory
used_memory:1048608
used_memory_human:1.00M
.

.
```

Now, we're going to create a second function based upon the add_id and use a new add_id_expire function to set an expiration time of 300 seconds on the first 75 keys we create.

```
>>>def add_id_expire(redis_instance):
        count = redis_instance.incr("global:uuid")
redis_key = "uuid:{}".format(count)
redis_instance.set(redis_key, uuid.uuid4())
        if count <= 75:
redis_instance.expire(redis_key, 300)
```

Resetting our counter variable to zero and running our test again, we iterate through the loop 238 times, 57 more times than when we ran our Redis instance with the noeviction policy. The loop results are confirmed when we retrieve our global increment variable global:uuid, check if uuid:1 and uuid:75 still exist, and check if uuid:76 and uuid:238 exist with uuids in our datastore:

```
127.0.0.1:6379> GET global:uuid
"238"
127.0.0.1:6379> GET uuid:1
(nil)
127.0.0.1:6379> GET uuid:75
(nil)
127.0.0.1:6379> GET uuid:76
"9922e314-17f8-4630-a709-07a3c8a8019c"
127.0.0.1:6379> GET uuid:238
"1a1318ae-57b6-4a4a-a366-2727033a315d"
```

As we expected, the keys `uuid:1` to `uuid:75` don't exist and during the loop an additional 57 keys were created in the database compared to the default `noeviction` policy. We can also see that we didn't create an additional 75 uuids only 57 more. This is likely due to the fact that we ran out of memory after all of the keys with expiration times had been evicted as we tried to add more keys without accounting for the memory overhead needed for eviction.

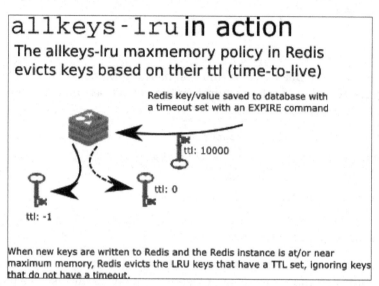

Now, the next LRU-style eviction policy, `allkeys-lru`, is recommended if you expect to add a power-law access `pattern1` to your Redis database. The `allkeys-lrupolicy` is a good initial choice if you are unsure of what eviction policy to use with this important caveat. The `allkeys-lru` can delete any key in Redis and there is no way to restrict which keys are to be deleted. If your application needs to persist some Redis keys (say for configuration or reference look-up) don't use the `allkeys-lru` policy!

To test `allkeys-lru`, we'll flush the data from our Redis instance, set the `maxmemory-policy` directive, and then run our original `add_id` function.

Running our experiment in Python with an infinite while loop using the original `add_id` function, we went through hundreds of thousands of iterations (615,094) before running out of memory. Running an `INFO stats` command in the Redis cli and looking at the number of evicted keys in with the `INFO stats`, we see the following:

```
127.0.0.1:6379> INFO stats
# Stats
total_connections_received:2
```

```
total_commands_processed:1230193
```

    .

    .

```
evicted_keys:264524
```

In the `allkeys-lru` policy, Redis was able to process 1,230,193 commands by evicting 264,524. Since all of our keys in this loop have the same usage (that is, we are not retrieving any of the keys after our initial SET command), the Redis estimation of LRU for the keys was consistent across the datastore. For our experiment, the `allkeys-lru eviction` policy was effective in freeing memory for additional keys by evicting stale keys in our datastore. To further test the `allkeys-lru` policy, we will restart our experiment and only iterate 200 times through our loop (more than our test of the `noeviction` policy but less then our `volatile-lru test`). The following are the results of this iteration:

```
127.0.0.1:6379> GET global:uuid
"200"
127.0.0.1:6379> INFO stats
# Stats
total_connections_received:2
total_commands_processed:614
```

    .

    .

```
evicted_keys:24
```

In this test, the `allkeys-lru` policy evicted 24 keys, we created the full 200 keys as we would expect going through 200 iterations of our loop, but the problem is that we don't know which of the 200 keys were evicted. To determine the missing keys, we'll need to loop through all of our keys and test if the key exists or has been evicted. This can easily be accomplished with the following Python code snippet:

```python
>>> for i in range(1, 201):
        key = "uuid:{}".format(i)
        if not local_redis.exists(key):
            print(key)
```

Here is the output of this code snippet (your' results from running this code should vary from this list, if only slightly because of the probabilistic nature of Redis's LRU algorithm):

```
uuid:15
uuid:17
uuid:23
uuid:29
uuid:39
uuid:46
uuid:50
uuid:57
uuid:67
uuid:68
uuid:83
uuid:86
uuid:89
uuid:110
uuid:116
uuid:121
uuid:128
uuid:130
uuid:146
uuid:147
uuid:150
uuid:151
uuid:175
uuid:176
```

There are a couple of things to note about these evicted keys that illustrate the RedisLRU algorithm; first, the RedisLRU algorithm is not exact, as Redis does not automatically choose the best candidate key for eviction, the least used key, or the key with the earliest access date. Instead, Redis default behavior is take a sample of five keys and evict the least used of those five keys. Going back to the preceding list of evicted keys, we can see the results of this sampling strategy. If we want to increase the accuracy of the LRU algorithm, we can the change the `maxmemory-samples` directive in either `redis.conf` or during runtime with the `CONFIG SET maxmemory-samples` command. Increasing the sample size to 10 improves the performance of the RedisLRU so that it approaches a true LRU algorithm but with the side-effect of more CPU computation.

Decreasing the sample size to 3 reduces the accuracy of RedisLRU but with a corresponding increase in processing speed.

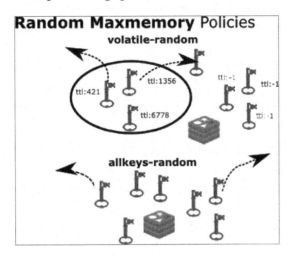

The next two maximum memory eviction policies—volatile-random and `allkeys-random`—mirror the `volatile-lru` and `allkeys-lru` policies but do not use the LRU algorithm. The volatile-random policy evicts a random key based on expiration status that have been set on any keys. The entire keyspace is open for eviction in the `allkeys-random` policy.

We can use both the `add_id` and `add_id_expire` functions to test these two policies. First we'll run through the volatile-random policy with our experiment using a modified version of the `add_id_expire` function that sets half of the Keys to an expiration time of 5 minutes, allowing us to compare the performance of the volatile-random policy to our other policies. Our results are different to the `volatile-lru` test when we created a total of 246 keys. Unlike the `volatile-lru` policy, we need to an **O(n)** operation to figure if a `uuid:1` through the last uuid key we created were evicted.

Running a sample run of 1000 iterations of the `add_id_expire` function results in the following performance:

```
127.0.0.1:6379> INFO stats
# Stats
total_connections_received:2
total_commands_processed:1805
.

.

expired_keys:0
evicted_keys:499
```

Notice that even though our `add_id_expire` function sets an expiration time on half of keys added to our Redis instance, the small size of our sample set was such that all of the keys were evicted before any of the keys expired under this test of the `volatile-lru` policy. Checking the state of our keyspace, we find the following:

```
127.0.0.1:6379> GET global:uuid
"652"
127.0.0.1:6379> GET uuid:1
(nil)
127.0.0.1:6379> DBSIZE
(integer) 153
127.0.0.1:6379> GET uuid:652
(nil)
127.0.0.1:6379> GET uuid:651
"e42ce917-efe9-4657-b2d6-cccd0f26b19c"
```

In this test of the `volatile-random` policy, we ran out of memory before we could complete the 1,000 iterations. During those 652 iterations – easily determined by our `GET global:uuid call` – of our test, we created and evicted 499 keys while retaining only 153 keys.

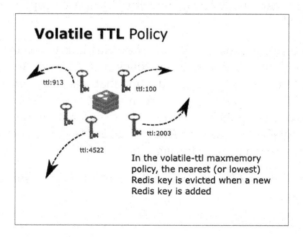

The last maximum memory policy is `volatile-ttl`. It is similar to `volatile-lru` but with the additional characteristic that Redis will try to evict those keys based on the **time to live** (TTL) of the key that is to be evicted from the Redis database.

Creating memory efficient Redis data structures

The following are some of the methods for memory optimization in Redis:

Small aggregate hashes, lists, sets, and sorted sets

For hashes, lists, and sorted sets, this special encoding is based on ziplist A Ziplist is described from `ziplist.c` as follows:

The ziplist is a specially encoded dually linked list that is designed to be very memory efficient. It stores both strings and integer values, where integers are encoded as actual integers instead of a series of characters. It allows push and pop operations on either side of the list in **O(1)** time. However, because every operation requires a reallocation of the memory used by the ziplist, the actual complexity is related to the amount of memory used by the `ziplist.2`.

Depending on the size, type, and contents of the data structure, the ziplist encoding offers significant memory savings for your Redis database. Redis dynamically switches between the ziplist and the default encoding for the data structure when the current limit for that Redis data type is reached. To see this switch in action, we'll create a Python function that displays this dynamic switch by printing the type of encoding and size for a hash key when its default threshold is met:

```
def dynamic_encoding_switch(instance):
  for i in range(515):
    instance.hset("test-hash", i, 1)
    if i> 510:
      debug = instance.debug_object("test-hash")
      print("Count: {} Length: {} Encoding: {}".format(i,
        debug.get('serializedlength'), debug.get('encoding')))
```

Running `dynamic_encoding_switch` results in the following output to our Python shell:

```
>>>dynamic_encoding_switch(local_redis)

Count: 511 Length: 2070 Encoding: ziplist

Count: 512 Length: 2439 Encoding: hashtable

Count: 513 Length: 2444 Encoding: hashtable

Count: 514 Length: 2449 Encoding: hashtable
```

Why does Redis dynamically re-encode the hash from a ziplist to a hash table in this case? This is because there is a trade-off between memory efficiency and performance. The ziplist implementation in Redis achieves it's small memory size by storing only three pieces of data per entry; the first is the length to the previous entry, the second is the length of the current entry, and the third is the stored data. This brevity comes at the cost of more computation (hence time) that is required for changing the size and retrieving the entry versus the larger linked-list based encodings that store additional pointers but is correspondingly faster in changing and retrieving at larger sizes.

For hashes, the `hash-max-ziplist-entries` directive sets the total number of fields that can be specially encoded as a ziplist with a default value of 512 fields. The `hash-max-ziplist-value` directive sets the maximum size before the hash is converted from a ziplist with a default size of 64. We can illustrate these two conditions with the following very simplistic examples.

To test the size difference between ziplist and linked list for hashes, let's spin up two identical instances of Redis. For our remaining tests in this chapter, we will keep our first instance's configuration directives using Redis's default values and modify the second instance's directives to force Redis to use the default encoding for each data type.

Alert

Be aware that if you're trying to improve the memory performance by adjusting the threshold values of sets, hashes, and lists with ziplist on an existing datastore, any pre-existing values will remain encoded in the original format. Changing these values' threshold values does not re-encode old values but only changes any new values that are added to Redis.

First, we'll set the `hash-max-ziplist-entries` to 0 for the second instance, create and populate a hash with 500 fields containing identical fields and integers values then compare the two using the `DEBUG OBJECT` command from the Redis-cli. for these two Redis hashes. First, we'll create a small Python function to create our hash:

```python
def plot_hashes(runs=500):
    reset()
    key = "test-hash"
INSTANCE2.config_set('hash-max-ziplist-entries', 0)
    run, zip_list, linked_list = [], [], []
    for i in range(runs):
        field = "f{}".format(i)
```

```
INSTANCE1.hset(key, field, i)
INSTANCE2.hset(key, field, i)
debug1 = INSTANCE1.debug_object(key)
zip_list.append(debug1.get("serializedlength"))
debug2 = INSTANCE2.debug_object(key)
linked_list.append(debug2.get("serializedlength"))
```

Now, we'll run our function and then examine the results of the `debug_object` command on `test-hash` for each object, as shown here:

```
>>>plot_hashes()
>>INSTANCE1.debug_object("test-hash").get("serializedlength")
3102
>>>INSTANCE2.debug_object("test-hash").get("serializedlength")
3764
```

If you compare the encoding size for these two identical hashes, you will find that the standard hashtable encoding for test-hash results in a serialized length of 3764 while the ziplist encoding for test-hash is 3102, a direct memory saving (when serialized) of 662 bytes. Graphing the results as presented in the following figure gives you only the memory savings but does not consider the additional computation time the ziplist encoding requires as the size of hash increases:

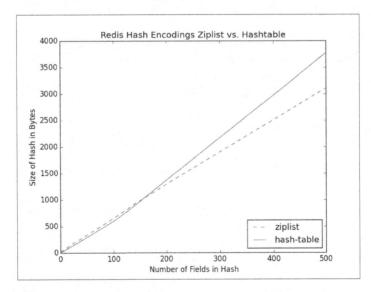

For lists, like hashes, the ziplist encoding is used for small lists with the thresholds being determined by the `list-max-ziplist-entries` and the `list-max-ziplist-value` with both directives having the same default values as the hash directives of 512 and 64 respectively. In the code file `small_types_tests.py`, there is a function that sets the `list-max-ziplist-value` to 0 for the second instance. The function then iterates through a number of runs, adding a random UUID to the same Redis key in each Redis instance, and then saving the serialized length of each instance as seen in this Python code snippet from the `small_types_tests.py`:

```
def plot_list_ziplist(runs=1000):
    reset()
INSTANCE2.config_set("list-max-ziplist-entries", 0)
    key = "test-list"
    run, zip_list, linked_list = [], [], []
    for i in range(runs):
run.append(i)
uid = uuid.uuid4()
INSTANCE1.lpush(key, uid)
INSTANCE2.lpush(key, uid)
debug1 = INSTANCE1.debug_object(key)
zip_list.append(debug1.get("serializedlength"))
debug2 = INSTANCE2.debug_object(key)
linked_list.append(debug2.get("serializedlength"))
```

We can see this difference between by comparing the two list encoding methods on `test-list` in both Redis instances:

```
>>>INSTANCE1.debug_object("test-list").get("serializedlength")
15756
>>>INSTANCE2.debug_object("test-list").get("serializedlength")
18946
```

For the first 512 UUIDs that are added to both lists, the size of the ziplist encoded value is 15,787 while the size of the linked-list encoded value is 18,946, a memory savings of 3190 bytes if using a ziplist.

While it may not be immediately apparent, but for very small lists, the linked-list encoding for Redis lists is actually more efficient. We can see this more clearly if we graph the first 50 list items as shown here:

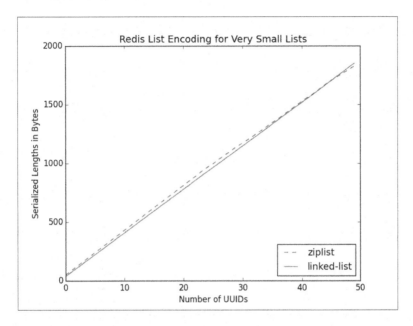

For small lists, the default linked list encoding is more efficient than the ziplist encoding but as the size of the list increases, the ziplist encoding becomes more efficient.

For sets the advantages of these special encodings only occurs if the set is small and contains only integers. The Redis directive, `set-max-intset-entries` with a default value of 512 will encode the set as an intset data type. Running the two Redis instances experiment with the Python function and then retrieving the output results in:

```
>>>INSTANCE1.debug_object("test-set").get("serializedlength")
1034
>>>INSTANCE2.debug_object("test-set").get("serializedlength")
2874
```

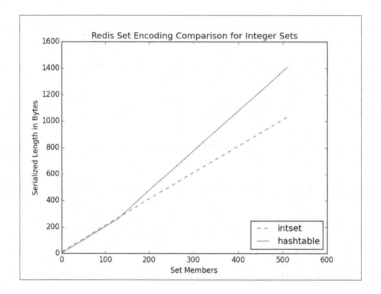

Finally, in examining and experimenting with the special encoding of sorted sets, we will use the same two Redis instances and set the `Rediszset-max-ziplist-entries` to 0 to force Redis to use a hashtable for the data encoding. For each ZADD command, the `plot_sortedset` function adds a UUID to each instance with the score set to 0 for lexical ordering of the UUIDs. To Author: Unclear? Please rephrase for more clarity.

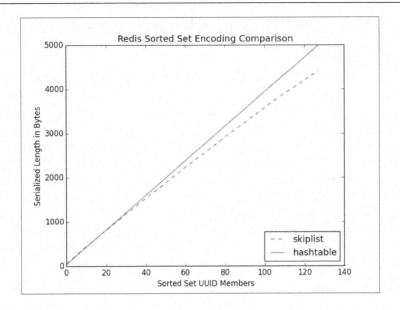

Comparing the results from our Python shell on the `test-sorted-set` in both instances results in the following:

```
>>>INSTANCE1.debug_object("test-sorted-set").get("serializedlength")
4421
>>>INSTANCE2.debug_object("test-sorted-set").get("serializedlength")
4994
```

For the ziplist implementation, the `test-sorted-set` serialized length is 4,421 bytes while the skiplist implementation serialized length of 4,994 a difference in favor of the ziplist encoding of 573 bytes.

For all the ziplist implementations, the computation time increases significantly as the size of the data structure grows larger. For your own Redis-based application, adjusting these thresholds is a matter of balancing memory size with performance realizing that any large ziplist data structure slows down when compared to equivalent default data structure for the Redis data type.

Bits, bytes, and Redis strings as random access arrays

In both chapters one and two, we talked about the use of bitmaps in Redis using various commands such as SETBIT, GETBIT, BITCOUNT, BITPOS, and BITOP. To illustrate the memory savings of using bitmap over a set, let's return to the tea example from earlier and look at how we could indicate whether a tea was decaffeinated or not, an important decision for those of us trying to wake up or fall asleep! A Redis set, with a key name of tea:caffeinated could easily solve this issue. We could store the key name of each tea with caffeine in the set with the SADD command. For the sake of this example, let's assume that we have over 10,000 teas and over 60% has some traceable level of caffeine. Continuing with our initial Redis key schema for teas and since we are using a unique incremental counter for each tea, the tea/caffeinated set could be populated from a Redis-cli like this (assuming tea:4 is something like green tea):

```
127.0.0.1:6379> SADD teas/caffeinated tea:1 tea:4
(integer) 2
```

To simulate our full 10,000 tea inventory, we'll use a function in the small_types_tests.py Python module, populate_tea, to compare our initial approaches:

```
def populate_tea(full=True):
    for i in range(10000):
        if random.random() <= .6:
            member = i
            if full:
                member = "tea/{}".format(i)
    INSTANCE1.sadd("teas/caffeinated", member)
    INSTANCE1.setbit("teas/caffeine", i, 1)
```

In populate_tea, we call the random.random() method to generate a random value between 0 and 1. To model our assumption that 60% of our teas have some caffeine, we check to see if the value is below .6, and add a tea with caffeine to both our set, teas:caffeinated and our bitmap teas:caffeine. Running this function we have over 10,000 variety of teas:

```
>>>INSTANCE1.debug_object("teas/caffeinated").get("serializedlength")
53879
>>>INSTANCE1.debug_object("teas/caffeine").get("serializedlength")
1252
```

To see how many teas in our inventory have caffeine, we can either run the SCARD command on the teas/caffeinated set or the BITCOUNT command on the teas/caffeine bitmap:

```
127.0.0.1:6379> SCARD teas/caffeinated
(integer) 6063
127.0.0.1:6379> BITCOUNT teas/caffeine
(integer) 6063
```

For our teas/caffeinated set, the serialized length is 53,879 bytes while our bitmap is stored as a raw string with a serialized length of 1,252 a significant memory savings of 52,627 bytes! Now, you might be wondering why we have the full parameter in our populate_tea function? With our initial implementation, we stored a string key for each tea. To reduce the size of the teas:caffeinated set, we set the function parameter full to False and then we only store the integer of the tea counter. So, running populate_tea with full=False, results in the following lengths for both teas/caffeinated and the teas/caffeine from the Redis-cli:

```
>>>INSTANCE1.debug_object("teas/caffeinated").get("serializedlength")
17800
```

By using integers instead of strings in our teas/caffeinated set, we were able to drop the size significantly from 52,879 to 17,800 bytes but our bitmap teas/caffeine is still orders of magnitude smaller than our set. However, using bitmaps is not necessarily a panacea. Sparse bitmaps that number in the hundreds of millions waste space as only the first bit is set per offset, leaving the remaining bits per entry not being used. Also, Redis integer sets and hashes provide additional functions that are difficult or require a lot of client code to work correctly with bitmaps.

Optimizing hashes for efficient storage

In the Redis topic on Memory Optimization, Salvatore Sanfilippo writes about a technique using Redis's hashes to implement a high-level and very memory-efficient key-value data storage using Redis hashes. To illustrate how to use this technique, we will return to the legacy representation of MARC records introduced in Chapter 1, *Why Redis?* and compare two approaches to storing MARC JSON serialization in Redis. In the first experiment we will simply use a one-to-one MARC redis key to MARC record JSON serialization stored as a string. For the second experiment, we will use hashes to store the same JSON serializations.

For both experiments, our Redis schema will use marc as a prefix, separated by a colon, followed by a unique progressive counter, overall a simple and common schema for Redis:

```
marc:25
marc:334
marc:8990
marc:122345
```

Our dataset will be just over 17,000 MARC21 records of the most popular material checked out by the patrons of a small academic library at a private liberal arts college. The ingestion algorithm we will use for each MARC record in our first experiment will be these three lines in the basic_ingestion function included in the following code:

```
def basic_ingestion(record):
    """Function takes a MARC record, converts it into JSON, and
then saves the result as string in Redis.
Args:
        record -- MARC21 record
    """
marc_json = record.as_json()
redis_key = "marc:{}".format(INSTANCE1.incr("global:marc"))
INSTANCE1.set(redis_key, marc_json)
```

Running this function from our Python command line starts with the popular_records Python list of MARC records that we read from the pymarc.MARCReader generator:

```
>>>marc_reader = pymarc.MARCReader(
        open('tutt-library-popular.mrc', 'rb'), to_unicode=True)
>>> for record in marc_reader:
base_ingestion(record)
```

The basic information about our Redis database after ingesting these MARC records looks like this from the Redis-cli:

```
127.0.0.1:6379> DBSIZE
(integer) 17145
127.0.0.1:6379> INFO memory
# Memory
used_memory:58283440
used_memory_human:55.58M
```

```
used_memory_rss:58118144

used_memory_peak:58283440

used_memory_peak_human:55.58M

used_memory_lua:35840

mem_fragmentation_ratio:1.00

mem_allocator:libc
```

Our Redis database contains 17,145 keys, with each key storing a JSON representation of our MARC record. The total size of the Redis database is 55.58 megabytes. Now, we'll store these same serialized JSON MARC records using an approach based on Redis hashes.

First, we'll use a simple algorithm to split our keys into two parts; the first part will be used as a key with the last two characters as a field name in a hash to a value. Further, we'll stipulate that all of `marc:{record-number}` keys will end in integers. Depending on what we use for our Redis schema (that is a Redis Object Mapper, client validation code, or external schema validator), this condition can be enforced as seen in this code snippet from the `marc_hash.py` module that can be downloaded from the book's website or at this Github repository— `https://github.com/jermnelson/marc-redis`.

```python
def split_key(redis_key):
    """"""
new_key, field = redis_key[:-2], redis_key[-2:]
    if not new_key.startswith('marc'):
        raise InvalidKeyError(redis_key, "Must start with marc")
    try:
int(field)
    except ValueError:
        raise InvalidKeyError(redis_key, "Last two characters must
            be integers")
    return new_key, field
```

After defining this function, we'll now test our ingestion with this second function that takes a `MARC21` record, serializes it to JSON, and then uses Python string formatting to increment a global MARC counter with the Redis instance:

```python
def hash_ingestion(record):
marc_json = record.as_json()
redis_key = "marc:{}".format(REDIS.incr("global:marc"))
```

The `split_key` function takes the existing Redis key and return the new field name made up of the last two digits of the `global:marc` counter and the field's value is the serialized json.

```
key, field =split_key(redis_key)
REDIS.hset(key, field, marc_json)
```

After defining these functions, running our test experiment on our MARC record collection results in the following from Redis-cli:

```
127.0.0.1:6380> DBSIZE
(integer) 174
127.0.0.1:6380> INFO memory
# Memory
used_memory:57823456
used_memory_human:55.14M
used_memory_rss:57851904
used_memory_peak:57836688
used_memory_peak_human:55.16M
used_memory_lua:35840
mem_fragmentation_ratio:1.00
mem_allocator:libc
```

Using this alternative method, storing these 17k+ MARC records are stored with only 174 keys and the memory used is 55.14 megabytes, resulting in a saving of 431,536k over the basic string implementation.

Hardware and network latencies

In your application, performance issues can easily be mistaken for out-of-memory issues with your Redis database when the problem may have to do more with hardware or network latencies between your client application and your backend server. Latency, as understood in the Redis community, is broken down in three ways:

- **Command latency**: This is the amount of time it takes to execute a command. Some commands are fast and operate in **O(1)** while other commands have **O(n)** time complexity and are thereby a likely source of this type of latency.

- **Round-trip latency**: The time between when a client issues a command and then receives the response from the Redis server that can be caused by network congestion.

- **Client-latency**: If multiple clients attempt to connect to Redis at the same time, concurrency latency can be introduced as later clients may be waiting in queue for early client processes to complete.

To help debug issues, Redis has a special mode for monitoring command latency that can be set in either `redis.conf` from issuing a `CONFIG SET` for the `latency-monitor-threshold` directive. The Redis `latency-monitor-threshold` directive sets a limit in milliseconds that will log all or some of the commands and activity (called events) of the Redis instance that exceed that limit with a default of 0, meaning Redis does not automatically run latency monitoring but must be actively set. Borrowing the example from Redis's official documentation on latency monitoring, first we'll set the `latency-monitor-threshold` directive to 100 milliseconds:

```
127.0.0.1:6379> CONFIG SET latency-monitor-threshold 100
```

Now we'll run a series of `DEBUG SLEEP` to demonstrate the various subcommands and functionality of Redis's latency monitor.

```
127.0.0.1:6379> DEBUG SLEEP 1
127.0.0.1:6379> DEBUG SLEEP .25
127.0.0.1:6379> LATENCY LATEST
1) 1) "command"
   2) (integer) 1433877394
   3) (integer) 250
   4) (integer) 1000
```

The `LATENCY` command with the `LATEST` subcommand returns the latest Redis commands that exceeded the latency threshold and includes the event name, UNIX timestamp when the latency event occurred, latest event latency in milliseconds, and the all-time maximum latency for this event. In our example, line 2) 433877394 is the timestamp of the latest `DEBUG SLEEP` command, line 3) 250 is the result of `DEBUG SLEEP .25`, and finally line 4) 1000 records our first `DEBUG SLEEP 1` command.

The `LATENCY HISTORY` command and subcommand returns the latest 160 latency events that are being tracked. Running this command from Redis-cli results in the following:

```
127.0.0.1:6379> LATENCY HISTORY command
1) 1) (integer) 1433877379
   2) (integer) 1000
2) 1) (integer) 1433877394
   2) (integer) 250
```

The results are tuples made up of the UNIX timestamp and the time in milliseconds for each event.

The LATENCY command with the RESET subcommand can either clear all latency events or just selected events by passing in one or more event names. The LATENCY GRAPH command produces an ASCII-style graph of the logged latency events since the last LATENCY RESET command. Here is the result from Redis-cli (some return values have been removed for brevity):

```
127.0.0.1:6379> DEBUG SLEEP .5
OK
(0.50s)
127.0.0.1:6379> DEBUG SLEEP .3
127.0.0.1:6379> DEBUG SLEEP .8
127.0.0.1:6379> DEBUG SLEEP .2
127.0.0.1:6379> DEBUG SLEEP .6
127.0.0.1:6379> LATENCY GRAPH command
command - high 800 ms, low 201 ms  (all time high 800 ms)
--------------------------------------------------------------------------
-------
   #
 _ | o
 | | |
|o|_|

55544
95170
sssss
```

Finally, the LATENCY DOCKER mode provides a rich set of human-readable (but with flashes of HAL 9000 from Stanley Kubrick's film 2001!) statistical data such as average time between latency spikes, median deviations of those spikes as well as human understandable analysis of the latency events and suggestions for reducing the latency.

Operating system tips

Redis is developed and runs most applications under POSIX supported operating systems like Linux and many of its distributions, Macintosh OS and other BSD derived operating systems, and other commercial UNIXes. The Redis project does not officially support Microsoft Windows, although Microsoft's Open Tech group develops and maintains a port to 64bit-based Windows. There have been experiments running Redis with Raspberry Pi4 and Android5.

Tips for running Redis on Linux

You should disable the transparent huge pages in your kernel by running the following:

```
echo never > /sys/kernel/mm/transparent_hugepage/
enabled
```

Set `vm.overcommit_memory` to 1 to avoid issues with background saving with your Linux virtual machine by swapping.

Summary

This chapter started with some memory-related directives that can be set and then we looked at the various policies for key eviction when Redis reaches the limits of its available memory. Different memory-efficient encoding for small hashes, lists, sorted sets, and sets under special conditions, sets were examined next. We then looked at using bitmap strings as random access arrays followed by using hashes more effectively as a high-level key-value store that is more memory efficient. Finally, we took a look at how to use the Redis latency monitor mode to track problematic and long-running Redis commands followed by a couple of tips for improving running Redis on Linux. The next chapter switches the focus to software development and starting with a tour of Redis's C source code and then switching to using Redis clients using three different programming languages.

4

Programming Redis Part One – Redis Core, Clients, and Languages

In this chapter, *Programming Redis Part One – Redis Core, Clients, and Languages*, we'll start with a tour of the Redis C source code, examining how the major Redis C header and code files interrelate and work with each other, followed by a high-level code execution flow so that we can implement our own new Redis command. Then, to prepare for the next section on using Redis clients of two different programming languages, we'll do a detailed breakdown of the **Redis Dump Binary (RDB)** format, the binary format Redis uses in persisting snapshots of its database on disk. We will also cover the Redis protocol specification, the low-level communication format that clients use to communicate with the Redis server. Finally, we'll use these Redis clients and programming approaches in different use cases.

Redis internals

As a network server, Redis's internal operations follow a basic execution flow where the server waits and listens for incoming connections on a port by accepting the connection if the inbound client communicates with the correct syntax and format called the **REdis Serialization Protocol (RESP)**. After accepting the socket connection, Redis yields a descriptor for nonblocking read and write operations on the in-memory state of the database.

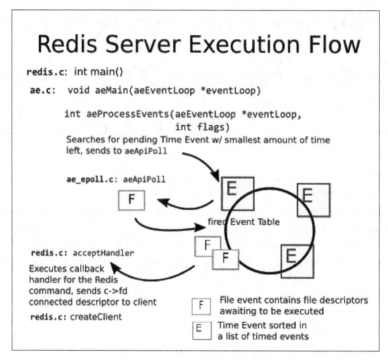

Redis Server Execution Flow

For the Redis server, the main function creates an event loop calling the `aeMain` function that creates an infinite `while` loop. This loop tests the event loop's `stop` property and exits if the test fails. Each iteration of the `while` loop in `aeMain` calls the `aeProcessEvents` function with a pointer to the event loop along with any flags. The `aeProcessEvents` function processes all the time-based events before processing all the file events. Remember that POSIX systems treat running processes as file descriptors, so even to read the values from memory, Redis treats these reads as file descriptors in the event management code. In Redis, time-based events control when the event loop processes its events depending on the flags passed to the `aeProcessEvents` function. The events range from immediately, to the shortest time possible, to blocking and waiting forever, all of which are set with a time value structure.

Using the LLDB debugger on a running Redis instance, we can trace the execution flow for a Redis session up until this point by looking at each frame. In the following backtrace, we start with the most recent frame:

```
(lldb) thread backtrace
* thread #1: tid = 0xf41e, 0x00000001000047ef redis-
server`aeProcessEvents [inlined] aeGetTime(milliseconds=<unavailable>) +
8 at ae.c:186, queue = 'com.apple.main-thread', stop reason = step in
```

With Redis being a single-threaded server application, we start in thread #1 and halt execution of the Redis server at a predefined breakpoint. Working backwards from the most recent frame, we'll trace the history of this execution path back to the beginning in frame #5.

```
  * frame #0: 0x00000001000047ef redis-server`aeProcessEvents [inlined]
aeGetTime(milliseconds=<unavailable>) + 8 at ae.c:186
```

As shown in the preceding code, starting with most current frame #0, the aeGetTime function is called from the current aeEventLoop struct in frame #1.

```
  frame #1: 0x00000001000047e7 redis-server`aeProcessEvents + 108 at
ae.c:304
```

frame #1 is in our processTimeEvents function's while loop that calls the aeGetTime function from frame #0 with two time reference parameters. The processTimeEvents was called from frame #2's aeMain function.

```
frame #2: 0x000000010000477b redis-server`aeProcessEvents(eventLoop=
0x0000000100323150, flags=<unavailable>) + 651 at ae.c:423
```

In frame #2, the aeProcessEvents function is called with the current point to eventLoop in aeMain, whose return value will eventually increment our processed variable in the aeProcessEvents function.

```
frame #3: 0x0000000100004a1b redis-server`aeMain(eventLoop=
0x0000000100323150) + 43 at ae.c:455
```

In frame #3, we are in the while loop in aeMain that was called with a pointer to the current eventLoop struct created in frame #4:

```
frame #4: 0x000000010000f1a8 redis-server`main(argc=<unavailable>,
```

In frame #4, the main function starts on line 3892 in redis.c followed by a call to the ae.c's aeMain function:

```
argv=0x00007fff5fbffb20) + 1256 at redis.c:3892
  frame #5: 0x00007fff900185c9 libdyld.dylib`start + 1
```

For `frame #5`, we see that the Redis server is being launched by the operating system.

The `aeEventLoop` struct contains two important structures: an `aeFileEvent` that contains the event loop's registered events, and a pointer called to the `aeFiredEvent` struct. The `aeFiredEvent` struct contains two variables: one for the file descriptor, and a bitmask describing the event. In the `aeProcessEvents` function, each `FileEvent` uses the Linux `epoll_wait` system call through the `aeApiPoll` function, which waits for any I/O activity on the file descriptors. This is a blocking call. The `aeApiPoll` is implemented in `ae_poll.c`. When a read or write I/O operation occurs on the `aeFileEvent`, the `aeProcessEvents` will eventually add an additional entry to the fired struct.

The `call` function's first parameter is a pointer to the active `redisClient` along with a flags integer. Within the `call` function, the command is sent to any client that is in monitor mode before executing the command. The command is then executed by calling the `proc` function on the active `redisClient` struct. The execution flow is now dependent on the Redis command that has been received. One of the simplest Redis commands is the `PING` command. This command causes the server to replay the *PONG* response. The `PING` is implemented by the `pingCommand` function in `redis.c`.

Running the LLDB debugger from the root directory of our Redis directory, we will launch a running instance of Redis and set a breakpoint on `pingCommand`:

```
$ lldb
(lldb) file src/redis-server
Current executable set to 'src/redis-server' (x86_64).
(lldb) breakpoint set -f redis.c -l 2482
Breakpoint 1: where = redis-server`pingCommand + 9 at redis.c:2484,
address = 0x0000000100007639
```

Issuing the run command in our debugging session will launch Redis server, getting the ascii screen of Redis.

```
(lldb) run
Process 642 launched: '/Users/jeremynelson/redis-dev/src/redis-server'
(x86_64)
642:C 08 Jul 06:54:17.092 # Warning: no config file specified, using the
default config. In order to specify a config file use
/Users/jeremynelson/redis-dev/src/redis-server /path/to/redis.conf
642:M 08 Jul 06:54:17.093 * Increased maximum number of open files to
10032 (it was originally set to 2560).
```

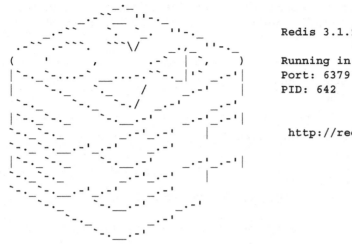

```
                                    Redis 3.1.999 (8f302e56/1) 64 bit

                                    Running in standalone mode
                                    Port: 6379
                                    PID: 642


                                    http://redis.io
```

```
642:M 08 Jul 06:54:17.097 # Server started, Redis version 3.1.999
642:M 08 Jul 06:54:17.103 * DB loaded from disk: 0.006 seconds
642:M 08 Jul 06:54:17.103 * The server is now ready to accept connections
on port 6379
```

Next, we will open a second terminal window, launch redis-cli, and issue a PING
command:

```
$ src/redis-cli

127.0.0.1:6379> PING
```

Switching back to our running debugger terminal window results in the following
output:

```
Process 642 stopped
* thread #1: tid = 0x18cff, 0x0000000100007639 redis-server`pingComman
d(c=0x0000000103000000) + 9 at redis.c:2484, queue = 'com.apple.main-
thread', stop reason = breakpoint 1.1
frame #0: 0x0000000100007639 redis-server`pingCommand(c=
0x0000000103000000) + 9 at redis.c:2484
   2481  * in Pub/Sub mode. */
   2482 void pingCommand(redisClient *c) {
   2483     /* The command takes zero or one arguments. */
-> 2484   if (c->argc > 2) {
   2484         addReplyErrorFormat(c,"wrong number of arguments for
'%s' command",
   2486               c->cmd->name);
   2487     return;
```

With our execution halted at pingCommand, we examine the state of redisClient by issuing the frame variable LLDB command and then by looking at the value of c->argc:

```
(lldb) frame variable c
(redisClient *) c = 0x0000000103000000
(lldb) frame variable c->argc
(int) c->argc = 1
```

Here is the relevant snippet of the c source code with the line numbers for the pingCommand function in redis.c:

```
2481 void pingCommand(client *c) {
2482     /* The command takes zero or one arguments. */
2483     if (c->argc > 2) {
2484         addReplyErrorFormat(c,"wrong number of arguments for '%s'
command",
2485             c->cmd->name);
2486         return;
2487     }
2488
2489     if (c->flags & CLIENT_PUBSUB) {
2490         addReply(c,shared.mbulkhdr[2]);
2491         addReplyBulkCBuffer(c,"pong",4);
2492         if (c->argc == 1)
2493             addReplyBulkCBuffer(c,"",0);
2494         else
2495             addReplyBulk(c,c->argv[1]);
2496     } else {
2497         if (c->argc == 1)
2498             addReply(c,shared.pong);
2499         else
2500             addReplyBulk(c,c->argv[1]);
2501     }
2502 }
```

From our code at line 2483, we can see that redisClient fails the if (c->args > 2) condition.

We can also examine our execution history by issuing the thread backtrace command; we will omit the frames we've already examined:

```
(lldb) thread step-in
Process 642 stopped
* thread #1: tid = 0x18cff, 0x000000010000765f redis-server`pingComman
d(c=0x0000000103000000) + 47 at redis.c:2490, queue = 'com.apple.main-
thread', stop reason = step in
```

```
frame #0: 0x000000010000765f redis-server`pingCommand(c=
0x0000000103000000) + 47 at redis.c:2490
2486        return;
2487      }
2488
-> 2489 if (c->flags & REDIS_PUBSUB) {
2490        addReply(c,shared.mbulkhdr[2]);
2491     addReplyBulkCBuffer(c,"pong",4);
2492        if (c->argc == 1)
```

Stepping over lines 2489-2496 results in the following output (omitting some of the output for brevity):

```
(lldb) thread step-over
.
.
.
2497      } else {
-> 2498  if (c->argc == 1)
2499              addReply(c,shared.pong);
2500          else
2501              addReplyBulk(c,c->argv[1]);
(lldb) frame variable c->argc
(int) c->argc = 1
```

Just to confirm, we displayed the value of the c->argc variable as 1, so the conditional then executes the addReply function. The addReply function then runs the prepareClientToWrite function. The prepareClientToWrite function is called when we expect new data to be sent to the calling client along with a REDIS_OK return value and a write handler socket to write to the eventLoop. The execution flow returns to the call function after the prepareClientToWrite function is completed. After the command has finished processing, the call function returns to the processCommand function. The processCommand function then returns a REDIS_OK or REDIS_ERR status to the processInputBuffer function, thereby calling the resetClient command. After the client has been reset, the processInputBuffer function returns control to the aeProcessEvents function. Finally, the control is returned to the aeMain event loop of the running Redis server instance.

Understanding redis.h and redis.c

A significant benefit of Redis being an open source project is that its C source code is available for you to download, examine, and experiment as you learn and understand Redis. Our survey of Redis source code starts by examining two code files, redis.h and redis.c. These contain the primary source code to run the server.

In the following paragraphs, we'll start by examining a few defined constants, structures, and macros in `redis.h`.

At the beginning of the `redis.h` header file, the `includes` directive imports header files from the standard C libraries such as `stio.h`, `stdlib.h`, and `time.h` as well as other header files from dependencies such as `pthread.h` for Linux threading, `syslog.h`, and `lua.h`. Next in `redis.h`, the `mstime_t` millisecond time type is defined as a long signed integer type that is under 64 bits and can range in size from $-9,223,372,036,854,775,807$ to $+9,223,372,036,854,775,807$. However, since we are storing milliseconds, negative time values are not valid in this context and therefore are not used in the Redis server or client code. After defining `mstime_t`, the various helper macros, functions and API function interfaces used in the running and managing of your Redis instances are defined by the local header files for Redis's event library (`ae.h`), dynamic safe strings (`sds.h`), hash tables (`dict.h`), linked lists (`adlist.h`), and a version of `malloc` that is aware of the total memory available (`zmalloc.h`). Other header file that are defined for networking (`anet.h`), ziplists, and integer set structures (`ziplist.h` and `intset.h` respectively), that were introduced in the last chapter and finally, by the `version.h`, `util.h`, `latency.h`, and `sparkline.h` header files.

After these `include` statements, `redis.h` defines the `REDIS_OK` constant as `0` and the `REDIS_ERR` constant as `-1`. These two constants are used extensively in the implementation code of the Redis commands contained in other source code files in the Redis project. Next in the `redis.h` header file, default server configuration values are defined and used in the absence of a Redis configuration file. For example, the `REDIS_SERVERPORT` is defined as `6379`, the maximum number of connected Redis clients is set to 10,000 with the `REDIS_MAX_CLIENTS` defined as `constant` and `REDIS_DEFAULT_RDB_FILENAME` is `dump.rdb`. Other look-up, metrics, and I/O-related definitions follow the Redis default configuration values that lead up to a listing of Redis command flags in `redis.h`.

These command flags in the `redis.c` code file are members of the `redisCommand` struct. This struct is passed to the `processCommand` function that we'll discuss later in this chapter. All the Redis commands (that is, GET, SET, HSET, and so on) are stored in `redisCommandTable`, a C struct, that is defined in `redis.c`. In `redisCommandTable`, each command is in a separate row that contains a number of settings specific to the Redis command.

Each command row has the following fields (in order from left-to-right):

- Command name: The lowercase string name of the command.
- Function pointer: A pointer to the function that implements the command.
- Function arity: The number of arguments that the command function expects.
- Function sflags: The sflags field contains the strings for all the different Redis command fields.
- The string values in the previous fields (sflags) and computes a bitmask using the constants defined in redis.h.
- An optional function to extract and/or compute a command's key arguments.
- The index of an argument in a listing of arguments passed to the Redis command, that is, the Redis key for the data structure value.
- The index of the argument that is the last key; this allows us to have Redis commands that operate on multiple keys at a time.
- The total time in microseconds of the execution time of the command. This is calculated by Redis and should always be set to 0.
- The total number of calls made by the command. This is mutable and is calculated at runtime and should always be set to 0.

The following are the row entries for the GET and SET commands:

```
{"get",getCommand,2,"rF",0,NULL,1,1,1,0,0},
{"set",setCommand,-3,"wm",0,NULL,1,1,1,0,0},
```

For the first fields in the example, the lowercase command strings are get and set. The second field in our example is for pointers to the getCommand and setCommand functions. The third field, airty, for getCommand is 2; for setCommand we see -3, which means that the number of arguments is greater than or equal to 3.

For the fourth field, the GET command has the rF flags, where r means a read command with F denoting that it is also a fast command. This means that its big O notation is either *O(1) or O(log(N))*. For such fast commands, the Redis server event loop should never delay the execution of a command—in this example, the GET command—if the kernel scheduler continues to provide time to the running Redis server. The SET command values are as follows: w means this command is a write command, m means that this command increases the memory used and is not allowed to be used if Redis is out of memory. There are twelve other commands flags for things such as random R, s for sort command, lowercase s to prohibit the command to be called in a script.

The fifth field takes the string values from the previous field (sflags) and computes a bitmask for rF and wm. The sixth field is set to NULL for both of these commands. This means that neither GET nor SET requires optional functions for retrieving key arguments. The seventh field is the index of the argument. This is a key, and it's value is 1 for both GET and SET. The seventh and eight fields, getCommand and setCommand, are both 1, so each of these commands only accept one key in the first argument of the argument list set in the command. For the ninth and tenth fields, the values are set to 0 as should be the case because these are dynamic fields whose values are calculated by running Redis.

These constants are first used in the redis.c header's processCommand function that we first encountered in the previous function. The processCommand function takes a pointer to a redisClient struct. The struct is fundamental in Redis, as it describes the state of the communication between the internal Redis processes in the server and the outside world. The networking.c createClient function takes a single parameter, int fd, allocates memory, and stores the pointer to the struct. The createClient then continues and initializes all of its important variables such as pointers to the current active Redis database (redisDb). Also, other important properties will be noted as we go through the following selected lines from redisClient in redis.h:

```
529 typedef struct redisClient {
530     uint64_t id;                /* Client incremental unique ID. */
531     int fd;
532     redisDb *db;
```

Line 530 defines a unique 64-bit integer ID, t_id, line 531 is the file descriptor integer ID, and line 532 is a pointer to the Redis database:

```
537     int argc;
538     robj **argv;
```

Line 537 argc is the # of args for the command, and line 538 argv is a reference to the return values from the command:

```
539     struct redisCommand *cmd, *lastcmd;
```

Line 539 defines the *cmd pointers to the current redisCommand struct and the *lastcmd pointer to the previous redisCommand struc.

```
550     int flags;                  /* REDIS_SLAVE | REDIS_MONITOR | REDIS_
MULTI ... */
```

Line 550 is the `*flags` bitmask containing the operating mode of the Redis server:

```
554     int repldbfd;              /* replication DB file descriptor */
555     off_t repldboff;           /* replication DB file offset */
556     off_t repldbsize;          /* replication DB file size */
```

Lines 554, 555, and 556 are variables for the master-slave database file that is replicated from the master instance to the all of its slaves.

```
564     char replrunid[REDIS_RUN_ID_SIZE+1]; /* master run id if this
is a master */
565     int slave_listening_port; /* As configured with: SLAVECONF
listening-port */
```

Line 564 is the master, run ID if the running Redis instance is a master, and line 565 is the port number that a Redis slave instance is listening on.

```
571     list *watched_keys;        /* Keys WATCHED for MULTI/EXEC CAS */
572     dict *pubsub_channels;  /* channels a client is interested in
(SUBSCRIBE) */
573     list *pubsub_patterns;  /* patterns a client is interested in
(SUBSCRIBE) */
```

Line 571 is a pointer to the `*watched_keys` linked list if the Redis instance is in multi/exec mode. Lines 572 and 573 are both pointers to linked lists that store subscribed channels and patterns when Redis is in pub/sub mode.

```
576     /* Response buffer */
577     int bufpos;
578     char buf[REDIS_REPLY_CHUNK_BYTES];
```

Lines 577 and 578 store the RESP from the server executing the commands.

The `processCommand` function starts by first checking whether a `quit` command was sent to the server and if it was, returning `REDIS_ERR` (the `quit` command is handled in a separate function). Additional error checking is done in `processCommand` as it checks whether the command even exists or if the command has the wrong number of arguments. Instead of returning `REDIS_ERR` for these errors, the function calls `addReplyErrorFormat` with a pointer to the command and an error message before returning an `REDIS_OK` status because the Redis server is still functioning correctly with the calling client. If the command requires authentication and the client has not authenticated to the server, an `addReply` function is called with a no authentication message and returns `REDIS_OK`. Following the authentication check, `processCommand` redirects the command to a cluster shard or adds an error and returns to the calling client.

In the `processCommand` function, after the cluster error checking, the function checks and handles the various cases when the Redis server is out of memory. First, after trying to free up memory by removing volatile keys, the function returns if no memory is available and the `REDIS_CMD_DENYOOM` constant is set. This function continues with three distinct checks to see whether any write commands will be accepted. This depends on the fact that the Redis instance is a slave and the `min-slaves-to-write` has been set, or if there are problems persisting to disk, or if the Redis instance is slave and is read only.

The next sections in the `processCommand` function handle special operating modes of the Redis instance; in particular, the operations are restricted to only the `SUBSCRIBE`/ `UNSCRIBE` commands if Redis is in pub/sub mode. More error checks are done for special cases, such as when the Redis instance is a slave and is disconnected from the master, by restricting the available commands to `INFO` and `SLAVEOF`. For the special edge case, when a Lua client's scripts are running too slow, the function flags the command, calls `addReply` with an error message, and returns back to the calling client. Finally, after all these error checks, `processCommand` actually executes the command as either a singleton or as part of a `MULTI`/`EXEC` transaction.

Starting at line 1791, `redis.h` defines the five fundamental Redis object types as follows:

```
/* Object types */
#define REDIS_STRING 0
#define REDIS_LIST 1
#define REDIS_SET 2
#define REDIS_ZSET 3
#define REDIS_HASH 4
```

Elsewhere in Redis's source code when we see an object type assigned to a Redis object, we now know that this object type has integers values ranging from 0 through 4. After these Redis object type definitions, in `redis.h`, the Redis object encoding types, such as Redis's hashtable, linked-list, ziplist, and intset, are assigned integer values 0 through 8. These means that we can combine the object type with the encoding type to reflect the actual data structure that is stored in a Redis key. So, a small hash value would be `REDIS_HASH` with an encoding of `REDIS_ENCODING_ ZIPMAP` reflected as two integer values, 0 and 3.

Next, the sizing and other settings for both the Redis persistence modes are defined in `redis.h`. For the snapshot RDB mode, Redis dynamically allocates bit size and shrinks the size if the Redis key is small using the first two significant bits of the key. If both the bits are set for these significant bits, `redis.h` defines four different encodings constants:

- **8 bit signed integers**: **REDIS_RDB_ENC_INT** with a value of 0
- **16 bit signed integers**: **REDIS_RDB_ENC_INT16** as 1

- **32 bit signed integers**: **REDIS_RDB_ENC_INT32** 2 as 2
- **Compressed strings**: **REDIS_RDB_ENC_LZF** 3 as 3

For AOF persistence mode, redis.h defines three states, REDIS_AOF_OFF, REDIS_AOF_ON, and the state where Redis is waiting to be appended to the AOF file. This is defined as 2 for REDIS_AOF_WAIT_REWRITE.

With a variety of different types of Redis clients, redis.h defines nineteen different flags to set a bit to 1 using the << bitwise left-shift operator so that a client information can be represented in a single byte. This bitmask sets a byte that allows the Redis commands and other operational code in the code base to quickly calculate and determine whether the client is a Redis slave or master, or whether the client is monitoring in multiexecution mode with REDIS_MULTI, or whether it is connected to REDIS_LUA_CLIENT with a Unix domain socket and is read-only with REDIS_READONLY, or whether the client is in pub/sub mode using the bitmasks for REDIS_PUBSUB. After the different client flag offset definitions, redis.h sets other Redis client constants for client aspects such as the client block types, client request types, client classes, and the slave replication states from both the slave and master perspectives.

Defined in the next section of redis.h are the four different logging levels for Redis: REDIS_DEBUG, REDIS_VERBOSE, REDIS_NOTICE, and REDIS_WARNING, with REDIS_NOTICE set to the default logging level with the REDIS_DEFAULT_VERBOSITY constant and a special raw log mode with REDIS_LOG_RAW that does not log a timestamp.

Interspersed in the same section as the logging directives are the settings for the different data structures and encodings used in Redis. For example, REDIS_HEAD and REDIS_TAIL are defined as 0 and 1 respectively for Redis lists; different sorting options for sorted lists are defined, for example REDIS_SORT_ASC is defined as 1, REDIS_SORT_DESC as 2, and REDIS_SORTKEY_MAX is set to 1024. In the previous chapter, we explored the different performance trade-offs for special encoding of lists, hashes, sets, and sorted sets and saw how to set directives such as hash-max-ziplist-entries and hash-max-ziplist-value. The default values for these directives are set in redis.h under the REDIS_HASH_MAX_ZIPLIST_ENTRIES and REDIS_HASH_MAX_ZIPLIST_VALUE constants. Finally, Redis set operations are provided constants with REDIS_OP_UNION set to 0 for the union operator, REDIS_OP_DIFF set to 1 for the difference operator, and REDIS_OP_INTER set to 2 for the intersection operator.

The different caching policies for Redis are assigned with progressive integers starting with REDIS_MAXMEMORY_VOLATILE_LRU set to zero and finishing with REDIS_MAXMEMORY_NO_EVICTION set to 5. The default caching policy, REDIS_DEFAULT_MAXMEMORY_POLICY, is set to REDIS_MAXMEMORY_NO_EVICTION in redis.h. Following this trend of defining various settings for Redis operation, such as Lua scripts timeouts, unit definitions, and shutdown flags, a lot of other settings are further defined in the redis.h source code file.

We'll skip the persistence, replication, multiexec, and clustering settings being set in redis.h as we'll be covering the configuration of these different Redis operations in future topics. Hopefully, you now have an idea of where the default values for your Redis instances are being set and used in the Redis code base.

Getting ready for Redis development with Git

With Salvatore Sanfilippo licensing Redis under the Three Clause BSD Open Source license and with the Redis code repository hosted on Github, we can actually make a copy of the Redis source code and fork our own development version of Redis. First, we'll open the command line in our Linux system and make sure we have Git installed:

```
$ sudo apt-get install git
```

Next, we will go to the Redis Github repository at https://github.com/antirez/redis/. To create a fork, first log in to GitHub (you will need to create a free account if you don't already have an account), look in the upper-right corner and click on the **Fork** button. Take a look at a close-up screenshot of the **Fork** button:

Redis Fork Button on Github

Now you will be re-routed to your own fork of Redis and then you'll clone your fork by doing the following (substitute your GitHub username for `jermnelson`), and you should see a similar screen output as follows:

```
$ git clone https://github.com/jermnelson/redis.git redis-dev
Cloning into 'redis-dev'...
remote: Counting objects: 20195, done.
remote: Total 20195 (delta 0), reused 0 (delta 0), pack-reused 20195
Receiving objects: 100% (20195/20195), 9.62 MiB | 433.00 KiB/s, done.
Resolving deltas: 100% (13515/13515), done.
Checking connectivity... done.
```

You'll can keep your Redis fork in sync with the main Redis repository with the following commands:

```
$ cd redis-dev
```

```
$ git remote -v
origin  https://github.com/jermnelson/redis.git (fetch)
origin  https://github.com/jermnelson/redis.git (push)
```

Next, we'll add an upstream sync so that we can pull changes from the Redis main repository:

```
$ git remote add upstream https://github.com/antirez/redis.git
```

```
$ git remote -v
origin  https://github.com/jermnelson/redis.git (fetch)
origin  https://github.com/jermnelson/redis.git (push)
upstream    https://github.com/antirez/redis.git (fetch)
upstream    https://github.com/antirez/redis.git (push)
```

Now, when I want to pull any changes from the upstream unstable branch, I will run the following command:

```
$ git fetch upstream
```

For our development on the Redis core repository, we'll create a new `local-dev` branch:

```
$ git checkout -b local-dev
```

Finally, we'll merge any upstream changes with the following:

```
$ git merge upstream/unstable
```

Our forked version of Redis is now up-to-date with the latest unstable changes, and we're ready to look at creating a new Redis C command in the next section.

Exercise – creating your own redis command

One of the tutorials on the Redis website is on the implementation of an autocomplete function using sorted sets in Redis. By improving partial word matches in a Redis autocomplete approach, we can use English word metaphones — a number of different algorithms to create sound-like representation of words. This method normalizes both the user input that matched is then matched to indexed words.

Instead of implementing the Lawrence Philip's double-metaphone algorithm from the ground up; we will base our new Redis command on the C source code of a preexisting open source project located at `https://bitbucket.org/yougov/fuzzy/`. We will first create two files, a `double_metaphone.h` as a header file and a `double_metaphone.c` C source file. When we want to store a metaphone of an existing word, we'll create two new Redis commands: GETDBLMETAPHN an SETDBLMETAPHN. The SETDBLMETAPHN command takes a Redis hash key and a English word, converts the word to a double-metaphone, and stores the result as either one or two fields in the Redis hash with the value being the original word. Our second Redis command, GETDBLMETAPHN, will take a pair of strings, convert the word to a metaphone, and return either one or two fields that best match the term.

The syntax for SETDBLMETAPHN is this:

```
"SETDBLMETAPHN <key> <string>"
```

The syntax for GETDBLMETAPHN is as follows:

```
"GETDLBMETAPHN <key>" :
```

To add these commands to our Redis fork, we'll add go through the following steps:

1. Add our `getMetaphone` and `setMetaphone` function prototypes at the end of our `redis.h` header file. Adding our function prototypes in this file allows all other code that includes `redis.h` to use our functions.

2. Copy `double_metaphone.h` and `double_metaphone.c` to our `src` directory.

3. Add the `getMetaphone` and `setMetaphone` functions commands as two new commands to `redisCommandTable` in `redis.c`.

4. Edit `double_mectaphone.c` and create a placeholder function for `getMetaphone`.

5. For the `getMetaphone` function, we will retrieve the string value found at the Redis key by calling the standard `getGenericCommand` implemented in the `t_string.c` c code file.

6. Continue editing `double_metaphone.c` and create a placeholder function for the `setMetaphone` function.

Double Metaphones

The Double Metaphone is a phonetic encoding algorithm that converts a string into a primary and secondary codes for a string. Here are examples using two books and their authors:

Infinite - **PRIMARY**: ANFN **SECONDARY**: ANFN
Jest - **PRIMARY**: JST **SECONDARY**: AST

David - **PRIMARY**: TFT **SECONDARY**: TFT
Foster - **PRIMARY**: FSTR **SECONDARY**: FSTR
Wallace - **PRIMARY**: ALK **SECONDARY**: FLK

Pride - **PRIMARY**: PRT **SECONDARY**: PRT
and - **PRIMARY**: ANT **SECONDARY**: ANT
Prejudice - **PRIMARY**: PRJT **SECONDARY**: PRJT

Jane - **PRIMARY**: JN **SECONDARY**: AN
Austen- **PRIMARY**: ASTN **SECONDARY**: ASTN

Now, after compiling Redis, GETDBLMETAPHN will behave exactly as the GET command if we run the following `redis-cli` session:

```
127.0.0.1:6379> SET metaphone:1 "Star Trek"

OK

127.0.0.1:6379> GETDBLMETAPHN metaphone:1 "Star Trek"

127.0.0.1:6379> GET metaphone:1 "Star Trek"
```

The function prototype for the `getMetaphone` function we added to `redis.h` takes a pointer to `redisClient` and returns void or nothing. Expanding on our initial implementation of just doing a call-out to `getGenericCommand`, we'll add a new functionality to handle a case where the Redis key is not found. That is, we will return the metaphones of the requested key. This provides us a quick and dirty way to generate a double metaphone of a string if the string is not an existing Redis key in the data store.

This new behavior for getMetaphone would likely be not what we would design and engineer in a production instance, but is suitable for the purpose of illustrating what is possible in custom commands. With our knowledge of RESP, we can parse the return buffer from our command and if the string returned is $-1, we'll call the DoubleMetaphone function with our Redis key and an output code string. This string will contain our phrase that has been converted to a double metaphone.

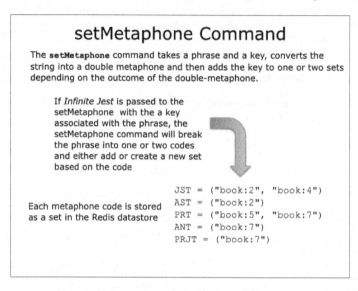

To handle the case of a missing Redis key, our getMetaphone function will return the double metaphone of the Redis key:

```
void setMetaphone(redisClient *c) {
    c->argv[2] = tryObjectEncoding(c->argv[2]);
    setGenericCommand(c,1,c->argv[1],c->argv[2],NULL,0);
}
```

A future enhancement for the Double-Metaphone commands would be to change NewMetaString and DestroyMetaString and other functions so that we can use Redis's Simple Dynamic Strings that is defined in sds.h with the source code in the sds.c file. These sds string structures are used extensively in the Redis code base to support not only Redis keys and simple strings, but also Redis's data types such as lists, sets, sorted-sets, hashes, and more complex value types. By refactoring our metaphone code to use Redis's Simple Dynamic Strings, we eliminate the need to implement a custom string type for our metaphone commands while leveraging the existing simple dynamic strings in the Redis core code base.

Redis Serialization Protocol (RESP)

The Redis server communicates with its clients using the Redis protocol specification or RESP. While Redis is the primary user of RESP, Salvatore Sanfilippo's latest project Disque uses RESP but not Redis itself. In the Redis official documentation, RESP is referred to as a **Domain Specific Language** (DSL). It is helpful to think of RESP in this way, especially when we discuss the details of the specification as it relates to all the different available clients for Redis in many different programming languages. RESP serializes all the Redis data types and can easily represent different data types such as simple strings, errors, integers, bulk strings, and arrays.

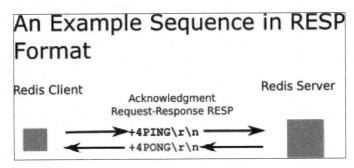

RESP Client-Server

Although not specifically restricted to TCP, RESP is often used within the context of the Request-Response model supporting client-server applications. There are exceptions to the Request-Response model RESP that supports such as:

- Pipelining when the client sends multiple commands to the server without waiting for a response for each command

Pub/sub push channels when the server sends notifications to a channel with one or more subscribers. While interacting with Redis, the client sends a command to the Redis server as an array of bulk strings. The Redis server parses this using RESP and responds with one of the following RESP types, depending on the command. The Redis server response is one of these five types and is determined by the first byte:

1. A simple string indicated by +.
2. An error string is indicated by -.
3. An integer string is indicated by :.
4. A bulk string is indicated by $.
5. An array is *.

The RESP termination characters are carriage return or line feed, traditionally represented in ASCII as \r\n (CRLF).

For RESP simple strings, the beginning character is the plus sign character, +, followed by string characters that cannot contain either a carriage return or line feed at the end because the simple string is terminated with CRLF:

```
+OK\r\n
```

When the Redis server sends a simple string to a calling client, the client should return the characters between the initial + and the \r\n that terminates the return response. If a nonsensical command such as NOPE is sent from a client to the Redis server, the RESP response would be as follows:

-ERR unknown command 'NOPE'\r\n. In case of an error, the Redis server returns a RESP error that starts with a negative sign character, -, followed by an error message and is again terminated with \r\n. The client typically raises an exception on receiving a RESP error for conditions such as a wrong type of operation on a data type or if the client sends a unknown command to the Redis server.

For more specific error conditions such as when, a LPUSH command is executed on a hash key. This would result in the WRONGTYPE RESP error followed by the message in the preceding response.

When a client issues the INCR and INCRBY commands, the server returns an RESP integer like the following using redis-cliclient:

```
127.0.0.1:6379> INCR global:counter
:1\r\n
127.0.0.1:6379> INCRBY global:counter 10
:11\r\n
```

The RESP integer type starts with a colon byte, :, followed by an integer and again is terminated with a CRLF (""). The returned integer string is a signed 64-bit integer that can have any number of different values depending on the Redis client commands.

In a RESP bulk string, the first byte is the dollar sign, $, with an integer length of the contained string followed by a CRLF. Next, the actual string data and the RESP bulk string are terminated with a second CRLF. Here are some examples of the RESP bulk string:

```
$-1\r\n
```

A RESP bulk string used to represent a null value has the length value of -1.

`$0\r\n\r\n`

An empty string has an integer length of 0 followed by two CRLFs.

`$25\r\nA world of handmade sound\r\n`

For the preceding sample string, "A world of handmade sound", the Redis bulk string with that encoded data has a length of 25 and is surrounded by a pair of CRLF.

Clients communicate with the Redis server using RESP arrays, and for certain types of responses from the Redis server also RESP Arrays are used. RESP Arrays are collections of other RESP types such as RESP simple strings, integers, and bulk strings. The first byte in a RESP Array is an asterisk, *, followed by an integer indicating the total number of commands, with CRLF terminator characters. Each element in the RESP Array is a RESP type and does not have to be the same type. This results in RESP Arrays that have multiple RESP types for elements. RESP Arrays can also be made up of RESP Array elements as well thereby creating a simple data hierarchy or a tree structure in RESP. RESP elements can also be null. This can be done using the syntax for specifying null bulk string of `$-1\r\n`.

For example, a RESP Array of two RESP integers, 3 and 56, would look like as follows:

`*2\r\n:3\r\n:56\r\n`

A mixed RESP Array consisting of a RESP string, an RESP integer, and a RESP error would be as follows:

`*3\r\n$5\r\nhello\r\n:3\r\n-ERRWrong Type\r\n`

Finally, a RESP array containing other RESP arrays would look like this:

`*2\r\n*3\r\n:1\r\n$3\r\nAND\r\n$-1\r\n*2\r\n:3\r\n+OK\r\n`

A better illustration of RESP arrays and subtypes can be seen in this illustration:

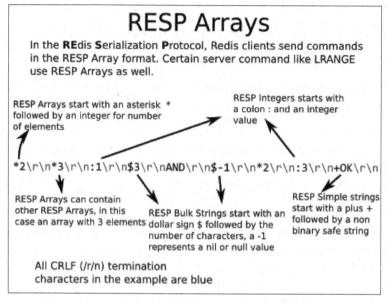

RESP Array

Pipelining

A network optimization technique that uses RESP between Redis clients and servers enables a client to issue multiple commands to a server without waiting for a corresponding reply or acknowledgment from the server. Pipelining in Redis attempts to reduce the **Round Trip Time (RTT)** between the server and client by eliminating the need for the client to receive a server acknowledgment for each issued command. In pipelining, the client parses the server response after sending multiple commands at once. You can use pipeling mode directly from the Netcat UNIX program or through a Redis client that supports Pipeling.

For example, you could send multiple commands to your running Redis server in a pipeline for activities such as initializing a Redis key schema. We can demonstrate this by sending the RESP to our running Redis server using Netcat by issuing the following command that redirects its input to the locally running instance:

```
$ (printf "INCR\r\nglobal:book\r\nHMSET\r\n"; sleep 1) | nc localhost
6379
+ 1
+ OK
```

We received `+1 +OK` as a single response back from our Redis server. This method of pipelining shows the RTT savings as we make 1 RTT verses making three separate calls if we issued each command separately from `redis-cli`:

```
127.0.0.1:6379> INCR global:book
(integer) 1
127.0.0.1:6379> HMSET book:1 title "Go Set a Watchman" creator "Harper
Lee"
OK
```

We can also use pipelining with a Redis client. This can be demonstrated using the recommended client for Python, `redis-py`, available at `https://github.com/andymccurdy/redis-py`.

Redis RDB format

Redis uses a binary format called RDB to persist snapshots of its in-memory data. This is because the default mode for persistence in Redis RDB allows the entire data set that is held in the memory to be restored if Redis unexpectedly quits, or to load an existing dataset when Redis initializes. We'll examine the format of the RDF file by first launching a Redis instance, saving a number of different keys using various data structures, and using a hex editor along with Sripathi Krishnan's Redis RDB tools found on GitHub at `https://github.com/sripathikrishnan/redis-rdb-tools` Python module to examine in detail the format and structure of the RDB format.

The RDB format does not use newline characters or spaces as delimiters. To examine the specifics of some common Redis data structures, we'll issue the following commands from the `redis-cli` (the return codes have been omitted for this example):

```
127.0.0.1:6379> INCR global:book

127.0.0.1:6379> HSET book:1 author "Jane Austen"

127.0.0.1:6379> LPUSH book:1:edition:2 "copy 2" "copy 4"

127.0.0.1:6379> EXPIRE book:1:edition:2 400
```

After these commands have been issued, we'll investigate dump.rdb by first opening the file with vi in hex mode and then copying and examining the selected hexadecimal characters and corresponding values from each line in the following tables:

Hexadecimal	Value	Description
52	R	The first five bytes of every RDB file represents the string REDIS. This is useful for the parser to confirm it is a Redis binary dump. file format.
45	E	
44	D	
49	I	
53	S	
30	0	The next bytes, 30 3030 36, signifies the RDB version number in big endian format 006, so this is version 6.
30	0	
30	0	
36	6	
fe	\xfe	fe 00 indicates that the database selector code fe is 0.
00	\x00	
00	\x00	The 00 is a one byte flag indicating the value type.
0b	\x0b	
67	g	The string global:book is stored in hexadecimal as the key with the value set to 0.
6c	l	
6f	o	
62	b	
61	a	
6c	l	
3a	:	
62	b	
6f	o	
6f	o	
6b	k	
31	1	

Hexadecimal	Value	Description
10	\x10	This byte denotes the type of encoding for the value stored in the string and is one of the following: 0: String 1: List encoding 2: Set encoding 3: Sorted Set encoding 4: Hash encoding 9: Zipmap encoding 10: Ziplist encoding 11: Inset encoding 12: Sorted Set in Ziplist encoding 13: Hashmap in Ziplist encoding
62	b	The next Redis key and value stored in our dump.rdb file is the book:1:edition:2 list
6f	o	
6f	o	
6b	k	
3a	:	
31	1	
3a	:	
65	e	
64	d	
69	i	
74	t	
69	i	
6f	o	
6e	n	
3a	:	
32	2	
00	\x00	The next two elements are the contents of the Redis list with the size for the list member being 6.
06	\x06	
63	c	The list value of copy 4 stored as a string.
6f	o	
70	p	

Hexadecimal	Value	Description
79	y	
20		
34	4	
08	\x08	08 is the value type of 0, with 06 representing the length of the next list member.
06	\x06	
63	c	The list value of copy 2 stored as a string.
6f	o	
70	p	
79	y	
20		
32	2	

Coroutines using Redis and Python

At the 2015 Open Repositories conference in Indianapolis, I was approached by Mark Matienzo, Director of Technology at the Digital Public Library of America, to join a team for pitching ideas at a contest sponsored by the conference. Our pitch was for a Linked Data Fragments Server with caching that would enable people and organizations to provide a simple and well-understood service to query and get back RDF triples from a graph database instead of supporting full resource-heavy SPARQL endpoints that even for the largest website is difficult to keep and run for users. Linked Data Fragments, first proposed by Ruben Verborgh at Ghent University in Belgium, constructs a triple pattern fragment made up of a subjects, predicates, and object statements that combine to query a Linked Data store and returns a Linked Data Fragment made up of triples matching the query along with metadata and paging information.

Although our team did not win the pitch contest, with Mark's encouragement along with the collaboration help of Aaron Coburn of Amherst College, I started a new open-source project using Python and Redis that implements the Linked Data Fragments specification. The source code repository is at https://github.com/jermnelson/linked-data-fragments, with the first version being used in two active projects, the Islandora eBadge and bibcat.org. The Islandora eBadge project allows organizations to issue Mozilla Open Badges for users while storing the resulting Open Badges in a digital repository. The bibcat.org project is the result of a contract I had with the Library of Congress to design and implement a Linked Data-based search and display system for the Library of Congress's new BIBFRAME Linked Data vocabulary.

My primary reasons for starting and continued development of the Linked Data Fragments server centered around its obvious utility in the digital library systems I was working on. The Linked Data Fragments server would also help other organizations that deal with much larger scales such as the Library of Congress and the Digital Public Library of America. Another important secondary reason was that I was interested in a new Python module called asyncio for Asynchronous I/O that offered a new (to me) model for network programming.

The first concept behind the asyncio module and this programming model is that the scalability of a network program should be limited by the number of open sockets, instead of by the availability of free threads in a modern POSIX-based operating system. Most modern POSIX operating systems can easily handle thousands of open socket connections, but are limited by the number of threads they can support at any one time, typically in the range of a hundred. The second concept in the Python asyncio module is in explicit cooperative multithreading, where events are dealt with immediately or wait for additional events to occur while an erroneous call blocks the execution of the entire application. This leads to many subtle multithreading bugs such as incorrect manipulation of shared data structures between threads.2 In the asyncio module, Python adds additional syntax and operators that expand the existing Python decorators to build explicit event-driven network code. This code is scaled out based on I/O limits instead of the available threads in the operating system's multithreading environment.

The Linked Data Fragments server contains two main files, server.py and cache.py. The server.py implements a socket server to which clients send triple Subject-Predicate-Object requests. These are parsed using a simple algorithm that generates a triple pattern to search the Redis cache. In cache.py, we use the aioredis-based and the asyncio-based Redis client. This we'll use to interact with our Redis cache instance. The aioredis project's Git repository is available at https://github.com/aio-libs/aioredis/. The primary developer of aioredis is Alexey Popravka.

The aioredis module's main Python module—__init__.py—is available at https://github.com/aio-libs/aioredis/blob/master/aioredis/__init__.py. This imports a number of supporting Python for different components of this library including connection.py, pool.py, util.py, and errors.py. The connection.py Python module defines a create_connection function with a asyncio.coroutine Python decorator. The first parameter to c address is a Python list, a tuple that represents a host or port par, or a string for a Unix domain socket path on the running Redis server followed by optional db, password, encoding, and loop parameters.

The `create_connection` first yields a Python `StreamReader` and `StreamWriter` from either a Redis open connection using the `asyncio.open_connection` in the case of an address host and port, or an `asyncio.open_unix_connection` for a Unix domain socket. Next, a connection instance of a `RedisConnection` class is created using both the reader and writer from the previous steps along with the other `create_connection` parameters.

The `RedisConnection` class provides a `_read_data` coroutine to respond to the output from the Redis server along with two important methods, `execute` and `execute_pubsub`. The lower-level parsing of the RESP requests and responses is accomplished using the `hiredis` Python module that wraps the Hiredis Redis c client. The execute method first checks whether the `RedisConnection` instance is in PUBSUB mode, returns an error if it is before creating an `asyncio.Future` with the executed Redis command. The `execute_pubsub` method instead of creating a future object, with the Redis server that returns an `asyncio.gather` coroutine for coordinating both publication and subscription channels and their associated patterns.

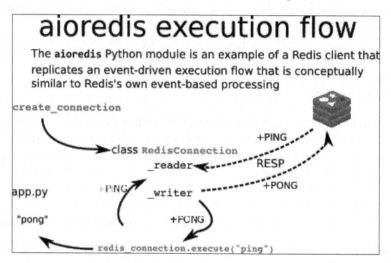

The commands module is made up groupings of related commands for hashes (`hash.py`), lists (`list.py`), strings (`string.py`), sets (`set.py`), sorted sets (`sorted_set.py`), and code files of other data structures. The commands module supports generic commands in the `generic.py` file, publish/subscribe channel support in `pubsub.py`, Lua scripting support with `scripting.py`, and Redis transactions with `transaction.py`.

The Linked Data Fragment server uses the aioredis module to manage and respond to network requests that follow a simple subject, predicate, object triple format. Although the Linked Data Fragments server could run on other web protocols than HTTP, the initial design of the Linked Data Fragment server follows a simple HTTP GET request using a URL pattern similar to this: `http://linked-datastore-example.com/serv er?predicate=schema:creator&object=Mark+Twain`, where the missing element, in this case a subject, does a search for all the subjects that match a `schema:creator` value of Mark Twain. The Linked Data Fragment server then responds with a list of subject-object-triples that match this triple fragment.

Supporting this design with the aioredis module, the Linked Data Fragment server implements a simple Redis key schema. In our RDF implementation, we assume that our triples must follow these constraints:

- A subject can either be a blank node or a valid URL (although the URL can use a namespace prefix for brevity)
- A predicate must be a valid URL
- An object can be either a Blank Node, a valid URL, or a string literal

The Redis key schema uses the `sha1` hash of each individual subject, predicate, or object as a simple string key that stores the serialized value. We then store each triple key in the following format—subject `sha1`: predicate `sha1`: object `sha1`, with the value being the JSON-linked data representation of the triple. We could have just as easily stored the RDF XML, Turtle, or other N-triples serialization. However, for the convenience of implementation we use JSON, as it is the most commonly requested output. Most of the triple singleton and triple keys are set with a TTL of one week so that we can use our Redis LRU volatile algorithm for our caching.

For triples using a namespace prefix, we expand the prefix to complete the URL before calculating the `sha1` hash. Using `sha1` hashes for our keys, we normalize our URL and literal strings to a single identifier key. For example, if we wanted to store a simple RDF graph of Mark Twain's three books: Adventures of Tom Sawyers, Huckleberry Finn, and Roughing It, they would be stored with these keys:

Triple type	Value	sha1 hash key
Subject URL	`http:// books.com/ adventures-of- tom-sawyer`	`9192f6c2ea49440a15aa72c7d9c8c74f77ba2bf9`
Predicate URL	`http://schema. org/creator`	`e7c68409090a3d30933a819b3654b659c94cbc39`
Object literal	Mark Twain	`2b22164235bb360ad57c73ffffbd6550ddb366ef`

In our Redis database, we would store the triple as a key with an integer one. We can replicate this Redis key schema from the redis-cli:

```
127.0.0.1:6379> SET 9192f6c2ea49440a15aa72c7d9c8c74f77ba2bf9 http://
books.com/adventures-of-tom-sawyer
OK

127.0.0.1:6379> SET e7c68409090a3d30933a819b3654b659c94cbc39 http://
schema.org/creator
OK

127.0.0.1:6379> SET 2b22164235bb360ad57c73ffffbd6550ddb366ef "Mark Twain"
OK

127.0.0.1:6379> SET 9192f6c2ea49440a15aa72c7d9c8c74f77ba2bf9:e7c684090
90a3d30933a819b3654b659c94cbc39:2b22164235bb360ad57c73ffffbd6550ddb36
6ef '[\n  {\n      "@id": "http://books.com/adventures-of-tom-sawyer",\n
"http://schema.org/creator": [\n        {\n           "@value": "Mark Twain"\n
}\n    ]\n  }\n]'
OK
```

From the `cache.py` module, the current implementation uses the Redis SCAN command to search for any given triple fragment pattern. The following is `get_triple` coroutine:

```python
@asyncio.coroutine
def get_triple(subject_key=None, predicate_key=None, object_key=None):
    redis = get_redis()
    pattern = str()
    for key in [subject_key, predicate_key, object_key]:
        if key is None:
            pattern += "*"
        else:
            pattern += "{}".format(key)
    pattern = pattern[:-1]
    yield from redis.scan(pattern)
    redis.close()
```

Using this single function, we can now match any of the following triple search patterns:

For a subject search with a `schema:creator` predicate and a the string `Mark Twain`:

```
*:7c68409090a3d30933a819b3654b659c94cb
```

Todo list application using Node.js and Redis

Amir Rajan, the author of the `node.js` Todo list application, uses Redis to add and update a simple Todo web application. The Todo application uses the node.js and `expresses` and `redisses` modules. We will first clone and then install all the dependencies of the application including Express, a fast and minimalist web framework for node.js and the Redis node.js client:

```
$ git clone https://github.com/amirrajan/nodejs-todo.git
$ cd nodejs-todo
$ npm install
```

After launching a Redis instance running on the default port `6379`, we'll run the `server.js` with `node.js` from the command line:

```
$ node server.js
```

Now, we'll open up a second terminal window and run a redis-cli session by first checking the size of the Redis database and then running the MONITOR command:

```
127.0.0.1:6379> DBSIZE
(integer) 1
127.0.0.1:6379> MONITOR
OK
```

We'll then open `http://localhost:3000` in a web browser and submit our first **Todo Redis** as shown in this screenshot:

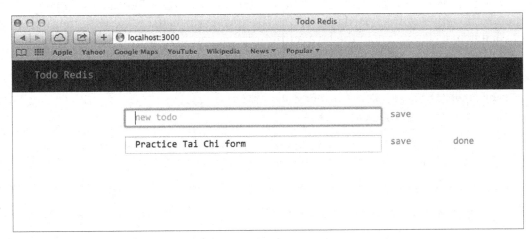

ToDo Redis Screenshot

The resulting `todos` hash value was set with our first Tai Chi form event with an `uuid` Redis key:

```
1436158403.745530 [0 127.0.0.1:61551] "hset" "todos" "c93e53d4-4284-43f1-
a3ef-d350ca805bbc" "Practice Tai Chi form
```

If we shut down our Redis server, we get an `unhandledexception` in our `node.js` application:

```
events.js:72
        throw er; // Unhandled 'error' event
        ^

Error: Redis connection to 127.0.0.1:6379 failed - connect ECONNREFUSED
    at RedisClient.on_error (/Users/jeremynelson/2015/nodejs-todo/node_
modules/redis/index.js:189:24)
    at Socket.<anonymous> (/Users/jeremynelson/2015/nodejs-todo/node_
modules/redis/index.js:95:14)
    at Socket.EventEmitter.emit (events.js:95:17)
    at net.js:440:14
    at process._tickCallback (node.js:415:13)
```

The functionality of Rajan's todo `node.js` is limited. By tracking two additional pieces of information about our `todo` items, creation time and time completed or canceled, we can note when items were initiated, when items were completed, and the time of completion by comparing the two values for any particular todo item. To capture these values as well as provide some additional functionality, we'll create two Redis sorted sets: `created:todos` and `completed:todo`. When adding a new member to either of the sorted sets, the UNIX timestamp as the score with the UUID of each item as the value. In the JavaScript function handler for the `/todos/create` route, we'll add the following call to the redis module after the `todo` item is saved to the original hash value:

```
client.hset("todos", id, req.body.description);
client.zadd("created:todos", Date.now(), id);
```

We will then add a similar ZADD command to the JavaScript function handler for the `/todos/delete` route:

```
client.hdel("todos", id);
client.zadd("completed:todos", Date.now(), id);
```

To test our code additions to this application, we'll first save `server.js`, restart the node, and then add two new items: Morning Code Review with Mike and Tai Chi 13 Posture Practice, to our item listing. We'll then click the `done` link in the web UI for Morning Code Review with Mike. With our `redis-cli`, we first check to see whether our two new sorted sets are present:

```
127.0.0.1:6379> KEYS *
1) "completed:todos"
2) "created:todos"
3) "todos"
```

Second, retrieve the values in each sorted set:

```
127.0.0.1:6379> ZRANGE created:todos 0 -1 WITHSCORES
1) "2b7dd99a-c1b3-4130-9372-00ea15f648f1"
2) "1436447038668"
3) "3a874008-7983-4861-b774-18baa5207fb3"
4) "1436447053529"
127.0.0.1:6379> ZRANGE completed:todos 0 -1 WITHSCORES
1) "2b7dd99a-c1b3-4130-9372-00ea15f648f1"
2) "1436447057307"
```

To calculate the total completion time for a `todo` item we can retrieve the score for our Morning Code Review with Mike item, 1436447057307-1436447038668; a highly unlikely total time of 1.8639 seconds for any code review!

Replication and public access

Now, let's add redundancy to our `todo` application's datastore and create a slave instance that we'll use as a backup for our todo list. We'll create a new `ReadOnly` function in the `Node.js` `server.js` file that will display a list using our Redis slave instance. First, we'll create an Express route that maps the `/readonly` route to our function:

```
function ReadOnly(req, res) {
  res.render('readonly');
}
app.post('/readonly', ReadOnly(req, res));
```

We'll next create a copy of `redis.conf` for our slave instance and run it on port `6380`. Our new function can then be run by passing in a `readonly` argument when running the `server.js` code file:

```
$ node server.js readonly
```

Summary

This chapter started with an in-depth exploration of how Redis handles and responds to client requests defined in multiple C header and code files. Then, we took a detailed look at the source code. We examined the `processCommand` function that works in relation to other functions and operations in Redis. We then went through an exercise where we added two new Redis commands by coping and retrofitting existing C code into our own development Redis branch.

The next sections were on the Redis Serialization Protocol and thewith a detailed byte-level examination of the Redis binary persistence format. We then looked at two different projects that use different Redis client implementations in Python and Node.js.

Now that you have a better understanding of what is under the hood of Redis, in *Chapter 5, Programming Redis Part 2 – Lua Scripting, Design Patterns, and DevOps*, we will show how to add complex server-side Lua programs to Redis instead of creating custom Redis commands. *Chapter 5, Programming Redis Part 2 – Lua Scripting, Design Patterns, and DevOps* also introduces some popular design patterns for building applications using Redis. The chapter finishes up with an overview of using Redis in various DevOps circumstances.

5
Programming Redis Part Two – Lua Scripting, Administration, and DevOps

In this chapter, we will first focus on the capabilities and limitations of server scripting in Lua. Lua scripts provides us with options to add complex behavior to Redis without the need to modify the Redis source code. We will revisit some of the examples from the previous chapters and see how these applications can be improved and simplified with the use of Lua scripts. From there, we will slightly switch gears to focus on how the two administration topics-Redis master-slave replication and transactions-impacts your application designs. We'll finish the chapter by examining the role of Redis in a typical DevOps environment, which many organizations of all sizes are adopting to improve their delivery of information and computing resources.

The use of Lua in Redis

In his original 2011 blog post about the addition of server-side scripting to Redis, Salvatore Sanfilippo lists three reasons why:

- Scripting increases the speed of Redis for some tasks by reducing the bandwidth between the server and client, that is separate calls are sent to Redis to read a value, apply some client-side computing to the value, and then add the value back to Redis

- As most workflows in Redis tend to be I/O bound and not CPU bound, scripting provides a better balance between the two

- Scripting allows the Redis server code base to remain fast and lean for general abstractions, while giving users the ability to add specific server-side functionalities

The entire post can be found here: `http://oldblog.antirez.com/post/redis-and-scripting.html`.

Later, server-side scripting was officially added to Redis using the Lua programming language in version 2.6. Lua is a fast and lightweight-programming language designed to be embedded into programs or added as a scripting environment for other programming languages, particularly C and C++ programs as well as for scripting gaming environments. Lua, "Moon" in Portuguese, has been designed, sponsored, and maintained by LuaLab at the Pontifical Catholic University of Rio de Janeiro in Brazil. Lua is used to extend the functionality of a Redis server by allowing more complex logic and operations to be embedded into a running Redis instance. A difference between Lua and other scripting languages, such as Python, Perl, and Ruby, is that Lua is very fast and small compared to these other languages. Lua is licensed under the MIT open source license and the source code for the language is available for downloading at `http://www.lua.org/`.

Installing Lua

Installing Lua on your computer varies (of course!) according to the operating system. For Linux and other POSIX-derived operating systems including Mac OS X, you can follow these steps outlined on Lua's website1:

```
curl -R -O http://www.lua.org/ftp/lua-5.3.1.tar.gz
tar zxf lua-5.3.1.tar.gz
cd lua-5.3.1
make {os-code} test
```

 This will download the 5.3.1 version of Lua, extract, and then build it for your system. To verify that Lua is complied and installed correctly, change the locations of the directories so that they are inside the Lua `root` directory and then run the test that will display the following:

```
$ make test
src/lua -v
Lua 5.3.1 Copyright (C) 1994-2015 Lua.org, PUC-Rio
```

After successfully executing the preceding test, you will learn and experiment with a lot of of Lua' syntax and types by invoking the Lua interpreter in interactive mode:

```
$ lua-5.3.1/src/lua
Lua 5.3.1  Copyright (C) 1994-2015 Lua.org, PUC-Rio
>
```

While Lua scripts can be invoked directly with the Lua interpreter and run as a standalone program, Lua really proves to be useful when it is embedded into other programs. With Redis, Lua scripts are run inside the event loop of the Redis server. These scripts are run after being loaded from the client and are either evaluated directly with the EVAL or invoked later through a SHA1 digest of the Lua script that is run with the EVALSHA command. The syntax of the EVAL command is as follows:

```
EVAL lua_script number_of_keys key [key..] arg, [arg ...]
```

In the preceding command, the lua_script argument is a string of the Lua 5.1 script that is run within the context of the Redis server. The number_of_keys parameter is the number of the arguments that follow. They represent Redis keys. Next in the command are the Redis keys used in the Lua script. Finally, there are zero or more additional arguments that do not represent keys and are the last arguments passed to the EVAL command.

To understand the syntax of Lua that is needed for Redis scripts as well as to understand the limitations Redis imposes on scripting, we'll start with a simple example and move on to a more involved example of Lua scripting.

From a Python shell, we will import the redis module, create a Python Redis client, and then we will create a Lua script: first_script, that returns the Hello Redis string without any keys or options passed to EVAL and with the required number of keys argument set to 0:

```
>>> import redis
>>> datastore = redis.StrictRedis()
>>> first_script = """return "Hello Redis" """
>>> datastore.eval(, 0)
b'Hello Redis'
```

The Lua core syntax is deliberately kept small. Lua ignores spaces and new lines except when the space is used as a delimiter between names and keywords. The comments between tokens (or other lexical elements) are created by surrounding the text with --[[and]]--. Lua accepts any combination of letters, digits, and underscores for use as an identifier for variables, table fields, and labels except that a variable name cannot begin with a digit. Lua has approximately 22 reserved keywords that cannot be used as a name in Lua functions, and this includes typical control flow keywords such as if else, elseif, while, and for and keywords for defining functions such as goto, end, and return. Lua is case-sensitive, so the addPerson and AddPerson functions would be interpreted in Lua as two different functions. Another Lua convention for variable names is avoiding names that start with underscore _. The underscore character followed by uppercase characters is a convention that is used for Lua environmental variables such as version— _VERSION.

Using the `print` keyword in a Redis Lua script to the standard output. If you include a print statement in your Lua script, the output will show up in the standard output of Redis. We may the following Lua script that starts with a comment describing what we're doing, followed by printing what version of Lua is running from our Python shell:

```
>>> second_script = """--[[ Prints Lua Version to Redis Output ]]--
print(_VERSION)"""
>>> datastore.eval(second_script, 0)
```

In this case, we will display the following in the terminal window in which Redis is running:

```
1139:M 27 Nov 12:03:49.640 * The server is now ready to accept
connections on port 6379
ions on port 6379
Lua 5.1
```

Notice that our comment is not displayed in the Redis server's output but the 5.1 version of Lua that is embedded in Redis is displayed by printing the `_VERSION` global variable. If we use Lua's print statement, it will provide us with a quick method to see the value of a variable in our Redis Lua script; however, it isn't the greatest method to debug errors in our Lua scripts. Starting with Redis 3.2, an integrated Lua debugger is now available in Redis and we will use it later in this chapter.

Lua variables are all first-class values and can be one of these eight different types: `number`, `string`, `boolean`, `function`, `nil`, `userdata`, `thread`, and `table`. The `number` type can be either `integers` or `floats` with Lua's default use of 64-bit integers and double-precision 64-bit floats although Lua can be complied to use 32-bit. From our third Lua script, you can see how a Lua number can be either an `integer` value or a `float` value and how Lua can seamlessly convert between the two. The following Lua script first creates two local variables, a and b, and displays the Lua types using Lua's type function:

```
>>> third_script = """--[[ Demos Lua int and float number type ]]--
local a = 10
print(a)
print(type(a))
local b = a + 3.123
print(b)
print(type(b))"""
>>> datastore.eval(third_script, 0)
```

This results in the following output from our Redis server:

```
10

number

13.123

number
```

Because Lua scripts are run in a strict mode in Redis, all script variables need to be localized in the scope of the script. Redis does not allow global variables to be used in Lua scripts. By default, Lua assumes all the variables are global. Since Redis rejects global variables, all variable declarations in Lua must use the **local** keyword. Let's see whether we can run the following Lua script snippet without the local keyword for an a variable:

```
>>> datastore.eval("""a = 10

print(a)""",0)

Traceback (most recent call last):

  File "<pyshell#48>", line 2, in <module>

    print(a)""",0)

  File "/Library/Frameworks/Python.framework/Versions/3.4/lib/python3.4/
site-packages/redis/client.py", line 1899, in eval

    return self.execute_command('EVAL', script, numkeys,
      *keys_and_args)

  File
    "/Library/Frameworks/Python.framework/Versions/3.4/lib/python3.4/
site-packages/redis/client.py", line 565, in execute_command

    return self.parse_response(connection, command_name, **options)

  File
    "/Library/Frameworks/Python.framework/Versions/3.4/lib/python3.4/
site-packages/redis/client.py", line 577, in parse_response

    response = connection.read_response()

  File
    "/Library/Frameworks/Python.framework/Versions/3.4/lib/python3.4/
site-packages/redis/connection.py", line 574, in read_response

    raise response

redis.exceptions.ResponseError: Error running script (call to f_928273b0
02b0116d3428bab44baa7c2af82dddf3): @enable_strict_lua:8: user_script:1:
Script attempted to create global variable 'a'
```

Lua supports string-to-number type coercion where a number is converted from a string as well as a function to number that takes a string and returns a number. This is useful to convert the values that you may pass to your script as arguments. These optional values are accessible in a Lua script through a table called **ARGV**. Note that all the ARGV argument values are passed to your Lua scripts as strings, so you'll need to either convert or coerce the value to a Lua number if you want to perform numerical operations on the value in your script. Here is what happens when we pass 1 as an optional argument when running fourth_script:

```
>>> fourth_script = """--[[Demostrates string-to-number using ARGV[1]
]]--
print(ARGV[1].." is a "..type(ARGV[1]))
local a = tonumber(ARGV[1])
print(a.." is a "..type(a))
print(ARGV[1] + 2)"""
>>> datastore.eval(fourth_script, 0, 1)
```

The preceding code results in the following output from the Redis server:

```
1 is a string
1 is a number
3
```

The fourth_script introduces the .. string concatenation operation that allows you to combine strings together in your scripts, Lua's string type is an 8-bit immutable sequences of bytes with the strings being encoding agnostic. Boolean and nil are similar to other programming languages with a Boolean being either a true value or a false value and the nil representing a non-existent value, which evaluates to a boolean false value. Lua strings can be delimited with either single ' or double " quotes and support C-like escape sequences such as form-feed \f, newline \n, carriage return \r, or vertical tab \v. Lua 8-bit strings can contain any byte in a literal string using it's numerical hexadecimal value. We can illustrate this by running the following Lua script in Redis.

```
>>> datastore.eval("""return "\x48\x45\x4C\x4C\x4F\x20\x57\x4F\x52\x4C\x44" """, 0)
b'HELLO WORLD'
```

The table in Lua is a type of associative array object that has a richer data structure than a simple variable. Lua tables are a generic aggregate datatype that are also used as sets and lists. Lua makes no distinction between these different types of collections unlike other programming languages that have separate data types for lists and sets. A Lua table offers index-based access to it's members as well as a dictionary-like syntax where named keys can be used to retrieve specific values from the table. In your Redis Lua scripts, the KEYS and ARGV variables are Lua tables that store the Redis keys and optional arguments that you pass to both the EVAL and EVALSHA command calls. A word of caution, Lua tables do not start with an index of 0 but with an index of 1, which can cause confusion when you first learn Lua tables. Also, the index cannot be a nil or NaN (not a number) value.

To illustrate the use of KEYS and ARGV as Lua tables, we will run a Lua script that prints the type of the KEYS and ARGV variables:

```
>>> datastore.eval("""print("KEYS type="..type(KEYS))
print("ARGV type="..type(ARGV))""", 0)
```

This prints the following to the Redis server output:

```
KEYS type=table
ARGV type=table
```

We can also create new tables in our Redis Lua script by assigning a variable to an empty table using curly brackets. In fifth_script, we will create an empty table book, assign the first ARGV variable to the bf:Title property, and then return the bf:Title property:

```
>>> fifth_script = """--[[ Creates a Table for a Book based on ARGV ]]--
local book = {}
book["bf:Title"] = ARGV[1]
return book["bf:Title"]"""
>>> datastore.eval(fifth_script, 0, "Breakfast of Champions")
b'Breakfast of Champions'
```

When a Lua table is used as an array, the same underlying table syntax remains. Creating an array with a list of values in Lua is simple; in our sixth_script, we will define a local table for a work week that returns the day based on the value we pass to the Redis Lua script. Notice that we need to convert our ARGV[1] string to a number in order to use the index-based Lua table notation:

```
>>> sixth_script = """--[[ Work Week Script takes number ARGV[1] and
returns day ]]--
local work_week = {"Monday", "Tuesday", "Wednesday", "Thursday",
"Friday"}
```

```
return work_week[tonumber(ARGV[1])]"""
```

```
>>> datastore.eval(sixth_script, 0, 2)
```

```
b'Tuesday'
```

```
>>> datastore.eval(sixth_script, 0, 0)
```

If the index doesn't exist, a `nil` value is returned and nothing happens. Sending in 4 as the `ARGV[1]` property returns the expected value from the `work_week` table:

```
>>> datastore.eval(sixth_script, 0, 4)
```

```
b'Thursday'
```

Tables have many roles in Lua and spending some to learn the nuances of tables will benefit and improve your understanding when running Lua scripts on Redis server. More information on Lua tables can be found at `http://lua-users.org/wiki/TablesTutorial`.

The function type allows Lua programs to manipulate both Lua as well as C functions. As first-class functions, Lua functions are passed by reference instead of by value, making them more memory efficient than copying the value. A Lua function has the following syntax:

```
functioncall ::= prefix_expression arguments
```

If the `prefix_expression` is of the `function` type, then this function (in the `prefix_expression` slot) is called with the `arguments` parameter. If the `prefix_expression` is not of a function type, then the `prefix_expression _call` metamethod is called with the `prefix_expression` being the first parameter with the remaining parameters being the original arguments. Defining a function in Lua starts with the function keyword, followed by the arguments in brackets ( ) with the body of the function finally terminating in the `end` keyword. A Lua function may or may not return a value using the `return` keyword. An example of a Fahrenheit to Celsius temperature conversion Lua function is demonstrated in the `seventh_script` as follows:

```
>>> seventh_script = """--[[ Fahrenheit to Celsius Temperature Converter
]]--
local ftoC = function(f)
 return (f-32) * (5/9)
end
return ftoC(ARGV[1])"""
```

Now we can run `seventh_script` on some example Fahrenheit temperature values:

```
>>> datastore.eval(seventh_script, 0, 95)
35
>>> datastore.eval(seventh_script, 0, 50)
10
>>> datastore.eval(seventh_script, 0, 32)
0
>>> datastore.eval(seventh_script, 0, 0)
-17
>>> datastore.eval(seventh_script, 0, -40)
-40
```

The syntax to call a function, in this case the local `ftoC` Lua function, is similar to other programming languages. In preceding the `seventh_script` example, the `ftoC` function is called on the `ARGV` value we passed as the third value in the `datastore.eval` calls using four different Fahrenheit temperatures. If your application requires unit conversions, you can add Lua scripts, similar to this Fahrenheit to Celsius unit conversion script, to normalize your data on the server-side instead of in your client code.

Unlike other programming languages such as C, in Lua, functions are values that can be assigned to a variable making the functions anonymous without requiring a function name beforehand. As Lua functions are evaluated as any other expression, functions are considered first-class and, as we can see from our example, we use brackets ( ) with zero or more arguments after the function-defined variables. If the Lua function has a variable number of arguments, the syntax is to use an ellipsis . . . followed by a closing bracket). Specific variables can be extracted using the select keyword or can be stored into a table by surrounding the ellipsis with the { } brackets. Lua functions can return any number of separate values that are distinct from each other instead of being part of a larger container object. The `eighth_script` starts by defining a local function called `olympicMetals` that returns three strings, one for each metal.

```
>>> eighth_script = """--[[ Lua function returning multiple variables
]]--
local olympicMetals = function()
  return "Gold", "Silver", "Bronze"
end
```

The Lua script now calls `olympicMetals` and assigns three variable before printing a message:

```
    local gold, silver, bronze = olympicMetals()
    print("1st="..gold.." 2nd="..silver.." 3rd="..bronze)"""
```

Switching back to the Redis server output, we will see the following:

```
1st=Gold 2nd=Silver 3rd=Bronze
```

Wrapping a function that returns multiple values with an outer set of brackets ( ) will discard all of the return values except the first, which we can see if we modify our eighth_script by wrapping the olympicMetals function with brackets and returning the results:

```
>>> eighth_script = eighth_script + "\nreturn (olympicMetals())"
>>> datastore.eval(eighth_script, 0)
b'Gold'
```

Because Redis only returns a single value, evaluating Lua scripts that return multiple values operates in a similar fashion by only returning the first value. We can get around this limitation in our Redis Lua scripts using curly brackets { } to wrap any function that returns multiple values as a Lua table instead. To see the contents of our calling olympicMetals function, we will modify our Lua script by removing the three metal variables and instead return the results as a Lua table, which the Python Redis client returns as a Python list with the following three items:

```
>>> eighth_script = """--[[ Lua function returning multiple variables
]]--
local olympicMetals = function()
  return "Gold", "Silver", "Bronze"
end
return {olympicMetals()}"""
>>> datastore.eval(eighth_script, 0)
[b'Gold', b'Silver', b'Bronze']
```

Using KEYS and ARGV with Redis

We have already been using the keys and optional arguments that are accessible as the KEYS and ARGV Lua tables in our Lua server-side scripts in Redis. To illustrate this, we'll run ninth_script that echoes back a Lua table with the KEYS and ARGS variables as members to the Redis client:

```
>>> ninth_script = """--[[ Returns all KEYS and ARGV as members of a Lua
Table ]]--
return {KEYS[1], KEYS[2], ARGV[1], ARGV[2]}"""
>>> keys_and_args = ["Airline:1", "Airline:2", "Singapore Airlines",
"Southwest"]
>>> datastore.eval(ninth_script, 2, *keys_and_args)
[b'Airline:1', b'Airline:2', b'Singapore Airlines', b'Southwest']
```

We can refactor this script—now called `tenth_script`—so that instead of requiring explicit keys for the Lua table, we can create a `for` loop that iterates through all of the values in KEYS and ARGV and returns the resulting Lua table:

```
>>> tenth_script = """--[[ Demostrates creating a Lua table with both
KEYS and ARGV ]]--
local airlines= {}
for i,k in ipairs(KEYS) do
  table.insert(airlines, k)
end
for i,k in ipairs(ARGV) do
  table.insert(airlines, k)
end
return airlines"""
>>> datastore.eval(tenth_script, 2, *["Airline:1", "Airline:2",
"Singapore Airlines", "Southwest"])
[b'Airline:1', b'Airline:2', b'Singapore Airlines', b'Southwest']
```

In this script, the `local` keyword precedes the `airlines` variable assignment to an empty table with curly brackets. We are using a function called **ipairs** to loop through both KEYS and ARGV that ensures the table is accessed in order starting at index 1, an important characteristic with a position-based EVAL command that assumes both KEYS and ARGS are accessed inside the Lua script in order.

Redis commands can be called within a Lua script using either the `redis.call` or `redis.pcall` functions that use the Redis Lua module. The major differences between these two Redis calls is how errors are handled. An error that occurs when executing the `redis.call` will pass through the error to the Redis client that issued the EVAL command. The `redis.pcall`, on the other hand, captures the error into a Lua table and returns the table to the calling client, making `redis.pcall` easier for error-checking and handling in the Redis client. If you're using a Redis client, the difference in your client application may be minimal. For instance, the Python Redis module raises a `redis.exceptions.ResponseError` regardless of you using `redis.call` or `redis.pcall` in your Lua script.

Because Lua and Redis data types are different, Redis needs to transform incoming data to the corresponding Lua type and then transform the results of the script execution to the RESP values of Redis. The following table shows the corresponding mapping between Lua and RESP values.

Redis Datatype	Lua Datatype
Redis integer reply	Number
Redis bulk reply	String
Redis multi bulk reply	Table
Redis status reply	Table with a single OK field
Redis error reply	Table with a single ERR field
Redis nil bulk reply	False Boolean value
Redis integer reply of 1	True Boolean value

A common pattern in Redis applications that we have discussed in earlier chapters is maintaining a global counter that is appended to a key pattern with a delimiter to make a unique key with which data is then inserted into Redis depending on the data structure. For example, we have a global book counter that is used to create a hash key where properties are stored. Using a Lua script we can reduce the number of Redis calls by half:

```
>>> add_book_lua = """local book_id = redis.pcall('INCR', 'global:book')
local book_key = "book:"..book_id
redis.pcall("HMSET", book_key, "title", ARGV[1], "author", ARGV[2])
return book_key"""
>>> datastore.eval(add_book_lua, 0, "Moby Dick", "Herman Meville")
b'book:1'
```

Now, we will retrieve all of the fields and values in our new Book hash:

```
>>> for field, value in datastore.hgetall('book:1').items():
  print(field, value)
b'author' b'Herman Meville'
b'title' b'Moby Dick'
```

While it is certainly feasible to use the EVAL command for Lua scripts, the preferred method to run Lua scripts is through Redis's script loading and execution. With simple Lua scripts, the overhead of sending the script on each invocation to the Redis server is acceptable and minimal; however, the downside is that the entire text of the script must be used every time this Lua script is used in the application. For more complex and larger Lua scripts, network latency may become a concern as each invocation now sends the entire script over the network.

Restrictions and considerations when using Lua scripts in Redis

Blocking: Be careful of long-running Lua scripts or when using larger and complex Lua scripts. Because of Redis's single-threaded nature, these scripts block execution for other clients until completed!

Atomaticy of scripts: To ensure that Lua scripts are pure functions when run on any Redis instance, that is, I need to be confident that running a particular Lua script on **Slave 1** and **Slave 2** is the same; otherwise, debugging side effects and constructing unit testing becomes a much greater challenge. Any Redis write command should perform in an identical fashion given the same arguments. Commands such as SPOP that randomly return a value and write back to Redis are prohibited and will cause an error if called from a Lua script.

Limited Lua libraries: The Redis Lua environment only includes the following Lua libraries: table, string, math, debug, cjson, and cmsgpack.

Cluster support: Lua scripts can be run on a Redis cluster as long as the script operates on keys that are on the same hash slot.

To provide a flexible method for loading Lua scripts once in the Redis server, Redis provides a SCRIPT LOAD command that takes the string of the Lua script and returns the SHA1 hash of the script. Clients can then call a hashed digest of the Lua script along with the KEYS and ARGV arguments using the EVALSHA command. The SCRIPT LOAD command syntax is as follows:

SCRIPT LOAD script

Redis computes the SHA1 of a Lua script that has been loaded into Redis using the SCRIPT LOAD command, which returns the SHA1 digest that can be executed using the EVALSHA command.

Along with the ability to load Lua scripts into a running Redis instance, Redis also provides three other SCRIPT subcommands to help manage these scripts in the Redis server's script cache:

SCRIPT EXISTS script_SHA1 [script_SHA1...]

The SCRIPT EXISTS command takes one or more SHA1 digest values and checks to see whether the script is the Redis server's script cache. This is done by returning an array of integers with a value of 1 for each SHA1 digest argument found and zero for the SHA1 digests that are absent from the script cache.

SCRIPT KILL

The SCRIPT KILL command is for long-running Lua scripts that may have an internal error or may be hung-up in a race condition. As the Redis server is single-threaded and blocks on each EVAL or EVALSHA call, the SCRIPT KILL command will interrupt the running process and return an error to the script and call client.

SCRIPT FLUSH

The final command, SCRIPT FLUSH, clears the Redis server script cache and any subsequent EVALSHA commands will return an error until a SCRIPT LOAD command is issued with a new Lua script.

Going back to our add_book_lua script, we can generate the SHA1 digest for the script with the following:

```
>>> add_book_sha1 = datastore.script_load(add_book_lua)
>>> add_book_sha1
'946ba456ead00a1787f6579097fc8df2fb30e17b'
```

With the SHA1 of this function, we can use this hash digest with a different client; in this case, our Redis-cli client. We will first check to see whether the script exists and then add a new book hash key by calling the EVALSHA command:

```
127.0.0.1:6379> SCRIPT EXISTS 946ba456ead00a1787f6579097fc8df2fb30e17b
1) (integer) 1
127.0.0.1:6379> EVALSHA 946ba456ead00a1787f6579097fc8df2fb30e17b 0 "I
Know Why the Caged Bird Sings" "Maya Angelou"
"book:2"
127.0.0.1:6379> HGETALL book:2
1) "title"
2) "I Know Why the Caged Bird Sings"
3) "author"
4) "Maya Angelou"
```

If the Redis script cache is flushed, we should get an error if we attempt to call the SHA1 digest of the Lua script with a third book:

```
127.0.0.1:6379> SCRIPT FLUSH
OK
127.0.0.1:6379> EVALSHA 18b5c2930c60be193478b990e2c8d5afda9116e4 0 "The
Adventures of Sherlock Holmes" "Sir Arthur Conan Doyle"
(error) NOSCRIPT No matching script. Please use EVAL.
```

Advanced Lua scripting with Redis

Now that we have a basic understanding of Lua scripting in Redis, we will see how we might refactor a few examples from the previous chapters to use Lua scripts. We'll also note potential problems that might occur while using Lua scripting including introducing hidden complexities and harmful performance implications of these changes. Lua scripting is a valuable tool, but must be used in the context of its limitations with server-side scripts in Redis.

In *Chapter 3, Managing RAM: Tips and Techniques for Redis Memory Management*, we will modified our tea and coffee Python code to use Lua scripts for bitmap operations, and finally, in *Chapter 4, Programming Redis Part One: Redis Core, Clients, and Languages*, we modified both the linked data fragments as well as our Node.js applications to use Lua scripts.

MARC21 ingestion

From our first chapter example of ingesting the MARC21 records into a Redis key schema structure, we'll use a loaded Lua script. The main reason why we might want to shift processing to the Redis server is to reduce the number of Redis commands issued between the client and server to a single call with EVALSHA that contains all the information that we want to populate a number of keys in our datastore. To start, we'll create a Redis Lua script called marc_ingestion_script_:

```
>>> marc_ingestion_script = """--[[ MARC ingestion Lua script ]]--
local marc_key = KEYS[1]
if redis.call("exists", marc_key) < 1 then
 marc_key = "marc:"..redis.call("incr", "marc")
end
```

The Lua script starts by assigning the marc_key variable to KEYS[1] and then checks for the existence of marc_key in the Redis. If the marc_key doesn't exist, then it is initialized with the marc: string that appends the integer returned by a Redis call incrementing a global MARC record variable.

```
local marc_fld_id = redis.call("incr", marc_key..":"..KEYS[2])
local marc_fld_key = marc_key..":"..KEYS[2]..":"..marc_fld_id
```

Next, a MARC field ID is created by incrementing a global variable that is created by combing the marc_key field with the value in the KEYS[2], which we assume is the MARC field code. We finish this by creating the MARC field key by concatenating the original marc_key, the MARC field code, and the MARC field id.

```
redis.call(elpushhall(elpush, marc_fld_key)
```

We then add the `marc_fld_key` to a `marc_key` list. This list collects all the fields in reverse order as they are added to the datastore.

```
for i,k in ipairs(KEYS) do
  if i > 2 then
    redis.call("HSET", marc_fld_key, k, ARGV[i-2])
  end
end
return marc_fld_key"""
```

Because the order of the remainder of the keys are the fields for the `marc_fld_key` hash matters, we will use the `ipairs` call to ensure that we start iterating through the KEYS at index 1. Since `KEYS[1]` and `KEYS[2]` are already in use, we will start to map each `key` starting with `KEY[3]` with a corresponding value in the ARGV table variable. The last line returns the new Redis key for the MARC field.

We will use this Lua script by saving the result of the SCRIPT LOAD command in a `marc_ingestion_sha1` variable in our Python shell:

```
>>> marc_ingest_sha1 = datastore.script_load(marc_ingestion_script)
>>> marc_ingest_sha1
'90eba74ace34ee70ad8705a9baab9e888c5c7740'
```

For our MARC record of David Foster Wallace's Infinite Jest, we will first define a Python list to store the keys and arguments for a MARC 100 field and then we would call `marc_ingestion_script` using the EVALSHA function with the `marc_ingest_sha1`, the number of keys set to 3, and the field list as parameters:

```
>>> field = [None, 100, "a", "Wallace, David Foster"]
>>> datastore.evalsha(marc_ingest_sha1, 3, *field)
b'marc:1:100:1'
```

The retrieval of the `'a'` subfield from the `marc:1:100:1` hash is confirmed by the following:

```
>>> datastore.hget('marc:1:100:1', 'a')
b'Wallace, David Foster'
```

For the entire MARC 245 field with multiple MARC subfields, we would first create the keys and arguments list and then call EVALSHA using `marc:1` as `KEYS[1]`:

```
>>> field245 = ["marc:1", 245, "a", "b", "c", "Infinite Jest :", "a
novel", "David Foster Wallace"]
>>> datastore.evalsha(marc_ingest_sha1, 5, *field245)
b'marc:1:245:1'
```

```
>>> datastore.lrange("marc:1", 0, -1)
[b'marc:1:245:1', b'marc:1:100:1']
```

The `marc_ingestion_script` allows us to reduce the number of round-trips between our Redis client and server from between 3 and 5 to a single EVALSHA call.

Online Storefront Paper Stationery

In *Chapter 2*, *Advanced Key Management and Data Structures*, we had an example of Online Storefront Paper Stationery. In this, we created a Redis key schema with accompanying logic relating keys together to manage the inventory of two types of paper that are updated when an online sale occurs in the online store. Just as a quick reminder, here is the graphic outline the example from *Chapter 2*, *Advanced Key Management and Data Structures*:

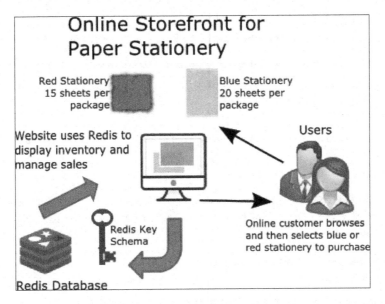

To shift the logic and key maintenance from the Redis client to the Redis server, we will create two Lua scripts to handle the Redis interactions and reduce the number of individual calls we make to the Redis instance. The downside of shifting to Lua scripts for these tasks may mean that the readability of the code in a Python application will decrease. Instead of seeing how the individual Redis calls relate to each other in Python, we now require the programmer to understand Lua as well. Another reason you may wish to shift logic and key management from Python code to Lua is if you are considering a switch in programming languages for the project. Your new application will not have to replicate the logic, but just call the EVALSHA with the proper Lua script digests with correct KEYS and ARGV.

We'll start refactoring the online storefront paper stationery example by creating a Lua script called `new_stationary_script` that takes zero Redis keys but four value arguments for the stationery color, width, height, and the number of sheets in a package of stationery. The Lua script will return the new stationery Redis key, as follows:

```
>>> new_stationary_script = """local stationery_key = "stationery:"..
redis.call("incr", "global:stationery")

redis.call("hmset", stationery_key, "color", ARGV[1], "width", ARGV[2],
"height", ARGV[3])

redis.call("incrby", stationery_key..":sheets", ARGV[4])

redis.call("set", stationery_key..":inventory", ARGV[5])

return stationery_key"""
```

Calling SCRIPT LOAD and saving the sha1 hash as the `new_stationary_sha1` variable, we can then call EVALSHA with the sha1 hash of this Lua script resulting in the following output when we send in the values for our blue and red stationery:

```
>>> new_stationary_sha1 = datastore.script_load(new_stationary_script)

>>> datastore.evalsha(new_stationary_sha1, 0, *['blue', "30 cm", "40 cm",
20, 100])

b'stationery:1'

>>> datastore.evalsha(new_stationary_sha1, 0, *['red', "45 cm", "45 cm",
15, 50])

b'stationery:2'
```

Now we will check to see whether the `new_stationary_script` worked correctly by first retrieving the `stationery:1` hash, the number of sheets for the `stationary:2` key, and the inventory for `stationary:2` using the following code:

```
>>> datastore.hgetall('stationery:1')

{b'height': b'40 cm', b'color': b'blue', b'width': b'30 cm'}

>>> datastore.get("stationery:2:sheets")

b'15'

>>> datastore.get("stationery:2:inventory")

b'50'
```

Now after these two stationeries have been added to Redis using this Lua script, we will next create a second Lua script called `record_sale` to record an online sale:

```
>>> record_sales = """--[[ Records a Stationery Sale ]]--
local sales_sorted_set = KEYS[1]..":sales"
```

```
redis.call("decrby", KEYS[1].."inventory", ARGV[1])
redis.call("zadd", sales_sorted_set, ARGV[2], ARGV[3])
return true"""
```

The `record_sale` Lua script takes the stationery's Redis key as `KEYS[1]`, the total number of packages sold in `ARGV[1]`, a UNIX timestamp from `ARGV[2]`, and the total sales amount in `ARGV[3]`. The script then decrements the inventory Redis key by the number of packages sold. The `record_sale` finished by adding a new entry to a sorted set of the stationery's sales using a sorted set with the score being the UNIX timestamp and the value of the sorted set being the sales amount. We'll record a sale in Python by first importing the time module to generate our UNIX timestamp:

```
>>> import time
>>> first_sale = ['stationary:1', 2, time.time(), 20]

>>> first_sale

['stationary:1', 2, 1448837693.338041, 20]
```

In the following code snippet, we have created a Python list for the first sale of two blue stationery packages:

```
>>> record_sales_sha1 = datastore.script_load(record_sales_script)
```

We can then test our Lua script by saving the SHA1 of this script as `record_sale_sha1` and then running EVALSHA with `first_sale`:

```
>>> datastore.evalsha(record_sales_sha1, 1, *first_sale)
1
>>> datastore.zrange("stationary:1:sales", 0, -1, withscores=True)
[(b'20', 1448837693.338041)]
```

With these two Lua scripts, this online stationery store implementation is simplified so that the application developer can focus on the web-specific interactions and the interface, while not needing to worry about data manipulation and the Redis key schema. While creating a consistent Redis key schema, an important role for Redis's Lua server-side scripting is that the Redis key creation and management can be handled for most cases within the application's Lua scripts and not in the client-side code, although most Redis object mappers continue to use client-side code to do this for their applications.

Interoperability using JSON-LD, Lua, and Redis

In *Chapter 3, Managing RAM – Tips and Techniques for Redis Memory Management*, we were using a Redis key schema to mirror a web service using forward slashes / as a key delimiter for a tea brewing service. Lua scripts running in Redis can directly use a smaller JSON structured as linked data. For our tea examples, we'll use the `https://schema.org/` and the `http://www.productontology.org/` JSON-LD vocabularies to store tea information. Instead of maintaining additional ingestion code to convert the JSON-LD into a Redis HASH, we'll create three JSON-LD strings for each tea type. Why might this be an advantage? First, by providing and using each of the three tea bag information stored as JSON-LD vocabularies, we will use this same format to interoperate with the tea suppliers downstream and upstream from customer demand. The following is the information for our tea brewing service structured as a `http://schema.org/` recipe for Earl Grey tea:

```
{
    "@context": {
        "": "https://schema.org",
        "pto": "http://www.productontology.org/id/"
    },
    "@id": "26bca550-db2b-445c-9253-4076e0bb968f",
    "@type": "Recipe",
    "cookTime": {
        "@type": "Duration",
        "@value": "PT5M"
    },
    "recipeIngredient": {
        "@type": "pto:Tea",
        "name": "Earl Grey"
    },
    "recipeInstructions": {
        "@type": "ItemList",
        "name": "Tea Box",
        "numberOfItems": 15
    }
}
```

The first Lua script that we will create adds a new brand of tea by storing the raw JSON data in an incremented global variable as string in our Redis datastore. This will also create supporting tea bags similar to individual tea boxes and bags stored as Redis list. The availability of JSON on the web, both publishing and consuming, means that you can provide easy interoperability with Redis using a Lua JSON library on the Redis server.

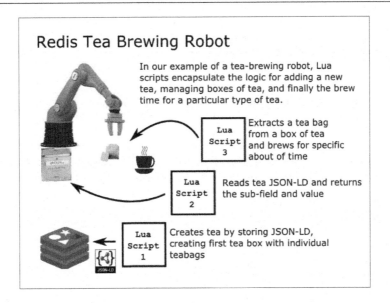

Our first Lua script will increment a global/tea variable, create and save a key for the tea with the JSON string passed as a string at the new key and finish by creating a list for the first tea-box populated with tea-bags using the `cjson` Lua library that is available for use in Redis Lua scripts:

```
local tea_key = "tea/"..redis.pcall("incr", "global/teas")
redis.pcall("set", tea_key, ARGV[1])
local box_id = redis.pcall("incr", "global/"..tea_key.."/box")
local box_key = tea_key.."/box/"..box_id
local box_json = cjson.decode(ARGV[1])
for i=1, box_json["recipeInstructions"]["numberOfItems"] do
  redis.pcall('rpush', box_key, i)
end
return tea_key
```

Once this Lua script is loaded with a return `SHA1` digest saved as a variable, we can then add our three examples by running the `addAllTeas` JavaScript function in the `load.js` Node.js file:

```
function addAllTeas(client) {
  console.log("Adding all Teas");
  fs.readFile("add-tea.lua", "utf8", function(err, data) {
    var add_tea_lua = data;
    client.script("load", add_tea_lua, function(err, data) {
      var add_tea_sha = data;
```

```
        var tea1 = addTea("earl-grey.json", add_tea_sha);
        var tea2 = addTea("lavender-mint.json", add_tea_sha);
        var tea3 = addTea("pepperment-punch.json", add_tea_sha);
    });
  });
  console.log("Finished");
  return true;
}
```

After running the `load.js` script from the command-line, we can examine the results with a new Redis Python client instance that we'll name as `tea_redis`:

```
>>> tea_redis.llen("tea/1/box/1")
20
>>> tea_redis.llen("tea/2/box/1")
20
>>> tea_redis.llen("tea/3/box/1")
15
```

Because the tea information is stored as a raw JSON string, we can decode the JSON string on the client-side using the Python JSON module:

```
>>> import json
>>> earl_grey = json.loads(tea_redis.get("tea/3").decode())
>>> earl_grey["recipeIngredient"]["name"]
'Earl Grey'
```

While this solution will work, we can also improve our tea application by decoding the JSON and returning the value of any JSON `hash` value by creating the following Lua script on the server-side:

```
if redis.call("exists", KEYS[1]) == 1 then
   local raw_json = redis.call("get", KEYS[1])
   local tea = cjson.decode(raw_json)
   return tea[ARGV[1]][ARGV[2]]
else
   return nil
end
```

Loading this script and then calling it from our Python shell provides us with a method to retrieve values from a smaller raw JSON. If our JSON objects are large, the Lua script may take too long to parse and return the value, as Redis will be blocked until the session is finished:

```
>>> with open("get-tea-info.lua") as fileobject:
raw_lua = fileobject.read()
>>> get_tea_sha1 = tea_redis.script_load(raw_lua)
>>> tea_redis.evalsha(get_tea_sha1, 1, "tea/1", "recipeIngredient",
"name")
b'Lavender Mint'
```

The final Lua script that we'll create for this example will wrap a tea brewing session by extracting the first tea bag from an existing box list and then steeping the tea for a predetermined time limit for each type. When the tea bag's time has expired, our application alerts the awaiting person that the tea is ready.

```
if redis.call("llen", KEYS[1]) < 1 then
  return nil
end
local tea_key = string.sub(KEYS[1], string.find(KEYS[1], "tea/%d+"))
local tea = cjson.decode(redis.call("get", tea_key))
local cook_time = tea["cookTime"]["@value"]
local brew_seconds = tonumber(string.sub(cook_time, string.find(cook_
time, "%d+"))) * 60
local bag_key = KEYS[1].."/bag/"..redis.call("lpop", KEYS[1])
redis.call("set", bag_key, 1)
redis.call("expire", bag_key, brew_seconds)
return bag_key
```

In our Lua script, we first check whether the tea box passed in as KEYS[1] is empty, and it returns nil if there are no teabags left in the list. Next, we will use the Lua standard string library to construct the tea key with a Lua pattern that matches the string.find function. This is passed to string.sub to get the tea key. We then decode the JSON value stored in the tea key, extract the number of minutes using the string.sub and string.find functions, and multiple by 60 to get the total number of seconds. Next, a bag_key is constructed from our second key, the tea box key, and then we construct our tea bag key with the key schema pattern of tea/{tea-id}/box/ {teabox-id}/bag/{teabag-id}. The tea-bag ID is obtained by running an LPOP command that returns the first element of the tea box list. We then set a timeout based on our brew_time local variable before returning the teabag key. This can be queried by our client with a ttl command until the key is evicted from our Redis instance.

To test our Lua script with Redis, we'll return to our Python shell and open our Lua script:

```
>>> with open("brew-tea.lua") as file_object:
  brew_tea_lua = file_object.read()
>>> brew_tea_sha1 = tea_redis.script_load(brew_tea_lua)
```

After saving the SHA1 in the `brew_tea_sha1` variable, we'll call EVALSHA and save the resulting tea-bag Redis key:

```
>>> tea_bag_key = tea_redis.evalsha(brew_tea_sha1, 1, "tea/2/box/1")
>>> tea_bag_key
b'tea/2/box/1/bag/1'
```

We'll query our Redis instance with the `ttl` command to see how much time is remaining:

```
>>> tea_redis.ttl(tea_bag_key)
159
>>> tea_redis.ttl(tea_bag_key)
59
>>> tea_redis.ttl(tea_bag_key)
-2
```

After the tea bag has been brewed, Redis returns a -2 to the client. As we have already noted in the previous chapter, having the client poll the server is not the optimal design for your application. Instead, using the Redis key expiration event notification feature, you can watch a key pattern have your application respond to the event when the `tea_bag` key has expired. In this case, the tea robot would remove the tea-bag. This example demonstrates how you can use JSON directly in your Redis application and perform more complicated workflows, such as brewing tea, on the server side.

Redis Lua Debugger

A major improvement new in Redis version 3.2 is a dedicated Lua debugger for troubleshooting problems with Lua scripts running on your Redis server. The Lua debugger runs in a forked server process from the main Redis event loop which means that multiple debugger sessions can be run simultaneously while other development is occurring on the server. By default, any data that was changed during the debugger session is roll-backed when the debugging session terminates or an alternative mode for the debugger can be enabled that persists data changes made in the Redis server's data during the debugging session (although this synchronous debugging mode blocks the Redis server through-out the debugging session). The Lua debugger for Redis uses a client-server model where the Lua debugger operates remotely on the with output from the debugger being feed back to the client, in this case a special mode of the Redis-cli client.

To illustrate the use of the Lua debugger, we'll need to have a running Redis 3.2 server and Redis-cli client. Next, we'll create a small Lua script that takes one or more e-mails, adds them to a chat room stored as a Redis list, and finally returns the total number of participants that are currently in the chat room. This Lua script, chatroom.lua, is available for download at the *Mastering Redis* website and is included as follows:

```
01 --[[ Lua script for simple chatroom management ]]--
02 local chatroom_key = KEYS[1]
03 for i, email in ipairs(ARGV) do
04   redis.call("LPUSH", chatroom_key, email)
05 end
06 return redis.call("LLEN", chatroom_key)
```

To start the Redis Lua debugger, we'll call this script from our Redis-cli with the -ldb and the -eval and the path to the chatroom.lua file option followed by a chatroom key, a comma, and three e-mail addresses stored in the ARGV:

```
~$ redis-3.2.0/src/redis-cli --ldb --eval chatroom.lua aikido-fan:456 ,
"mu@aiki.com" "at@maf.info" "kc@chiaikido.io"
Lua debugging session started, please use:
quit    -- End the session.
restart -- Restart the script in debug mode again.
help    -- Show Lua script debugging commands.


* Stopped at 2, stop reason = step over
-> 2    local chatroom_key = KEYS[1]
```

The Redis-cli is now in a special Lua debugger mode and no longer responds to Redis commands but to debugging commands. The Lua debugger starts in a stepping mode with the debugger stopping at the first line of Lua code, in this the setting of a local Lua variable for the KEYS[1] value. The step (alias is a single s character) command executes the Lua code, in this case line 2 in chatroom.lua:

```
lua debugger> step
* Stopped at 3, stop reason = step over
-> 3    for i, email in ipairs(ARGV) do
```

With line 2 executed, we can see the values of all local variables that are present in the current session with the print command (with a p character alias):

```
lua debugger> print
<value> chatroom_key = "aikido-fan:456"
```

Starting on line 3 in our Lua loop, we will iterate once through the loop and then issue another print command:

```
lua debugger> s
* Stopped at 4, stop reason = step over
-> 4      redis.call("LPUSH", chatroom_key, email)
lua debugger> print
<value> chatroom_key = "aikido-fan:456"
<value> (for generator) = "function@0x257ad70"
<value> (for state) = {"mu@aiki.com"; "at@maf.info"; "kc@chiaikido.io"}
<value> (for control) = 1
<value> i = 1
<value> email = "mu@aiki.com"
```

The result of issue the step command (using the s alias) twice and then a print command show the value of the variables, in this case we can see the loop values and the current iteration of the i counter variable is 1 and the current email variable value is mu@aiki.com.

Adding a break point with the Lua debugger is simple with the break command (with a b alias) followed by the line number in the Lua script. We'll add a break point at line 6 and then issue a continue (alias c) command to finish iterating through the for loop:

```
lua debugger> b 6
   5    end
  #6    return redis.call("LLEN", chatroom_key)
lua debugger> c
* Stopped at 6, stop reason = break point
->#6    return redis.call("LLEN", chatroom_key)
```

Separately, you can also add breakpoints in your Lua scripts by adding `redis.breakpoint( )` expression in your code. The `redis` (r alias) Lua debugger command allows you to issue Redis command to the server while in the Lua debugger, we can see the current elements in the `aikido-fan:456` Redis key with the **LRANGE** Redis command:

```
lua debugger> redis lrange aikido-fan:456 0 -1
<redis> lrange aikido-fan:456 0 -1
<reply> ["kc@chiaikido.io","at@maf.info","mu@aiki.com"]
```

Here we see the emails of the chat room's participants. Another useful Lua debugger command is the `trace` (t alias) that shows the current backtrace of the Lua debug session, the `list` (l alias) with optional line parameter for showing the source code around the current location:

```
lua debugger> t
In top level:
->#6    return redis.call("LLEN", chatroom_key)
lua debugger> list
    1    --[[ Lua script for simple chatroom management ]]--
    2    local chatroom_key = KEYS[1]
    3    for i, email in ipairs(ARGV) do
    4      redis.call("LPUSH", chatroom_key, email)
    5    end
->#6    return redis.call("LLEN", chatroom_key)
```

To exit the debug mode, we can either issue an `abort` (a alias) or a `continue` command that will drop your Redis-cli session back to it's normal Redis operation mode or the quit command to complete exit your session:

```
lua debugger> abort

(error) ERR Error running script (call to f_2c7fbbfbe9fe0c7d7cfe6a4a70212
a3147560f7d): @user_script:6: script aborted for user request

(Lua debugging session ended -- dataset changes rolled back)

127.0.0.1:6379>
```

The new Lua debugger should prove to be a particularly important tool as you develop and troubleshoot your Redis application's Lua scripts.

Programming Redis administration topics

Man Redis features and operational modes provide additional capabilities and restrictions when you are programming applications for your customers and stakeholders. As we have seen, adding Lua scripts to our application transfers even more business logic and data manipulation to the Redis instance, but with important restrictions and trade-offs. In the next sections, we'll do a tour of the administrative features of Redis that are pertinent to programming applications. First, we'll look at Redis's replication solution with Master-Slave instances, and then Redis transaction support and see how each of these features offer opportunities and trade-offs in our applications that have operational implications.

Master-Slave replication

A fundamental administrative topic to consider when programming with Redis is the decision about when to use Master/Slave replication for added stability, scaling, and performance, Redis data for application use. In replication, Redis instances designated as Masters have exact copies of their data stored on separate Redis instances designated as Slaves. This opens up a number of different possibilities of automatic backups, isolated write masters from more open slaves, and responding to spikes in user demand. We'll do a quick review of launching the simplest one-to-one Master/Slave setup

First, we'll launch our terminal and start up our master and slaves:

```
$ screen ../redis/src/redis-server
$ Ctrl-a
$ screen ../redis/src/redis-server --dbfilename slave.rdb --port 6380
$ Ctrl-a
```

In the preceding code, using the `screen` command, we first launched a new Redis instance with an empty datastore running on the default Redis port of `6379` and used the `dump.rdb` filename as it's snapshot. Then using the *Ctrl*-a C command, we created a new screen window and launched our second Redis instance that will be our slave, use as it's RDB filename `slave.rdb` as well as running on port `6380` to avoid a port conflict with the default master running on Redis default port. Finally, we created a new screen window on which we will run our Python command shell. We will create two Redis clients, one connected to the Master instance and another is `first_slave`, which is a client for the Redis instance that will replicate `first_master`:

```
>>> import redis
>>> first_master = redis.StrictRedis()
```

```
>>> first_slave = redis.StrictRedis(port=6380)
>>> first_master.dbsize()
0
```

Now we'll add some data to our new master. To make a larger dataset, we will create a Lua function that iterates a number of times through a variable that is passed to it and simply creates a string value as an incremented ID:

```
>>> increment_lua = """for i=1,ARGV[1] do local key='test:'..i redis.
call('SET', key, 'value='..i) end"""
>>> increment_lua = """for i=1,ARGV[1] do
    local key='test:'..i
    redis.call('SET', key, 'value='..i)
end"""
>>> first_master.eval(increment_lua, 0, 100000)
```

We will confirm that we have one hundred thousand keys in our master Redis datastore with the DBSIZE, as follows:

```
>>> first_master.dbsize()
100000
```

We will extract a few sample keys and confirm that our values are set according to what we specified in our Lua script by running the MGET command:

```
>>> for value in first_master.mget("test:1", "test:50000",
"test:100000"):
   print(value)
b'value=1'
b'value=50000'
b'value=100000'
```

We'll now return to `first_slave` and check whether this Redis instance is empty; we will issue a DBSIZE command and then issue the SLAVEOF command to begin the sync with the master that currently holds our 100,000 test keys:

```
.>>> first_slave.dbsize()
0
>>> first_slave.slaveof(host='localhost', port=6379)
True
>>> first_slave.dbsize()
100000
```

Using *Ctrl + A* to loop through our active screen windows, we will observe the running Master and see that a background fork started as soon as the SYNC command was received from our new slave:

```
1076:S 25 Jul 14:38:46.556 * SLAVE OF localhost:6379 enabled (user request)

1076:S 25 Jul 14:38:46.705 * Connecting to MASTER localhost:6379

1076:S 25 Jul 14:38:46.706 * MASTER <-> SLAVE sync started

1076:S 25 Jul 14:38:46.706 * Non blocking connect for SYNC fired the event.

1076:S 25 Jul 14:38:46.706 * Master replied to PING, replication can continue...

1076:S 25 Jul 14:38:46.706 * Partial resynchronization not possible (no cached master)

1076:S 25 Jul 14:38:46.706 * Full resync from master: 1b82a2315ec3c9daf5a37a7a11360469770494a7:1

1076:S 25 Jul 14:38:46.757 * MASTER <-> SLAVE sync: receiving 217808 bytes from master

1076:S 25 Jul 14:38:46.758 * MASTER <-> SLAVE sync: Flushing old data

1076:S 25 Jul 14:38:46.758 * MASTER <-> SLAVE sync: Loading DB in memory

1076:S 25 Jul 14:38:46.769 * MASTER <-> SLAVE sync: Finished with success
```

To see if our slave now has a copy for our Redis master, we will confirm whether the values are the same for both `first_master` and `first_slave`:

```
>>> for key in ["test:345", "test:67864"]:
print(first_master.get(key), first_slave.get(key))


b'value=345' b'value=345'
b'value=67864' b'value=67864'
```

A recent improvement to the resynchronization process for Redis's is it's implementation of the `PSYNC` command that improves durability and reduces network traffic if the replication link between the master and slave is broken during a standard `SYNC` command. If the `repl-backlog-size` directive is set and a size is specified, an in-memory backlog of the replication stream is saved by the master. This is done so that, if the replication link between it and the master's slaves is broken, the backlog allows the slave client to continue replicating the master's snapshot instead of beginning an entirely new replication process with the master. This feature reduces network traffic and improves stability if network latency exists between the Redis master and slaves.

Transactions with MULTI and EXEC

Transactions, where Redis commands are run in single sequential order by being sandwiched between the MULTI and EXEC commands. Redis transactions differ from the transactions used in SQL-based relational databases as they do not retrieve values to act upon, which is possible with SQL transaction. A more significant difference is errors can occur during the execution of a command and Redis will continue executing the remaining queued commands and not rollback the previous commands as it is done in a SQL relational database transaction.

To understand how Redis transactions are queued up and execute commands in order from our existing first_master Redis instance, we'll create a transaction for the movie-attendance Redis key and then we will increment movie-attendance in movie_attend_transaction:

```
>>> movie_attend_transaction = first_master.pipeline(transaction=True)
>>> movie_attend_transaction.incr("movie-attendance")
StrictPipeline<ConnectionPool<Connection<host=localhost,port=6379,db=0
```

In the second terminal window, we'll launch a second Python shell and create a Redis client for first_master2, and then retrieve the movie-attendance variable that was incremented in our first Python shell:

```
>>> import redis
>>> first_master2 = redis.StrictRedis()
>>> first_master2.get("movie-attendance")
```

Nothing was returned because we still haven't executed the transaction. We may issue our second Python shell as follows:

```
>>> first_master2.incr("movie-attendance")
1
```

Now in our original Python session, we will issue the EXEC command on movie_attend_transaction and then we'll see what is the value of movie-attendance with first_master:

```
>>> movie_attend_transaction.execute()
[2]
>>> first_master2.get('movie-attendance')
b'2'
```

Why is the value of movie-attendance 2 if we started the transaction before the first_master2 client was issued in the INCR command? The MULTI command is run when EXEC is issued on the transaction that was executed and not when the movie_attend_transaction issued the INCR command. By default, MULT/EXEC creates a queue of Redis commands that are executed during a blocking call when EXEC is issued. This may be very understandable if we want to lock the value, so if a movie-attendence variable is incremented in a transaction and the movie-attendence value is modified by another client, like we demonstrated, then the transaction will fail following an optimistic locking to Redis keys, such as movie-attendence, using the WATCH command with **check-and-set (CAS)** approach.

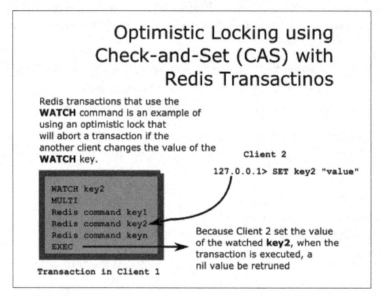

Optimistic Locking with CAS

To better illustrate the use of optimistic locking, we'll use telnet to access the master Redis instance and run WATCH with MUTLI and EXEC to illustrate optimistic locking with Redis transactions. First, we will return to our Python shell and remove the movie-attendance key:

```
>>> first_master.delete('movie-attendance')
1
```

Now we'll connect with telnet, use WATCH for the movie-attendance key, and then run the following transaction with MULTI-EXEC.

```
bash-3.2$ telnet localhost 6379
Trying ::1...
```

```
Connected to localhost.
Escape character is '^]'.
WATCH movie-attendance
+OK
MULTI
+OK
SET movie-attendance 15
+QUEUED
EXEC
*1
+OK
```

Now we'll check the value of movie-attendance from our Python shell:

```
>>> first_master.get('movie-attendance')
b'15'
```

The transaction executed correctly and set the movie-attendance value to 15 as we expected. Now we will repeat the telnet session using WATCH and see what happens:

```
WATCH movie-attendance
+OK
MULTI
+OK
SET movie-attendance 23
+QUEUED
```

Now, going back to our Python shell, we'll change the movie-attendance value and then go back and run EXEC in our telnet session:

```
>>> first_master.set('movie-attendance', 5)
True
```

Back to the telnet session, we get the following:

```
EXEC
*-1
```

Because we ran WATCH on movie-attendance, changing the value to 5 in the Python shell results in a -1 return when we attempt to run the transaction. Note that the Lua scripts running on Redis operate in a similar fashion: the operations in the script are atomic and if the script fails, changes to the datastore are aborted.

Redis role in DevOps

DevOps embraces a vision of enterprise technology that is a combination of traditionally siloed departments or divisions made up of **Software Development** (Engineering), **Technology Operations**, and **Quality Assurance**, where these three important functions are merged into a single organizational unit. This new unit emphasizes communication and cooperation among the various components while focusing on ways to automate and integrate development, quality testing, and production of technology services and resources. By focusing on these interrelated aspects of information technology, DevOps means to reduce the time-to-market or time-to-release of a new IT service, lower failure rates and runtime bugs, and increase recovery time if a product or service fails catastrophically.

Redis fits very well into this model due to a number of features including Redis's ease-of-deployment, rigorous unit and functionality testing of core and supplementary Redis technology, and the ease of automation through tools such as Chief, Ansible, Puppet, and Docker.

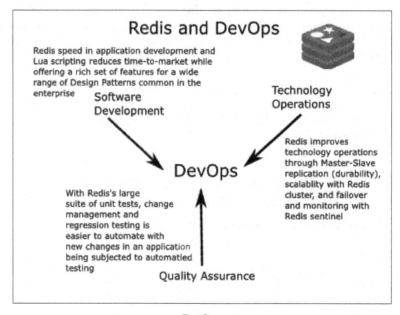

DevOps

Salvatore Sanfilippo writes about the use of Redis as a glue technology that complements if not supplements traditional databases or legacy systems in an enterprise. Over time, an organization accumulates a certain level of technical debt that is defined as the amount of effort required to fix or in some way remediate problems in a code base. CAST research labs estimate that the average cost to an organization per 300,000 lines of code is $1,083,000, or an average of technical debt per line of code can be $3.61.3. In a truly hybrid development-operations environment, operations code, such as a Lua scripts, introduce new avenues where source code can accumulate and contribute to the overall burden of maintainable code that the combined operations must address.

This is not to assert that incurring technical debt by introducing new code can be avoided. As an agile-based process with multiple development iterations of the code base, DevOps responsively adapts and changes with the business or operational environment shifts that happens with introductions of new competitors and strategic changes occurring within an organization's existing competition. The kind of code addition that is ideally minimizes in a functioning DevOps organization is in the growth of glue code for connecting directly incompatible vendor-siloed applications, legacy systems, and whatever current work-flow that is required by a business requirement. Redis offers an alternative by allowing the data to be structured so that it directly responds to new requirements. This can be a radical conceptual leap and offers something analogous to the Bridge4 structural design pattern for separating abstraction from it's implementation and the Adapter/Wrapper/Translator5 structural design pattern, which converts the interface of a class into another interface that the consuming client or process would expect.

Summary

This chapter started with a detailed examination of the Redis server scripting language called Lua before going into some examples of using Lua scripts with the EVAL command. This was followed by loading and then executing Lua scripts with the SCRIPT LOAD and EVALSHA commands. Next, we went back and saw how using Lua scripts can simplify the application logic in the earlier examples of the previous chapters, such the MARC21 ingestion, online stationery store, the linked data fragments server, and various node.js applications. The next section showed how in different Redis operational modes, such as Master-Slave replication and transactions, impact the Redis application design.

The final section was on how the role of Redis in the increasingly popular enterprise organizational structure called DevOps is flexible enough and well-suited for data storage and manipulation needs of both developers and operational staff.

In our next *Chapter 6, Scaling with Redis Cluster and Sentinel*, we will shift our focus to the more operational aspects of Redis; first with an exploration of the Redis cluster capabilities that allows large data problems to be spread across Redis instances, and second, with the monitoring and failover features of Redis Sentinel.

6
Scaling with Redis Cluster and Sentinel

This chapter first explores a crucial strategy of scaling large datasets with Redis by partitioning, or splitting up, the data across multiple Redis instances. By looking at various algorithms that different groups and projects have taken in sharding data, including one of the most successful efforts to do this with Redis, Twitter's Twemproxy project. This provides the background and history behind one of the biggest changes to Redis in the past few years; the inclusion of Redis cluster into the stable branch of Redis in version 3. We'll move from the Twemproxy approach to sharding Redis instances, to the strategy ultimately adopted and implemented in the Redis cluster. We will then experiment with using a Redis cluster with a couple of large datasets and see how client application code should be modified to be able to use the Redis cluster.

Regardless of the partitioning strategy taken to use Redis with large data, managing and supporting the large number of Redis instances led to the development and release of Redis Sentinel, a monitoring and failover program included with Redis that addresses the challenges of monitoring large number of running Redis instances, particularly when using Redis's master-slave replication.

Approaches to partitioning data

Partitioning data, where keys are divided and assigned to specific instances, is an important strategy for breaking up large databases or datasets that cannot be loaded into any single machine's available memory. With partitioning, computation and resources are no longer limited to what is available to a single Redis instance but expands and scales your application to include multiple processor cores and machines running and connecting to other Redis instances through network interfaces, routers, and adapters to other machines.

There are usually three different avenues for partitioning data with Redis — client-side partitioning, proxy assisted partitioning, and query routing. In client-side partitioning, the partitioning logic is contained in the client code that selects the correct partition or Redis node based on either an algorithm, storing extra information, or some combination of the two. With proxy-assisted partitioning, Redis clients connect to a proxy middleware that then routes the client's requests to the correct Redis node. We will be exploring one of the most popular projects that support this partitioning approach in a later section in this chapter on Twemproxy. The final implemented avenue for Redis partitioning is query routing where any client querying a random node in the cluster will be routed to the correct node containing the key, the approach taken in the current implementation of Redis cluster.

Range partitioning

Often, the simplest method to implement a partitioning strategy on either server or client-side, Range partitioning, does require management code and data structures to keep track of what key is assigned to a particular instance. At its core, Range partitioning assigns an incoming key to an instance based on whether the key is inside a particular range of values that have been assigned to an instance:

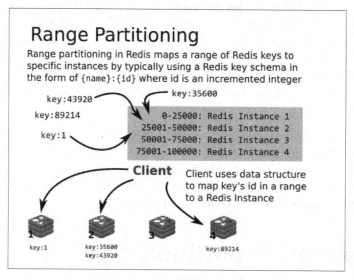

Range partitioning

A simplified version of a Range partitioning in Redis is to start with a defined number of Redis instances; in this example, we will arbitrarily pick five running Redis instances and assign a range of IDs to each instance. We will store a bitstring for each instance with a bit flipped to 1 for all IDs that are in the instance's assigned range. When a new key is created using a global increment, we will check each partition with a **GETBIT** call to see whether the new ID is in the assigned range for that partition and if it is, the key will be stored in the Redis instance for that partition.

Here is a short Python function, `set_range_partitions`, that sets the bits for our partitions:

```python
def set_range_partitions(datastore, partitions=5, size=20000):
    for i in range(0, partitions):
        key = "partition:{}".format(i+1)
        start = i*size + 1
        end = start + size
        for offset in range(start, end):
            datastore.setbit(key, offset, 1)
```

We now have five partition keys that store bitstrings for their range of keys. Because these keys do not take up much memory, we can store a copy on each of our five Redis instances. We'll first examine `partition:1` from a Redis-cli session:

```
127.0.0.1:6379> BITCOUNT partition:1
(integer) 20000
127.0.0.1:6379> GETBIT partition:1 1
(integer) 1
127.0.0.1:6379> GETBIT partition:1 20001
(integer) 0
```

As we would expect, `partition:1` size is `20000`, its first flipped bit starts at offset 1 and is as follows:

```
127.0.0.1:6379> BITCOUNT partition:5
(integer) 20000
127.0.0.1:6379> GETBIT partition:5 80000
(integer) 1
127.0.0.1:6379> GETBIT partition:5 99999
(integer) 1
```

To calculate which partition a new key will be stored at is a matter of performing a bitstring operation on the stored partition keys. The easiest method would be to issue a GETBIT command with the new key's numeric ID and see whether it is set to 1 for each of the partitions:

```
127.0.0.1:6379> GETBIT partition:1 568
(integer) 1
127.0.0.1:6379> GETBIT partition:2 568
(integer) 0
127.0.0.1:6379> GETBIT partition:3 568
(integer) 0
127.0.0.1:6379> GETBIT partition:4 568
(integer) 0
127.0.0.1:6379> GETBIT partition:5 568
(integer) 0
```

We would then use partition:1 for our key interesting-key:568:

```
127.0.0.1:6379> SET interesting-key:568 "Some data"
OK
```

For a second key with an ID 83697, we would repeat the process of checking each partition bitstring (the first three GETBIT checks are omitted):

```
127.0.0.1:6379> GETBIT partition:4 83687
(integer) 0
127.0.0.1:6379> GETBIT partition:5 83687
(integer) 1
```

The second key is stored in the fifth running Redis instance of our ad hoc cluster and is running on port 6382, which we connect to with a running a new Redis-cli session and using that Redis instance to set our second key:

```
127.0.0.1:6382> SET interesting-key:83697 "Another key with info"
OK
```

There are both positive and negative aspects when using the range partition approach to sharding a dataset. Conceptually, range partitioning is the easiest to comprehend and implement; however, as you can see we do incur an overhead cost both in tracking the partitions with a Redis bitstring data structures as well as developing custom client code to manage both the key assignment to the partition as well as retrieval and updating keys from the cluster of running Redis instances.

List partitioning

Similar to Range partitioning, List partitioning is where a partition is assigned a list of values and if the Redis key has one of the values in a list, it is assigned to that partition. To illustrate list partitioning, we'll start with a simple telephone application that stores the phone numbers from across the United States into one of three running Redis instances. What key is assigned to which of three running Redis instances will be based on a list of area codes assigned to each instance:

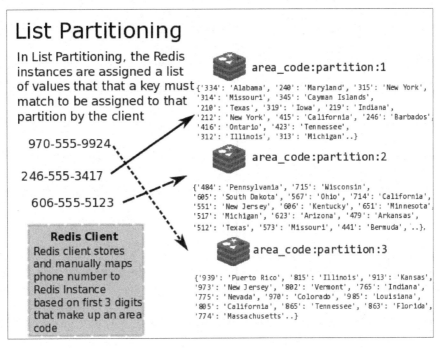

List partitioning

Like Range partitioning, using List partitioning requires intermediary data structures to support the assignment and tracking of keys in the datastore. In this case, we will populate three hashes, with each hash having the area code as the field and the geographic area (country or US state) as the value store for the area code. Because area codes are not necessarily numbered consecutively, we cannot use range partitioning.

We will first open a tab-delimited text file containing the area codes, extract the area code and geographic name from each row, and then assign the first 106 area codes to partition one, the next 106 area codes to partition two, and finally, the last 107 area codes to partition three. We will save the three Redis keys by following the schema `area_code:partition:{id}`, with our first Redis instance also functioning as the first partition:

```
def assign_codes_to_partitions(filename, datastore):
    with open(filename) as area_codes_file:
        area_codes = area_codes_file.readlines()
    area_code_shard1 = "area_code:partition:1"
    area_code_shard2 = "area_code:partition:2"
    area_code_shard3 = "area_code:partition:3"
    for i, row in enumerate(area_codes):
        fields = row.split("\t")
        code = fields[0]
        geo_name = fields[1]
        if i < 106:
            slot= area_code_shard1
        elif i >= 106 and i < 212:
            slot = area_code_ shard 2
        else:
            slot = area_code_ shard 3
        datastore.hset(hash_key, code, geo_name.strip())
```

To confirm that the first Redis node has three keys and the size of each hash is what we expect by using a Redis-cli session:

```
127.0.0.1:6379> DBSIZE
(integer) 3
127.0.0.1:6379> HLEN area_code:partition:1
(integer) 106
127.0.0.1:6379> HLEN area_code:partition:2
(integer) 106
127.0.0.1:6379> HLEN area_code:partition:3
(integer) 107
```

We will need a second function that takes a phone number, a list of values (name, address, mobile, or landline) and list of nodes in our cluster, looks up the area code to get which node to save the phone number hash to, and then saves the values to the sharded Redis instance node:

```
def save_phone_number(phone, values, cluster):
    area_code = phone[0:3]
```

```
if cluster[0].hexists("area_code:partition:1", area_code):
    shard = cluster[0]
elif cluster[0].hexists("area_code:partition:2", area_code):
    shard = cluster[1]
else:
    shard = cluster[2]
shard.hmset(phone, values)
```

Testing our first phone number from our interactive Python shell, we will execute the save_phone_number Python function like this:

```
>>> save_phone_number(
        "719 555 1212",
        {"name": "Jeremy Nelson",
         "type": "Mobile"},
        cluster)
```

Based on list partition, the phone number "719 555 1212" is saved as a hash in node 3 of our ad hoc cluster:

```
127.0.0.1:6379> HEXISTS area_code:partition:2 719

(integer) 1
```

We can confirm by opening a second terminal window to a Redis-cli session with our third node and retrieving all of the fields and values from our "719 555 1212" key:

```
$ ~/redis/redis-cli -p 6381
127.0.0.1:6381> hgetall "719 555 1212"
1) "type"
2) "Mobile"
3) "name"
4) "Jeremy Nelson"
```

With this setup, we should be able to distribute a large number of phone numbers across our three shards. What is missing from our sharding strategy is the means to easily add additional shards as our dataset grows. Because our algorithm is based on the distribution of area codes, we cannot just add more nodes as needed without restructuring our lists. Our strategy also assumes that North American phone numbers are equally distributed among the area codes, with new area codes being added when the existing number of area codes in a region by the **North American Numbering Plan Administration (NANPA)**. While not impossible, we could manually implement a resharding approach so that when the NANPA adds a new area code, an equal number of area codes are moved from their respective node and reassigned to a new node. Unlike the range partition, we do not require the area codes to be ordered or continuous but we do need to add custom client sharding code for managing our small cluster of Redis instances.

Hash partitioning

In Hash partitioning, a hash algorithm calculates what shard a key is assigned to the datastore. A typical `hash` function calculates a value from a key and performs a modulo operation on the value based on the number of shards or instances available in the datastore. In a 2011 blog post titled, *Redis Presharding1*, Salvatore Sanfilippo outlines a basic and simple hashing algorithm that takes a Redis key, hashes it with something like the SHA1 or CRC, and then does a modulo operation to calculate a location or node to store the key in. Sanfilippo encourages an approach of running many different instances of Redis when creating a cluster, he uses 128 Redis instances in his example for hashing Redis keys on the client side:

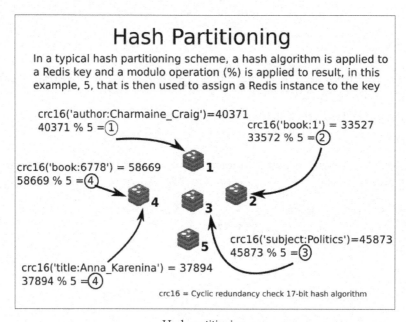

Hash partitioning

In the Java programming language, hashing is widely used with a required `hashCode()` method for classes that create a single 32-bit signed hash value when digesting the data stored in a class instance. In one example of using a Java client and Redis for hash sharding, a key made up of an e-mail address is routed to a Redis instance in a cluster by calling the Java `hashCode()` method of the e-mail string and storing the key in an *email bucket2*.

Composite partitioning

In a composite partitioning strategy, keys are assigned to an instance by different combinations of Range, List, or Hash partitioning. Redis cluster uses a form of composite partitioning called **consistent hashing** that combines features of the Hash and List partitioning to calculate a key's instance or node in Redis cluster terminology. Called a **hash slot**, it is the key's CRC16 hash value and then a computation of a modulo using 16384. The specific algorithm used by Redis cluster to calculate the hash slots for a key is simply the **cyclic redundancy check (CRC)** using a polynomial length of 17-bits or CRC16 with a theoretical maximum number of cluster nodes 16,284 with each node being a running Redis instance. To effectively use Redis cluster's consistent hashing algorithm, a minimal three Redis nodes are necessary in your Redis cluster.

For a three-node Redis cluster, the hash slots are assigned with the following:

- The first master having hash slots 0 to 5500
- The second master node being assigned hash slots 5501 to 11,000
- The third master having the remainder of 11,001 to 16,384 hash slots

The actual hash slot for the key is calculated as the modulo of CRC16 of the key divided by `16384` like this:

```
HASH_SLOT = CRC16(key) modulo 16384
```

The official Redis cluster specification provides a reference implementation of the CRC16 XModem, refer bullet point number 3 in *Appendix, Sources, Chapter 6: Scaling with Redis Cluster and Sentinel*, that is also available in the Redis source code directory in the `crc15.c` code file. We can see the hash slot allocation in action if we connect to a running 3-node Redis cluster using our Redis-cli with the `-c` parameter:

```
127.0.0.1:9001> SET book:1 "Mason and Dixon"
OK
127.0.0.1:9001> SET book:2 "Centennial"
-> Redirected to slot [12948] located at 127.0.0.1:9003
OK
```

Our first key, book:1, the hash slot is calculated as crc16("book:1") modulo 16384 is 759. In this particular cluster, the master node residing at port 9001 is allocated hash slots 0 to 5500 so with the client issuing the SET command stays on the same node. In our second key, book:2, the hash slot is calculated to be crc16("book:2") modulo 16384 to be hash slot 12938, which is allocated to the master node at 9003. Instead of doing this hash slot calculation manually, Redis provides a convenient command CLUSTER KEYSLOT that will perform this calculation for you:

```
127.0.0.1:9001> CLUSTER KEYSLOT book:1
(integer) 759
127.0.0.1:9001> CLUSTER KEYSLOT book:2
(integer) 12948
```

Key hash tags

An important exception to the Redis cluster's standard hash slot allocation discussed previously is the use of hash tags in the Redis key string that is restricted to the calculation of the hash slot to the characters just within the hash tag. In a Redis key, the hash tags are the characters contained between the first occurrence of the opening brace { and the closing brace }. This forces keys to reside in the same in the hash slot and Redis node in the cluster. This is important because the Redis cluster only offers limited support for multi-key commands while still completely supporting the core Redis commands for the entire cluster. If multi-key commands are needed, all of the keys must reside on the same node so the hash slot calculation can be restricted to just the hash tag. We can test this by returning to our Redis-cli session by first trying to issue a MSET command with keys that do not use the hash tags:

```
127.0.0.1:9001> MSET book:3 "Shogun" book:4 "Gone Fishin"
(error) CROSSSLOT Keys in request don't hash to the same slot
```

This is because the hash slot for book:3 is calculated as crc16("book:3") modulo 16384 is 8885 and the hash slot for "book:4" is crc16("book:3") modulo 16384 is 4690. Now, we'll try the same command but use hash tag "{book}":

```
127.0.0.1:9001> MSET {book}:3 "Shogun" {book}:4 "Gone Fishin"
OK
```

In this example, we want both book keys to reside on the same node so we created the {book} hash tag and issued two SET commands, the first redirected us to the first node because "book" hash slot, crc16("book") modulo 16384, is 1337 and the second key resides on the same node that we can confirm by the following:

```
127.0.0.1:9001> keys *
1) "{book}:3"
2) "book:1"
3) "{book}:4"
```

Clustering Redis with Twemproxy

Twemproxy is an open source project released by Twitter for creating a caching proxy between a client and backend made up of either Memcache or Redis instances. Twemproxy separates the client calls, in our case any suitable Redis client, from the datastore backend through the use of an intermediary middleware. This middleware then implements a sharding strategy based on your preferences that are set in a configuration YAML file. Twemproxy supports twelve different hash functions including md5, crc16, two versions of crc32, four variants of the **Fowler-Noll-Vo** (**FNV**), among others with the default being a fnv1a_64 hash functions.

With Twemproxy being a C program such as Redis, the steps to get Twemproxy running require a couple of different methods. To get started quickly, go to https://github.com/twitter/twemproxy/releases and download Twempoxy's distribution tarball. (You can also download a source tarball or clone the repository with Git, both requiring the additional step of running autoconf before running the following configure command):

```
$ tar xvf nutcracker-0.4.1.tar.gz
$ cd nutcracker-0.4.1/
$ ./configure
$ make
$ sudo make install
```

Before running Twemproxy, we will need to update and configure the proxy to use Redis, and map our running Redis instances as Twemproxy's backend cache servers:

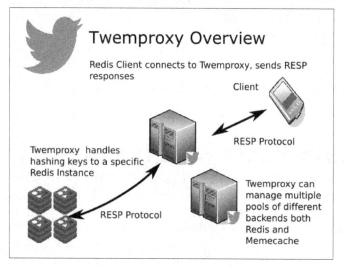

Twemproxy overview

Testing Twemproxy with Linked Data Fragments server

To start our testing of Twemproxy with Linked Data Fragments server, our backend Redis cluster will be made up of four Redis instances. Two Redis instances will be master nodes for our Linked Data cache. The remaining Redis instances will replicate the master nodes by running as slave nodes. We added and implemented a lightweight REST API for our Linked Data Fragment server project by using a Python framework for building REST APIs that were released and maintained by Rackspace called Falcon.

In the `api.py` Python module, a new class for a Triple REST endpoint is implemented with two methods; an `on_get` method for HTTP GET call that returns a serialized JSON of a simple RDF graph of the triple stored at the key in this syntax of `{subject sha1}:{predicate sha1}:{object sha1}` and an `on_post` method for creating a new triple based on the `sha1` digests of the subject, predicate, and object and then storing a `1` integer as a value. In the client code, if the triple key is found to exist, then a JSON Linked Data representation of the triple is generated by first splicing the key into its three digest values for the subject, predicate, and object, retrieving those values held at the `sha1` digest keys, and constructing the return JSON string on the fly.

Comparing the performance of the Linked Data Fragments server involved the creation of test data sets made up of BIBFRAME-based RDF graphs from two sources:

- Library of Congress MARC records for all records matching the terms "Mark Twain" and the "Bible"
- All MARC21 records of the most popular material at Colorado College's library based on the number of checkouts

Altogether, the two datasets represented a total of over 50,000 distinct graphs made up over 5,000,000 individual triples.

We will extend and continue to isolate our Redis-based code in our project by first creating a cache directory and moving and renaming our cache.py to the new directory and renaming it as aioredis.py. We will then create a new Python module in this same directory, and call it twemproxy.py.

To begin our testing, we'll first need to modify Twemproxy's YAML configuration file located at nutcracker-0.4.1/conf/nutcracker.yml. We'll be creating a simplified configuration with single server pools, alpha, for our Redis nodes running on ports 6379 through 6383. Here is the YAML configuration for alpha:

```
alpha:
  listen: 127.0.0.1:22121
  hash: fnv1a_64
  distribution: ketama
  auto_eject_hosts: true
  redis: true
  server_retry_timeout: 2000
  server_failure_limit: 1
  servers:
     - 127.0.0.1:6379:1
     - 127.0.0.1:6380:1
     - 127.0.0.1:6381:1
     - 127.0.0.1:6382:1
```

To connect to alpha, we will use the Twemproxy port 22121. Under the servers setting, the Redis instances are listed and mapped to the remaining ports. In the hash option, we selected fnv1a_64, the 64-bit variant of the FNV has function. The FNV hash function is fast but is not suitable for cryptographic use because of the chance of brute-force collusion detection. Other choices for the hash function that Twemproxy provides are CRC (which we already discussed) as well as others. Choosing a hash function will depend on a few factors including the speed of computation and the likelihood of hash collusion.

The distribution option in `alpha` is set to `ketama`, a hash distribution algorithm that hashes keys to unsigned integers on a circle continuum. Each number links to the server it is hashed with. A specific key's integer is matched to the closest higher number that circle backs to the first number in the circle when a key integer exceeds the maximum value in the continuum. Other distribution options include modula, where the server for a particular key is computed from a modula operation and a random option that selects the server that the key is to be assigned randomly from the available Redis servers running in the backend. After launching four Redis instances, being sure to specify separate ports and RDB filenames for each Redis instance, we will open another command line window and launch Twemproxy:

```
$ ./src/nutcracker
[2015-08-17 06:30:52.957] nc.c:187 nutcracker-0.4.1 built for Darwin
14.0.0 x86_64 started on pid 626
[2015-08-17 06:30:52.958] nc.c:192 run, rabbit run / dig that hole,
forget the sun / and when at last the work is done / don't sit down /
it's time to dig another one
```

With Twemproxy running, we can connect to port `22121` with our Redis-cli and issue commands:

```
$ redis/src/redis-cli -p 22121
```

To use our Lua scripts in our Redis instances, we'll open a Python command line, and loop through all four of the running Redis instances and load the `add_get_triple.lua` into each instance:

```
>>> import redis
>>> with open("/linked-data-fragments/redis/add_get_triple.lua") as fo:
add_get_triple = fo.read()
>>> cluster = []
>>> for port in range(6379, 6383):
        instance = redis.StrictRedis(port=port)
        instance.script_load(add_get_triple)
        cluster.append(instance)
```

Switching back to the running Redis-cli session that is connected to Twemproxy and calling the EVALSHA with the sha1 hash of add_get_hash results in the following:

```
127.0.0.1:22121> EVALSHA a5bb6a5952e578bdd2ddd9ede268ab28c6b90eb4 3
http://example.com/book/1 http://schema.org/name "Origins Reconsidered"
```

```
"2c866521408acafb64b0e67d17822260d68aadde:30cd0bd17373373839fb3a0ffaa6bba
51a17ba6c:574dbf58ad0e51382993cadec21742ae4de5aef8"
```

After Twemproxy evaluated the Lua script, the returned string is a triple made up of the SHA1 of each value in the KEYS variable.. However, if we try to retrieve the sha1 key of 2c866521408acafb64b0e67d17822260d68aadde we get back a nil value in our Redis-cli session:

```
127.0.0.1:22121> GET 2c866521408acafb64b0e67d17822260d68aadde
```

```
(nil)
```

So what happened? Because our Lua script populates the sha1 keys for each subject, predicate, and object in our RDF triple, it bypasses Twemproxy even if we directly connect to our first Redis instance; we can confirm the three keys have been set in only one instance and have not been proxied as follows:

```
127.0.0.1:6379> KEYS *
```

```
1) "30cd0bd17373373839fb3a0ffaa6bba51a17ba6c"
```

```
2) "2c866521408acafb64b0e67d17822260d68aadde"
```

```
3) "574dbf58ad0e51382993cadec21742ae4de5aef8"
```

```
127.0.0.1:6379> MGET 2c866521408acafb64b0e67d17822260d68aadde
30cd0bd17373373839fb3a0ffaa6bba51a17ba6c
574dbf58ad0e51382993cadec21742ae4de5aef8
```

```
1) "http://example.com/book/1"
```

```
2) "http://schema.org/name"
```

```
3) "Origins Reconsidered"
```

Using Twemproxy in the Linked Data Fragments server means that the current Lua scripts for creating and populating the RDF triples is not possible; therefore, the logic that exists in the Lua scripts would need to be added to the `twemproxy.py` module. Since this logic was added in the original implementation of the Redis cache but removed when Lua scripting was implemented in the project, we'll add the `sha1` hashing logic back to the `twemproxy.py` module. This illustrates an important point about using Twemproxy and Redis in your project—all interactions between your client code and your cache must be run through the proxy and not through direct writes to the Redis instances themselves:

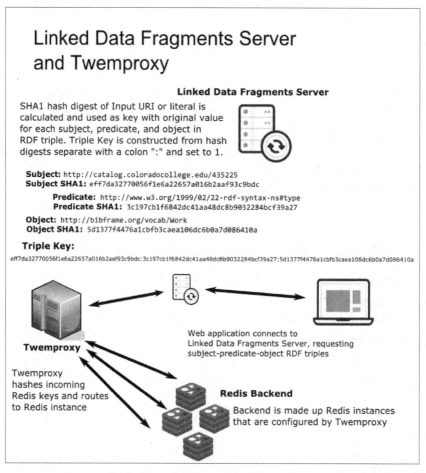

Linked Data Fragments server Twemproxy

After updating `twemproxy.py` with the additional code to create our `sha1` hashes for each triple, we can then retest the performance of Twemproxy. First, we will create a new Lua script—`get_triple`—that takes a triple and returns a string JSON-LD representation of the triple:

```lua
local subject_sha1, predicate_sha1, object_sha1 = split(KEYS[1], ":")
local output = '[{"@id": "'
output = output..redis.pcall('get', subject_sha1_)..'",'
output = output..redis.pcall('get', predicate_sha1)..'":[{'
local object = redis.pcall('get', object_sha1)
if string.sub(object,1,string.len("http")) == 'http' then
    output = output..'"@id": "'
else
    output =  output..'"@value": "'
end
output = output..'"'..object..'"}]}]'
return output
```

Next, we will load our Colorado College MARC21 test record test into our Twemproxy that is running with four Redis instances. After the test records are loaded, we will connect to each of the Redis instances with Redis-cli to determine the size and amount of memory being used in each of the instances:

```
127.0.0.1:6379> DBSIZE
(integer) 903287
127.0.0.1:6379> INFO memory
# Memory
used_memory:176939920
used_memory_human:168.74M
127.0.0.1:6380> DBSIZE
(integer) 836812
127.0.0.1:6380> INFO memory
# Memory
used_memory:164487104
used_memory_human:156.87M
127.0.0.1:6381> DBSIZE
(integer) 942231
127.0.0.1:6381> INFO memory
# Memory
used_memory:184067520
```

```
used_memory_human:175.54M
127.0.0.1:6382> DBSIZE
(integer) 879448
127.0.0.1:6382> INFO memory
# Memory
used_memory:172414320
used_memory_human:164.43M
```

Our Twemproxy Linked Data Fragments has a total of 3,561,778 separate keys with a total memory used between the four instances of 665.58 MB. Before the Redis Cluster was developed and released for both beta testing and finally into production with Redis version 3, Twemproxy was the preferred method for clustering your Redis data. With the large momentum behind the release and testing of the Redis cluster and the relative lack of development activity being done on Twemproxy, you would be better off using the Redis cluster instead of Twemproxy.

Redis Cluster background

The beginning of what eventually became the Redis cluster started with an announcement by Salvatore Sanfilippo in 2011 to the Redis e-mail list and a subsequent blog post, refer bullet point number 4 from *Appendix, Sources, Chapter 6: Scaling with Redis Cluster and Sentinel*. Earlier discussions about Redis clustering support started in 2010 with the first mention of the term *redis-cluster* in an e-mail message to the Redis-db listserv, refer bullet point number 5 in *Appendix, Sources, Chapter 6: Scaling with Redis Cluster and Sentine*. Development and testing of the Redis cluster continued from 2011 through 2015. In an October 2014 follow-up blog posting, Sanfilippo relates how over the 4+ years since his first commit in March 2011 related to Redis Cluster, he had to redesign, implement, and test the functionality of Redis Cluster on numerous occasions as he became more familiar with the challenges surrounding distributed computing at scale. During those years of development, the Redis community tried and often failed to effectively handle two issues; the first was how to shard data across *N* number of Redis instances and second, how to gracefully handle a failed node under certain conditions. In response to the second issue, Sanfilippo started Redis monitoring and failover work into what became Redis's high availability solution, Redis Sentinel, the final topic of this chapter.

Although Redis Cluster does offer a mechanism for increasing the size and scale of the dataset that can be managed by Redis, Redis Cluster cannot offer a strong consistency guarantee that data will not be lost when propagating data. As a distributed system, a write to a Redis master node is acknowledged immediately to the calling client before the master node propagates the data to its slaves. If the master node fails before the new data is propagated to its slaves and a slave node is promoted to master, then the data is lost.

With Redis Cluster default operating propagation mode as an asynchronous process (Redis Cluster continues to write and operate during client interactions), the cluster's performance is favored over data consistency in the masters and slaves nodes. If data consistency is more important to your application over raw performance, Redis Cluster offers the WAIT command that changes the data propagation to more of a synchronous process where the client is blocked until a specified number of slaves acknowledge any write commands or a timeout has occurred. Using WAIT only improves Redis Cluster data consistency and safety but still cannot guarantee the strong data consistency as a distributed data store.

Setting the configuration directive *node timeout* for Redis Cluster means that if the master node does not respond within the timeout window, the master node is considered as failing by the rest of the master nodes and is replaced by one of its slaves. The original master, in this scenario, stops accepting writes because it hasn't received any communication with the other master nodes in the cluster.

Overview of running Redis Cluster

Nodes in a Redis Cluster are Redis instances that are either masters or slaves. A master Redis instance is allocated one or more of the 16,384 available hash slots where Redis keys are assigned to a hash slot based on the CRC16 hashing of the key and taking the remainder of dividing the CRC16 by the number of masters. When a Redis cluster is running, each node has two TCP sockets open; the first is the standard Redis protocol for connecting clients, the default being port 6379 and the second port is calculated from the sum of the first port plus 10000 (16379 for the default port) that runs the Cluster's binary protocol for node-to-node communication. Clients should never need to connect directly with the cluster bus port but with the lower, standard port. Nodes in the Redis Cluster use the Redis cluster bus to connect with every other node in a mesh network topology. This means that for a Redis cluster of six nodes made up of three masters and three slaves, each node regardless of its replication status, has five outgoing and five incoming TCP connections. These connections are always alive and continually respond to pings from other nodes in the cluster. These messages, called *Heartbeat Packets*, contains a Node ID, currentEpoch, node flags, bitmap of hash slots served by the sender, TCP base port, sender's view of the state of the cluster (up, failing, and failed), and master node ID if the sender is a slave.

To avoid exponential growth of messages between nodes in the cluster, a gossip protocol is used that along with a configuration updating process contains the number of messages being sent between all of the nodes in the cluster's mesh:

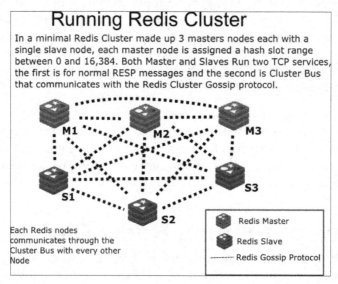

In a minimal Redis Cluster made up 3 masters nodes each with a single slave node, each master node is assigned a hash slot range between 0 and 16,384. Both Master and Slaves Run two TCP services, the first is for normal RESP messages and the second is Cluster Bus that communicates with the Redis Cluster Gossip protocol.

Each Redis nodes communicates through the Cluster Bus with every other Node

Running Redis Cluster

TCP connection requests through the Redis Cluster bus are always accepted by any cluster node but the node will only reply with information other than an acknowledgement response if the requesting node is part of the cluster. There are two ways for a node to be considered part of the Redis cluster. The first method of node cluster membership is if a first node sends a MEET message to second node, the second node must accept the first node as part of the cluster. The MEET command is set through the issuing of the CLUSTER MEET command. The second method of node cluster membership is a gossip algorithm based on a logical transitive relationship between nodes. If node 1 and node 2 are both part of the cluster and node 2 knows node 3, then eventually node 1 will exchange gossip message with node 2 about node 3, thereby node 1 registers node 3 as part of the Redis cluster. This allows for dynamic auto-discovery of other nodes in the cluster while providing for a more robust Redis cluster that does not need a significant overhead for coordinating adding new nodes to the cluster during runtime.

Understanding what is called an *epoch* in the context of Redis Cluster explains how Redis Cluster creates a version history throughout the lifespan of the running Redis Cluster. Epoch is a 64-bit unsigned integer that is incremented during such nodes events as adding a new master node. The *epoch* is stored in the `currentEpoch` variable that at the cluster's initialization, all master and slave nodes are set to 0. When a message is received using Redis's gossip protocol that includes the *epoch* in the message's header, if the receipt's *epoch* is less then message's *epoch* value, then the Redis receipt node updates it's currentEpoch value to the highest *epoch* value. In this way, the cluster eventually agrees upon the highest value for the *epoch* value and provides a linear path of events that significantly change the underlying composition of the master nodes in the cluster. When a slave is promoted to a master node as a failover event in the *epoch*, this means that slaves can be added incrementally on different running virtual machines without causing an updated *epoch* but when a slave is promoted to a new master, its is significant because such a promotion could potentially change the runtime characteristics of the entire node or have unexpected ramifications and consequences at a later time.

Using Redis Cluster

As a production-level clustering solution for an enterprise Redis cluster has a mature set of tools for performing management functions related to running cluster of Redis nodes. Redis cluster supports the following functions primarily through an included Ruby script, `redis-trib.rb` utility:

- Resharding and failover
- Moving or creating new allocations of hash slots in the cluster
- Handling error conditions such as master failing
- Adding or replacing master or slave nodes in the cluster
- Upgrading a master or slave instance

To test these various functions in Redis cluster, we will return to the area code example introduced earlier in the chapter and migrate our list-based solution to use Redis cluster instead of our custom client code. Building from the official Redis cluster tutorial example at `http://redis.io/topics/cluster-tutorial`, we will run the simplest recommended three master with three slave Redis cluster. The `create-cluster` utility bundled with Redis is the easiest method to run a Redis cluster, which we will use for the area codes. First, we'll create a new `config.sh` file for our specific Redis cluster options:

```
$ cd redis/utils/create-cluster
$ vi config.sh
```

```
#!/bin/bash
PORT=9000
TIMEOUT=2000
NODES=6
REPLICAS=1
```

Our cluster starts with port 9000, a latency time out of 2 seconds, six nodes made up of three master nodes, and three slave nodes. If we wanted to bump up the number replicas, increasing the replicas means each master will have that number of slave instances.

After saving our config.sh, first we need to install the Redis gem for Ruby:

```
$ sudo gem install redis
```

Now, we run the create-cluster script to create and start our cluster:

```
$ cd ~/redis/util/create-cluster
$ ./create-cluster start
Starting 9001
Starting 9002
Starting 9003
Starting 9004
Starting 9005
Starting 9006
$ ./create-cluster create
>>> Creating cluster
Connecting to node 127.0.0.1:9001: OK
Connecting to node 127.0.0.1:9002: OK
Connecting to node 127.0.0.1:9003: OK
Connecting to node 127.0.0.1:9004: OK
Connecting to node 127.0.0.1:9005: OK
Connecting to node 127.0.0.1:9006: OK
>>> Performing hash slots allocation on 6 nodes...
Using 3 masters:
127.0.0.1:9001
127.0.0.1:9002
127.0.0.1:9003
Adding replica 127.0.0.1:9004 to 127.0.0.1:9001
```

```
Adding replica 127.0.0.1:9005 to 127.0.0.1:9002
Adding replica 127.0.0.1:9006 to 127.0.0.1:9003
M: 9ed33dd148ba6546431b2439d1e85b3b742ef336 127.0.0.1:9001
   slots:0-5460 (5461 slots) master
M: de3ec68f65de532080e296be3a2b1502e35fe281 127.0.0.1:9002
   slots:5461-10922 (5462 slots) master
M: c12d7eae35befeb8530d6fec366fb34aaed9eefc 127.0.0.1:9003
   slots:10923-16383 (5461 slots) master
S: 623b9338e6fc277634a741e7f56c8a08240ff7d0 127.0.0.1:9004
   replicates 9ed33dd148ba6546431b2439d1e85b3b742ef336
S: f6efd99a0505072ca3539a629674eb88ffaaa78f 127.0.0.1:9005
   replicates de3ec68f65de532080e296be3a2b1502e35fe281
S: b9656e82c01ca7d085b6386d7ca8383903897157 127.0.0.1:9006
   replicates c12d7eae35befeb8530d6fec366fb34aaed9eefc
Can I set the above configuration? (type 'yes' to accept): yes
```

Running the `create-cluster` command first connects to all six running nodes and then performs the hash slot allocation between the three masters running on ports `9001`, `9002`, and `9003`. Accepting this configuration, the `redis-trib.rb` script that the `create-cluster` script uses outputs the following:

```
>>> Nodes configuration updated
>>> Assign a different config epoch to each node
>>> Sending CLUSTER MEET messages to join the cluster
Waiting for the cluster to join.
>>> Performing Cluster Check (using node 127.0.0.1:9001)
M: 9ed33dd148ba6546431b2439d1e85b3b742ef336 127.0.0.1:9001
   slots:0-5460 (5461 slots) master
M: de3ec68f65de532080e296be3a2b1502e35fe281 127.0.0.1:9002
   slots:5461-10922 (5462 slots) master
M: c12d7eae35befeb8530d6fec366fb34aaed9eefc 127.0.0.1:9003
   slots:10923-16383 (5461 slots) master
M: 623b9338e6fc277634a741e7f56c8a08240ff7d0 127.0.0.1:9004
   slots: (0 slots) master
   replicates 9ed33dd148ba6546431b2439d1e85b3b742ef336
M: f6efd99a0505072ca3539a629674eb88ffaaa78f 127.0.0.1:9005
   slots: (0 slots) master
   replicates de3ec68f65de532080e296be3a2b1502e35fe281
```

```
M: b9656e82c01ca7d085b6386d7ca8383903897157 127.0.0.1:9006
    slots: (0 slots) master
    replicates c12d7eae35befeb8530d6fec366fb34aaed9eefc
[OK] All nodes agree about slots configuration.
>>> Check for open slots...
>>> Check slots coverage...
[OK] All 16384 slots covered.
```

To confirm that we have a six-node cluster running three masters and three slaves, we will start a Redis-cli session with a special parameter -c to run and be able to switch between the various master's hash slots:

```
$ ../../src/redis-cli -c -p 9001
127.0.0.1:9001>
```

Issuing the CLUSTER INFO command displays the state of our running cluster:

```
127.0.0.1:9001> CLUSTER INFO
cluster_state:ok
cluster_slots_assigned:16384
cluster_slots_ok:16384
cluster_slots_pfail:0
cluster_slots_fail:0
cluster_known_nodes:6
cluster_size:3
cluster_current_epoch:6
cluster_my_epoch:1
cluster_stats_messages_sent:5430
cluster_stats_messages_received:5430
```

Getting specific information from the running nodes is possible by issuing the CLUSTER NODES command:

```
127.0.0.1:9001> CLUSTER NODES
b9656e82c01ca7d085b6386d7ca8383903897157 127.0.0.1:9006 slave
c12d7eae35befeb8530d6fec366fb34aaed9eefc 0 1439299522348 6 connected
f6efd99a0505072ca3539a629674eb88ffaaa78f 127.0.0.1:9005 slave
de3ec68f65de532080e296be3a2b1502e35fe281 0 1439299522348 5 connected
de3ec68f65de532080e296be3a2b1502e35fe281 127.0.0.1:9002 master - 0
1439299522348 2 connected 5461-10922
c12d7eae35befeb8530d6fec366fb34aaed9eefc 127.0.0.1:9003 master - 0
1439299522348 3 connected 10923-16383
```

```
9ed33dd148ba6546431b2439d1e85b3b742ef336 127.0.0.1:9001 myself,master - 0
0 1 connected 0-5460
```

```
623b9338e6fc277634a741e7f56c8a08240ff7d0 127.0.0.1:9004 slave
9ed33dd148ba6546431b2439d1e85b3b742ef336 0 1439299522348 4 connected
```

Now, we will create a random phone number generator to populate our cluster; more realistically, this data could be generated from a CRM application or other source of customer data. We will use our existing North American area code data to start our ten digit random phone number generator:

```python
>>> import random
>>> def random_phonenumber(area_code):
        number = str(area_code)
        for i in range(7):
            number += "{}".format(random.randint(0,9))
        return number
```

Using the Redis cluster Python library — `redis-py-cluster` — available at `https://github.com/Grokzen/redis-py-cluster`, we will first import and then instantiate a Python Redis cluster to populate our *Area code* application:

```python
>>> from rediscluster import StrictRedisCluster
>>> startup_nodes = [{"host": "localhost", "port": 9001}]
>>> area_code_cluster = StrictRedisCluster(startup_nodes=startup_nodes)
```

We will then create a second function that imports our `area-code.txt` CSV file and returns a dictionary made up area codes mapped to a geographic region by first iterating through each line in the `for` text file object, creating a list of fields, and then converting the string of the area code to an integer and setting the Python dictionary value to the second element in our a field's list:

```python
>>> def area_code_dict(filepath):
        with open(filepath) as fo:
            lines = fo.readlines()
        area_codes = dict()
        for row in lines:
            fields = row.split("\t")
            area_codes[int(fields[0])] = fields[1].strip()
        return area_codes
```

Our final function randomly selects an area code from a list of code keys from the area code Python dictionary, calls the previously defined `random_phonenumber` function, and then saves the random phone number as a Redis hash to our running Redis cluster with a `geographicArea` field set to the value from `area_codes` dictionary:

```
>>> def populate_cluster(total):
        codes = list(area_codes.keys())
        for i in range(total):
            number = random.randint(0, len(codes)-1)
            area_code = codes[number]
            phone_number = random_phonenumber(area_code)
            area_code_cluster.hsetnx(phone_number, "geographicArea", area_
codes[area_code])
>>> populate_cluster(150000)
```

We then populate our Redis cluster with 150,000 random phone numbers. In the test run for this chapter (if you are repeating these exercises on your own, your distribution of keys in the hash slots will be different), our results are broken down like this:

	Master	Slave	Size
Hash slot one	127.0.0.1:9001	127.0.0.1:9004	50005
Hash slot two	127.0.0.1: 9002	127.0.0.1:9005	49971
Hash slot three	127.0.0.1:9003	127.0.0.1:9006	50020

From these results, we can see that our numbers are almost evenly distributed across all three hash slots with a total variance between the three master nodes is 49, less than `.01` percent difference between the three hash slots. Using these area codes as our test cluster, we will now go through a series of exercises to illustrate a number of important operations and features of using Redis cluster.

Live reconfiguration and resharding Redis cluster

Redis cluster offers a number of commands for adding and removing nodes at runtime. To add a new empty node to the cluster first requires the node to be added to the cluster and then one or more slots in the existing nodes to be reassigned to the new node.

The CLUSTER ADDSLOTS command is primarily used for the manual creation of a Redis cluster and assigns a subset of the 16,384 available hash slots while the CLUSTER DELSLOTS command is used for manually modification of the cluster or for testing and debugging.

The CLUSTER SETSLOT command is used in multiple ways depending on the use case. The CLUSTER SETSLOT {hash slot number} NODE {node-id} form is used to assign a slot to a specified node under limited conditions. Otherwise, the CLUSTER SETSLOT takes either a MIGRATING or IMPORTING form depending on whether you want to work with the destination node with MIGRATING or with the source node with IMPORTING. For the CLUSTER SETSLOT {hash slot number} MIGRATING {desination node id} command and subcommand, the node will continue to accept queries for keys in it's assigned hash slots but redirects the calling client for key requests that don't exist in the node to the new hash slot on a different node. If command contains multiple keys then the behavior varies depending on whether the key exists or not or emits a TRYAGAIN error.

Likewise, when CLUSTER SETSLOT is set to the IMPORTING mode, the source node will refuse any requests about the hash slot and a MOVED redirection that is preceded by the ASKING command. The ASKING command sets a one-time flag on the client that forces the node to send only the next query to the specified node and not permanently redirect to the node with the assigned hash slot as is the case with a MOVED error.

To test the live configuration commands, we will spin up a new Redis master node running on port 9007 that has the configuration directive cluster-enabled set to yes and then, we'll add the new node to our area code cluster with new Redis-cli session using the CLUSTER MEET command:

```
127.0.0.1:9007> CLUSTER MEET 127.0.0.1 9002
OK
```

We can confirm that our new node is part of the cluster by running the CLUSTER INFO command again and noting the cluster_known_nodes values:

```
127.0.0.1:9007> CLUSTER INFO
cluster_state:ok
cluster_slots_assigned:16384
cluster_slots_ok:16384
cluster_slots_pfail:0
cluster_slots_fail:0
cluster_known_nodes:7
cluster_size:3
```

```
cluster_current_epoch:6
```

```
cluster_my_epoch:3
```

```
cluster_stats_messages_sent:1037
```

```
cluster_stats_messages_received:1037
```

We will manually transfer one slot to prepare for the migrating any keys to the new master node that has a random ID of ed862747677b458cf6c79f58b29b4e4c09a9603b:

```
127.0.0.1:9007> CLUSTER SETSLOT 12000 NODE
ed862747677b458cf6c79f58b29b4e4c09a9603b
OK
```

To double check, running CLUSTER SLOTS will now show the slot assignments (although no keys have been migrated to the new master node):

```
127.0.0.1:9007> CLUSTER SLOTS
1) 1) (integer) 0
   2) (integer) 5460
   3) 1) "127.0.0.1"
      2) (integer) 9001
   4) 1) "127.0.0.1"
      2) (integer) 9004
2) 1) (integer) 10923
   2) (integer) 16383
   3) 1) "127.0.0.1"
      2) (integer) 9003
   4) 1) "127.0.0.1"
      2) (integer) 9007
   5) 1) "127.0.0.1"
      2) (integer) 9006
3) 1) (integer) 5461
   2) (integer) 10922
   3) 1) "127.0.0.1"
      2) (integer) 9002
   4) 1) "127.0.0.1"
      2) (integer) 9005
```

From this output, we can see that our new node has indeed been assigned to the correct hash slot range.

Although the current CRC16-based composite hashing with Redis cluster does an acceptable job of equally distributing keys across all of its master nodes, your actual application's data may require you to reshard your cluster to better balance the load between the cluster's nodes. Fortunately, this process is relatively simple using the `redis-trib.rb` Ruby-based utility included with Redis:

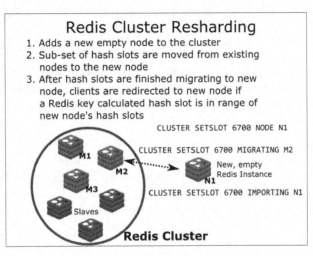

Redis cluster resharding

Failover

With Redis cluster running multiple masters with corresponding one or more slave nodes, normally when a master node fails, any of it's slaves will automatically be elected to replace the master node. This slave election starts when the slave's master is in a FAIL state, the master is assigned one or more hash slots, and the length of time between the last successfully connection between the slave and master is below a calculated threshold using the cluster-slave-validity-factor configuration directive. When a master has multiple slaves, a rank is calculated among the slaves with the highest rank given to the slave the most complete replication of the master's contents. After the slave has been promoted to the new master, the cluster's *epoch* is incremented and the change to the new master is propagated to the other nodes in the cluster through the gossip protocol.

An important aspect of how Redis cluster improves reliability of a running cluster is in the slave node distribution among Redis masters. In our simple three masters and three slaves setup, a slave replacing a master due to the master failing means that the new master does not have a backup slave instance. If the new master fails, the cluster can no longer read or write from the hash slots served by failed master so the cluster itself will fail and data that was in those hash slots will no longer be available and perhaps even worse, permanently lost. In more durable setups, masters will have multiple slaves and if the master fails, the highest ranked slave is promoted to the new master with the remaining slaves switching over and becoming slaves of the newly promoted master.

To illustrate the Redis Cluster failover mode, we will rerun our area code example, only this time we will increase the number of slaves per master to two, bring the total number of nodes in our cluster to 9 in the `config.sh` file. To start with an empty Redis Cluster, we run the following command to the `create-cluster` script:

```
$ ./create-cluster clean
```

Now, we will issue the `create-cluster` start and `create-cluster create` commands to start up our new 9-node Redis cluster. We will again execute the `populate_cluster` function to populate our cluster with 150,000 North American phone numbers that have been sharded between the three master instances but now being backed up by two slave replicas instead of one.

After the cluster has been populated, we now connect with a Redis-cli session using the –c parameter to run in cluster node and issue the CLUSTER SLOT command to display the running master and two slave nodes:

```
127.0.0.1:9001> CLUSTER SLOTS
1) 1) (integer) 5461
   2) (integer) 10922
   3) 1) "127.0.0.1"
      2) (integer) 9002
   4) 1) "127.0.0.1"
      2) (integer) 9007
   5) 1) "127.0.0.1"
      2) (integer) 9006
2) 1) (integer) 0
   2) (integer) 5460
   3) 1) "127.0.0.1"
      2) (integer) 9001
   4) 1) "127.0.0.1"
```

```
      2) (integer) 9004
   5) 1) "127.0.0.1"
      2) (integer) 9005
3) 1) (integer) 10923
   2) (integer) 16383
   3) 1) "127.0.0.1"
      2) (integer) 9003
   4) 1) "127.0.0.1"
      2) (integer) 9008
   5) 1) "127.0.0.1"
      2) (integer) 9009
```

Now, we will open a second Redis-cli session connect to the master node running at 127.0.0.1:9003 that is assigned hash slots 10823 to 16383 and issue a DEBUG SIGFAULT command to simulate a master node failure:

```
127.0.0.1:9003> DEBUG SEGFAULT
Could not connect to Redis at 127.0.0.1:9003: Connection refused
(0.90s)
not connected>
```

Shifting back to our original Redis-cli session, if we reissue the CLUSTER SLOT command, we can see that the original master node running on port 9003 is no longer present and that its slave running on port 9009 has been elected as the new master (the other nodes have been omitted for clarity):

```
127.0.0.1:9001> CLUSTER SLOTS.
.
3) 1) (integer) 10923
   2) (integer) 16383
   3) 1) "127.0.0.1"
   2) (integer) 9009
   4) 1) "127.0.0.1"
   2) (integer) 9008
```

To improve the cluster's resiliency, Redis Cluster implements what is called a replica migration, an algorithm that reallocates the slaves to a different master node if the master node does not have a slave node. If, referring back to our preceding area code example, we experience a second failure of the master node serving hash slots `10923-16383`, our last slave running on port `9008` is promoted to master. Now, the new master does not have a slave node so Redis Cluster will migrate one of the other slaves of a different master node to the new master node so that at least one or more slaves are present for every node in the cluster. In this way, Redis Cluster through replica migration is able to eventually ensure that at least one slave covers all of the masters in the node. Typically, a master with multiple slaves will only migrate a single slave to a slave-less master; however, this behavior can change by adjusting the `cluster-migration-barrier` configuration directive that limits the number of slaves that can be migrated to another Redis master node in the cluster.

Replacing or upgrading nodes in Redis Cluster

There may come a time when you will need to manually replace a running master or slave node in your Redis Cluster. The Redis Cluster automatic failover process that promotes a slave node to master that we saw in the last section may not be sufficient for the operational needs in your application.

In long running applications, a role Redis excels at in the Enterprise, there may come a time when you need to update the version of Redis you're running either due to a critical bug fix or just to keep your running Redis cluster current with the latest Redis stable version. The process for upgrading a Redis node in the cluster is similar to the process of replacing a node. First, a CLUSTER FAILOVER command is issued to one of the slaves of the master node we are either replacing or upgrading that then turns the old master node into a slave while promoting the slave to master. Second, the old master (now a slave) is replaced with a new updated node.

When replacing or upgrading a node in Redis Cluster you can also issue a CLUSTER RESET command followed by either a SOFT or HARD parameter to remove an old master node or reassign it's hash slots. If the node is a slave, the command will turn the node into a master node discarding any data in the process. The CLUSTER RESET command all of the hash slots that were assigned are released and all of the other nodes in the node table so that the node does not know the state of other nodes in the cluster. In a HARD cluster reset, the epoch variables of the node — currentEpoch, configEpoch, and lastVoteEpoch — are all set back to 0 and the node ID is assigned a new random ID.

Finally, the old node's ID and IP address will still be remembered by other nodes in the cluster particularly if the reset was only a SOFT reset. As other nodes will still attempt to connect to the old node ID through the gossip protocol, issuing a CLUSTER FORGET Redis command that removes the old node ID from the node table and enforces a 60 second timeout to prevent the node with same node ID to be readded to the cluster. In the next section, we'll take a look at a more general solution for monitoring Redis instances with Redis Sentinel.

Monitoring with Redis Sentinel

Redis Sentinel is a special operating mode of Redis for monitoring running Redis master and slave instances. Redis Sentinel allows for a failing master instance to be replaced by a replicated slave and other types of failures thereby giving users of Redis a high availability option for their application. Beside monitoring and automatic failover, Redis Sentinel also provides notification options where Redis Sentinel will alert the system administrators or other programs through an API when a critical error occurs in a monitored Redis instance. Redis Sentinel also assists in operational management by being a configuration provider for client automatic discovery of services. While simple in theory, Redis Sentinel is used in very complex workflows and monitoring/failover scenarios in the Enterprise.

As a distributed system, Redis Sentinel requires at least three instances for a robust deployment. Multiple Sentinels cooperate to detect failing masters by requiring a majority of the Sentinels to agree that a failure has occurred as a technique to reduce false positives about a master's availability, that is, dropping a functioning master even though it's status is fine. Multiple Redis Sentinels also cooperate by continue functioning if one or more of the Sentinel instances themselves fail as a hedge against failures in the monitoring system. Unlike the Redis server, running a Redis Sentinel instance requires a configuration file to operate correctly with an example of sentinel.conf file that is included every Redis distribution.

Sentinel's default TCP port for communicating with other Redis Sentinels is port 26379 that must be open on any servers that are running a Redis Sentinel instance. Ideally, each Redis Sentinel should be run on separate physical or virtual machines with different operating characteristics, such as availability zones, for reducing the possibility of a single point of failure in the software stack, physical hardware, or network connections:

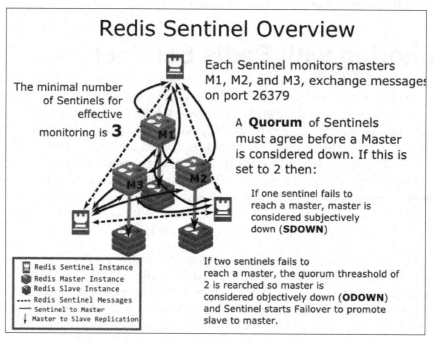

Redis Sentinel overview

Using Redis Sentinel does not guarantee strong consistency in data because Redis itself uses asynchronous replication in most master/slave and Redis Cluster setups. Proper deployment of Redis Sentinel can minimize the chances of writes being dropped by reducing the time window for such loss of writes to happen. Any Redis clients that are used in your application should be Redis Sentinel aware and most of the popular Redis clients already offer Redis Sentinel support.

As mentioned previously, a running Redis Sentinel instance requires a configuration file. In the example, `sentinel.conf`, there are a number of important configuration directives for customizing your Redis Sentinel setup depending on the organization and makeup of your Redis application. The first, the `sentinel monitor` directive specifies what Redis master this Sentinel instance will monitor and requires four parameters: a name for the master, an IP address of the master, the port number, and a quorum level.

Redis Sentinel automatically monitors any replicated slaves of a Redis master. The `sentinel down-after-milliseconds` directive and subcommand specifies the number of milliseconds that the Sentinel instance cannot communicate with a master before the master instance is considered down. These directives are repeated for each master that the Redis Sentinel is monitoring.

> **Redis Cluster quorum**
>
> When using Redis Sentinel, an important concept to understand is quorum—a threshold number required for Sentinel instances to agree that a master is down—set with the Sentinel monitor directive. When individual Sentinel instances attempt and fail to communicate with a master instance, they will send a PFAIL (possible fail) message to other Sentinels, when the number of Sentinel instances that fail to reach the master and send their own PFAIL messages reach the quorum number a FAIL message must sent by Redis Sentinel before any failover mitigation is attempted.

Another important function of Redis Sentinel is how to set up a notification message when a failure condition occurs in the masters that Redis Sentinel is monitoring. In the `sentinel.conf` configuration file, the `sentinel notification-script` configuration directive specifies a bash or other script to run in the case of a WARNING-level event. This script should accept two arguments—the event type and event description—that can then be launched to notify an administrator through whatever preferred communication channel used by the operations staff including e-mail, SMS, IRC, or even other monitoring systems through API calls. To use the notification script in Redis Sentinel, the script must exist in a location that the Redis Sentinel can access and the script must be set with the execute bit set to `True`.

While getting Redis Sentinel configured and running is relatively simple, deciding on a Redis Sentinel setup for your particular requirements is more challenging because of performance trade-offs, desired persistence, network partitioning, and machine resources availability. At the minimum, your Redis Sentinel setup should include at least three running instances that ideally would be running on separate physical machines; including any virtual machines dedicated to your client application such as the Web, database, and application servers. Going back to the different examples used in this chapter, we will now outline a Redis Sentinel setup for the Area Code List Partition.

Sentinel for Area Code List Partition

The Redis node setup for the Area Code List Partitioning example has three master Redis nodes and we will add three slave nodes that replicate these masters. To simplify our deployment, each master and corresponding replicated slave will run on a separate virtual machine. Our Redis Sentinel setup in this case is to implement the recommended minimum Redis Sentinel number with three Sentinels each running on the same VM as a master with the Redis Sentinel quorum set to 2:

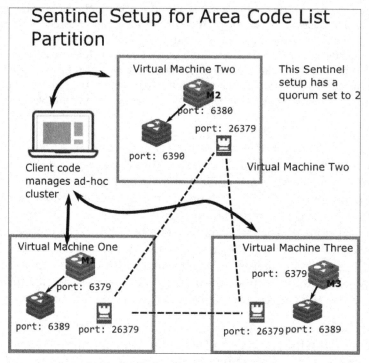

Sentinel setup for Area Code List Partition

After manually loading and launching two Redis instances and an instance of Redis Sentinel in each of our three test virtual machines, we will start a Redis-cli session and connect to the Redis Sentinel port of 26379 on VM2 (we will truncate some of the results and only display a few important properties):

```
127.0.0.1:26380> SENTINEL masters
1)  1) "name"
    2) "vm3"
    3) "ip"
    4) "172.26.6.145"
    5) "port"
```

```
 6)  "6379"
...
13)  "last-ping-sent"
14)  "421859"
15)  "last-ok-ping-reply"
16)  "421859"
...
25)  "role-reported"
26)  "master"
...
29)  "config-epoch"
30)  "0"
31)  "num-slaves"
32)  "1"
...
33)  "num-other-sentinels"
34)  "3"
35)  "quorum"
36)  "2"
2)   1)  "name"
     2)  "vm2"
     3)  "ip"
     4)  "127.0.0.1
     5)  "port"
     6)  "6380"
     ...
    13)  "last-ping-sent"
    14)  "0"
    15)  "last-ok-ping-reply"
    16)  "400"
     ...
    23)  "role-reported"
    24)  "master"
     ...
    27)  "config-epoch"
    28)  "0"
```

```
      29) "num-slaves"
      30) "1"
      31) "num-other-sentinels"
      32) "3"
      33) "quorum"
      34) "2"
    ...
3)  1) "name"
    2) "vm1"
    3) "ip"
    4) "172.29.40.33"
    5) "port"
    6) "6379"
    ...
    13) "last-ping-sent"
    14) "421859"
    15) "last-ok-ping-reply"
    16) "421859"
    25) "role-reported"
    26) "master"
    ...
    29) "config-epoch"
    30) "0"
    31) "num-slaves"
    32) "0"
    33) "num-other-sentinels"
    34) "3"
    35) "quorum"
    36) "2"
    ...
```

Summary

The biggest change to Redis in the release of the 3.x series is the inclusion of a working, stable, and production-ready Redis Cluster. Redis Cluster is the preferred method of scaling and splitting your data among different Redis instances running on separate machines. While Redis Cluster implements one method of hashing incoming keys through the use of a composite partitioning method and that combines features from hash and range partitioning, there are other options to scale your data through the use of client-side partitioning methods, a few which were illustrated in this chapter. We also examined a popular open source alternative for sharding and partitioning data from Twitter called Twemproxy that provides an intermediary proxy that handles the hash and assignment logic between the application and the Redis instance backends. We then turned back and examined in detail some of the features and functionality of Redis Cluster including its resharding, failover, replacing, and upgrading options that allow for long-running Redis Clusters handling large volumes of data. Finally, this chapter introduced some advanced usage of Redis Sentinel to monitor a range of different Redis application setups using examples from earlier in the chapter.

In *Chapter 7, Redis and Complementary NoSQL Technologies*, we see how Redis can complement other NoSQL technologies to provide a complete solution for your application needs.

7

Redis and Complementary NoSQL Technologies

While Redis and now, Redis Cluster fulfill many requirements for data storage in consumer and enterprise applications, other data-centered technologies may be required to completely meet the expectations and use cases of your projects. We'll start with a brief survey of the major types of data storage technology starting with a traditional SQL database followed by document and graph databases, search indexing, key-value, and the wide-column store. The upcoming sections will illustrate how Redis complements the NoSQL technologies of MongoDB, ElasticSearch, and Fedora Commons. In each case, we will see how Redis can be used to extend functionality or provide the "glue" technology to integrate with other systems by building upon your knowledge from previous chapters. We'll also examine some of the costs and possible hurdles with integrating Redis into another NoSQL or other data storage technology.

The proliferation of NoSQL

In the past ten years, a profusion of data storage technologies have emerged as options for data-intensive applications. Loosely broken down into major categories by how the technology stores, manipulates, and returns data, their popularity is tracked and ranked. Redis, as a key-value store, has improved in usage and popularity and now ranks in the top 10 data storage technologies, refer bullet point number 1 in *Appendix, Sources, Chapter 7: Redis and Complementary NoSQL Technologies*.

Relational databases, particularly those that support SQL, are the oldest and most popular data storage technologies. Starting with the large enterprise **Relational Database Management Systems (DBMS)** from Oracle and Microsoft, to the widely popular MySQL (now owned by Oracle) and Postgres open source systems, has become part of the mix of data storage technologies used by most enterprises. For smaller organizations, one of these DBMS may be the only data storage technology that they have available to use and often these databases are part of a larger customer management system, accounting, inventory, or other enterprise-level technology. In a relational database, data is organized into tables that generally represent a single entity with each row representing an instance of the entity with columns containing the entity's variables that can be required or not. The row has either a unique ID or a composite key made up of individual columns. Tables are related to each through the use of foreign keys, where the primary key of one table is stored in a column of a second table, and the application or database system is able to connect the data through joining the tables by these foreign key relationships. A relational database is normalized if data in individual columns is not duplicated in other tables. The most popular choice for structuring and querying relational databases is the declarative language SQL (structured query language) that has become the de-facto standard for most major databases with some variation on how each system implements and sometimes extends SQL:

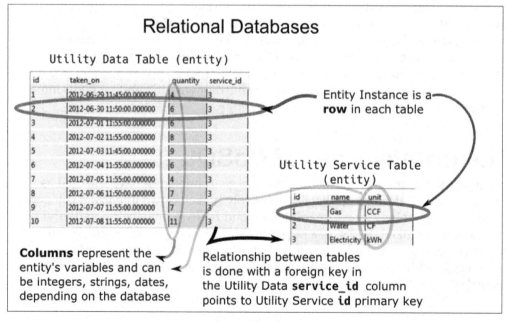

Relational Databases

Document-oriented databases, in contrast to relational databases, are based on managing and manipulating semi-structured data structures, informally called documents. In the next section, we will examine one of the most popular document stores called MongoDB but other document-oriented databases include CouchDB, Sedna, DocumentDB from Microsoft, Jackrabbit, and Informix from IBM, and MarkLogic. As long as the document has some type of structure, the format of the document can vary with such formats as XML, JSON, and YAML being common choices. Both XML and JSON formats are popular choices and have evolved into distinct niches within the broader document-oriented database. Regardless of the format, a document store typically relies on the structure of data to provide a method of querying or retrieving the document, with each document having a unique ID that represents the document itself. Many of the most-popular document-oriented databases have a custom query language for retrieving documents with the performance of these queries varying between the different document stores:

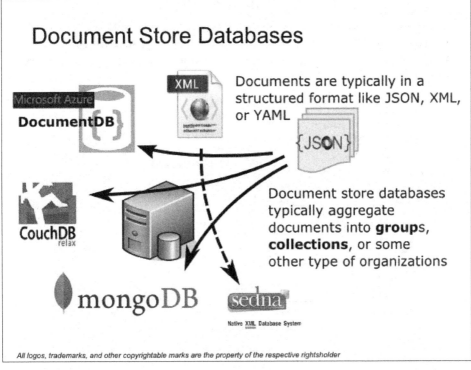

Document Store Databases

A graph database uses nodes, edges, and properties for storing and manipulating data. Nodes in a graph represent a subject or entity that contains one or more properties, with the edges being the connections or relationship between the different nodes in the database. A graph database allows for easier inference on the relationships between the different nodes through basic associative logic. Graph databases lack a formal schema that as a consequence allows for easier integration with heterogeneous data sources. Some well known graph databases include AllegroGraph, Blazegraph (formally BigData), InfiniteGraph, Neo4j, OpenLink Virtuoso, Oracle's NoSQL and Spatial products, OrientDB, and Stardog. The most popular method for retrieving and querying a graph database is through the graph database's implementation and support for SPARQL—the **SPARQL Protocol and the RDF Query Language**. SPARQL allows users to construct complex queries for retrieving nodes and for manipulating the properties and edges between nodes:

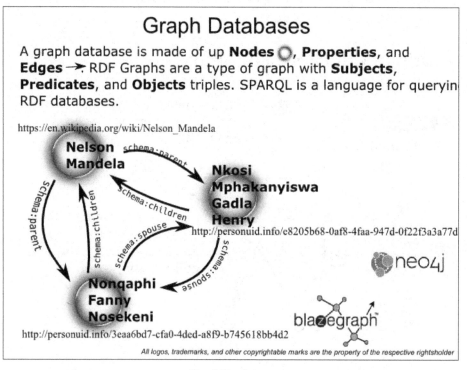

Graph Databases

Although technically classified as a subset of document-oriented database, full-text search data stores are focused on fast retrieval of results based on a user query without some of the more robust manipulation and management functionality seen in other types of document stores. Popular search-based systems based on Lucene are ElasticSearch and Solr, with other search oriented systems such as Sphinx and Xapian also available as a full-text search technology. Most of these search indexes take free-form user queries, tokenize or deconstruct the query, before performing a lookup into the search index. Most of these search data stores are missing transactional or other features used in more robust data technologies.

The next NoSQL type are key-value stores — with Redis being the most popular and widely used example of a key-value database — where keys are used to retrieve values, which are being increasingly used for a wide range of applications. While Redis, the topic of this book after all, offers a rich set of data types with supporting functionality, other key-value stores only implement a form of an associative array where a key retrieves an opaque value that is then used in the calling client code. Key-value stores can be broken down into different categories but not many of these key-value databases span multiple categories. For key-value databases that offer eventually consistency guarantees of if no updates occur, then the last-updated value will be available in all nodes in a distributed datastore. Examples of eventual consistency include Amazon's DynamoDB, Orcale's NoSQL Database, and Riak. The second category of key-value databases provide an ordering of the data by either the key or value with examples of ordered databases including Berkeley DB, HyperDex, InfinityDB, and LMDB. The third category of key-value datastore are memory-only with Redis being the most well known but other RAM databases include Aerospike, Oracle's Coherence, memcached, and OpenLink Virtuoso. The final category of key-value datastores are disk bound, either solid-drive or rotating disk where the data is read/write to disk. Examples of disk bound databases include BigTable, Hibari, LevelDB, and Tokyo Cabinet.

The final category of NoSQL databases is wide column store. Like relational databases, wide-columns have tables, rows, and columns but unlike a relational database the structure of the tables and columns can vary from row to row. Apache's Cassandra and HBase both are wide-column stores and both support MapReduce, a popular approach to distributed computing:

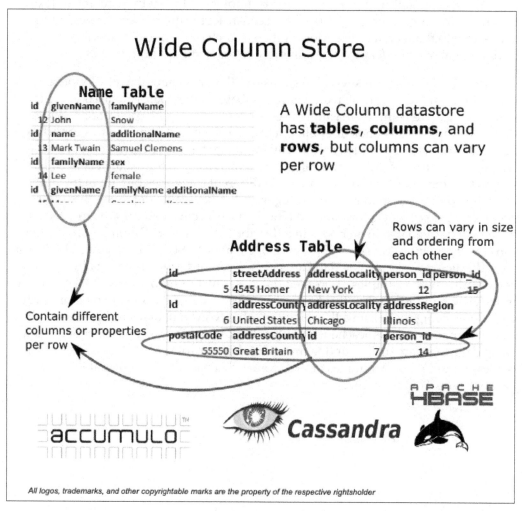

Wide Column Store

Redis as an analytics complement to MongoDB

As one of the most popular NoSQL data storages, MongoDB, is classified as a document store where the data is organized around manipulation and searching a variant of JSON-based documents called **BSON** (short for **binary serialized object notation**). MongoDB, the Mongo name is extracted from the word *humongous*, was started by the MongoDB Inc. company in 2007 and was released under an open source license in 2009. MongoDB is still sponsored and developed by MongoDB Inc with customers having the option to purchase enterprise support and hosting for MongoDB from the company:

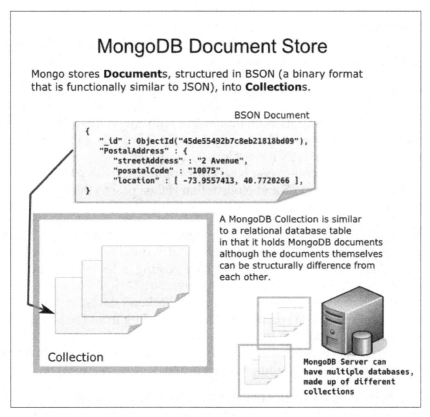

MongoDB Document Store

As a document-oriented data storage, MongoDB stores BSON objects instead of having rows and tables like a relational database. MongoDB does not provide a way to formally join different documents together nor does it support atomic transactions on multiple documents where all operations are guarantee to be executed. MongoDB does provide secondary indexes to improve search and atomic operations at the document-level and also has an expressive query language for retrieving documents from the datastore. Similar to Redis, MongoDB provides master-slave replication with automatic failover where a slave is promoted to master in the case of a master failing. MongoDB also supports the ability to shard across multiple nodes through a range-based partitioning. MongoDB organizes its BSON documents through the use of Collections that group together documents but unlike tables in a RDBMS system, the documents in a Collection do not need to have the same structure. MongoDB does not have a formal schema that has to be defined beforehand; instead MongoDB's dynamic schema is generated from the structure of the BSON documents that can be altered at runtime. MongoDB does cache documents in RAM but does not have a separate cache for application use.

As a general-purpose data store, MongoDB is used in a wide range of applications and is part of the MEAN stack made up MongoDB, ExpressJS, AngularJS, and Node.js. ExpressJS is a Node.js web application framework with AngularJS providing the dynamic client-side web frontend backed by MongoDB providing the application's storage needs. The use of MEAN has exploded in popularity with organizations interested in providing an end-to-end JavaScript application with JSON being stored and retrieved through ExpressJS and Node.js that is then passed through the rich-client HTML written with AngularJS.

Before MongoDB implemented a form of time-to-live (TTL) functionality, Redis was often used to trigger automatic deletion of MongoDB documents or collections in the datastore. As Cody Powell relates in a 2012 blog posting, refer bullet point number 2 in *Appendix, Sources, Chapter 7: Redis and Complementary NoSQL Technologies*, his use of a MongoDB as a cache was time-intensive, as a backend datastore for mobile gaming app recommendation engine, so although reading from the MongoDB was fast, inserting data took too long for his requirements. Later versions of MongoDB do implement TTL on collections so this use case for Redis and MongoDB is no longer necessary when performance-tuning an application.

In a pair of articles from 2014, refer bullet point 3 in *Appendix, Chapter 7, Redis and Complementary NoSQL Technologies* and 2015 refer bullet point 4 in *Appendix, Chapter 7, Redis and Complementary NoSQL Technologies*, DJ Walker-Morgan of Compose explores how Redis can complement MongoDB by shifting functionality and queries that MongoDB can do but is expensive both in terms of memory consumption and time but are easy to accomplish through Redis' built-in datatypes.

In the first article, Walker-Morgan relates how a client was experiencing bottlenecks in their MongoDB application when they needed to increment a per-customer counter in a MongoDB database. With each insert requiring a write to disk, the throughput for a single instance of MongoDB slowed down to around 1,500 writes per minute.

Instead of creating multiple MongoDB shards to support just this incremental requirement, using Redis for incrementing per-customer counters was much faster and did not require extensive refactoring of the MongoDB datastore for the client. In the second article, Walker-Morgan outlines how Redis' ability to directly manipulate data is a powerful addition to MongoDB. His first example returns to Redis' ability to quickly increment and store integers and how to model these increments through Redis' key schema conventions. In the second example, he goes through the process of setting and then later retrieving a count of users through the use of Redis' implementation of the HyperLogLog datatype:

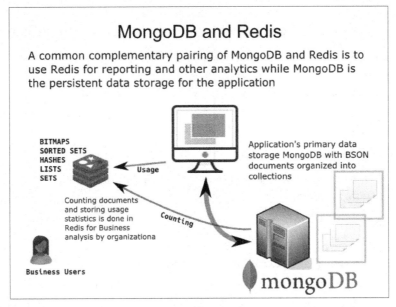

MongoDB and Redis

To experiment how Redis complements and extends MongoDB, we will model a use case where we take a MARC21 record, serialize it to JSON and store it in a single MongoDB instance. First, we'll use a Redis instance to store record usage counters using Redis bit-strings to provide a count of patrons per day that then are used to create aggregate metrics per arbitrary time periods.

By separating the metrics and analytics from the data storage, in this case using Redis for metrics and MongoDB for the data storage, this design encourages an approach that aligns with a librarian's ethos of concern for patron's privacy. An ethical design for a library catalog protects and limits the type and amount of identifiable information to protect the privacy of our patrons' information seeking behavior. There is often a tension between two library ideals, as codified in the American Library Association's code of ethics, where patron service and protection of privacy are at odds when we provide sub-par service by not tracking, analyzing, and then personalizing and customizing the search experience for our patrons. Using Redis in this context for user analytics, particularly through counting and activity metrics, means we can minimize the chance for privacy abuses by storing non-identifiable aggregate data in Redis while keeping MongoDB backend storage for permanent storage of the library system.

We'll start by downloading a MongoDB binary from www.mongodb.org (substitute your platform and the current MongoDB stable release), extracting the contents from the file, creating a data directory, and then running Mongo with its default settings:

```
$ wget https://fastdl.mongodb.org/osx/mongodb-{platform}-x86_64-{version}.tgz
$ tar -xvf mongodb-{platform}-x86_64-{version}.tgz mongodb
$ cd mongodb
$ mkdir -p data/db
$ ./bin/mongod --dbpath {path-to-data-db}/data/db
```

In a second terminal window, we will install the official Python client for MongoDB and launch a Python instance:

```
$ pip3 install pymongo
$ python3
Python 3.4.3 (v3.4.3:9b73f1c3e601, Feb 23 2015, 02:52:03)
[GCC 4.2.1 (Apple Inc. build 5666) (dot 3)] on darwin
Type "help", "copyright", "credits" or "license" for more information.
>>>
```

Now, we'll load a MARC21 file, pick a MARC21 record from the marc_records Python list, and then display our MARC21 JSON object:

```
>>> import json, pymarc
>>> marc_records = [r for r in pymarc.MARCReader(open("/var/tmp/sample-marc.mrc", "rb"), to_unicode=True)]
>>> sample_record = marc_records.pop(67)
```

```
>>> marc_json = json.loads(sample_record.as_json())
>>> marc_json
{'fields': [{'001': '4356682'}, {'008': ' eng  '},
            {'035': {'ind2': ' ', 'ind1': ' ', 'subfields': [{'a':
'.b10019947'}, {'b': 'tbp'}, {'c': '-'}]}},
            {'035': {'ind2': ' ', 'ind1': ' ', 'subfields': [{'a':
'(CoCC)102429'}]}}, {'040': {'ind2': ' ', 'ind1': ' ', 'subfields':
[{'a': 'MUU'}, {'c': 'MUU'}, {'d': 'm.c'}]}},
            {'049': {'ind2': ' ', 'ind1': ' ', 'subfields': [{'a':
'COCA'}]}},
            {'090': {'ind2': ' ', 'ind1': ' ', 'subfields': [{'a':
'PR2825.A2 B7 1967'}]}},
            {'100': {'ind2': ' ', 'ind1': '1', 'subfields': [{'a':
'Shakespeare, William,'}, {'d': '1564-1616.'}]}},
            {'245': {'ind2': '4', 'ind1': '1', 'subfields': [{'a': 'The
merchant of Venice /'}, {'c': 'edited by John Russell Brown.'}]}},
            {'250': {'ind2': ' ', 'ind1': ' ', 'subfields': [{'a': '7th
ed., rev.'}]}},
            {'260': {'ind2': ' ', 'ind1': ' ', 'subfields': [{'a':
'London :'}, {'b': 'Methuen,'}, {'c': '1964, 1967 printing.'}]}},
            {'300': {'ind2': ' ', 'ind1': ' ', 'subfields': [{'a':
'lviii, 174 p. ;'}, {'c': '22 cm.'}]}},
            {'490': {'ind2': ' ', 'ind1': '1', 'subfields': [{'a': 'The
Arden edition of the works of William Shakespeare.'}]}},
            {'490': {'ind2': ' ', 'ind1': '1', 'subfields': [{'a': 'The
Arden Shakespeare Paperbacks.'}]}},
            {'504': {'ind2': ' ', 'ind1': ' ', 'subfields': [{'a':
'Includes bibliographical references.'}]}},
            {'700': {'ind2': ' ', 'ind1': '1', 'subfields': [{'a':
'Brown, John Russell.'}]}},
            {'800': {'ind2': ' ', 'ind1': '1', 'subfields': [{'a':
'Shakespeare, William,'}, {'d': '1564-1616.'}, {'t': 'Works.'}, {'f':
'1954.'}]}},
            {'800': {'ind2': ' ', 'ind1': '1', 'subfields': [{'a':
'Shakespeare, William,'}, {'d': '1564-1616.'}, {'t': 'Works.'}, {'f':
'1954.'}, {'s': 'Paperbacks.'}]}},
            {'830': {'ind2': '0', 'ind1': ' ', 'subfields': [{'a':
'Arden edition of the works of William Shakespeare.'}]}},
            {'907': {'ind2': ' ', 'ind1': ' ', 'subfields': [{'a':
'.b10019947'}]}},
```

```
            {'902': {'ind2': ' ', 'ind1': ' ', 'subfields': [{'a':
'150104'}]}},
              {'999': {'ind2': ' ', 'ind1': ' ', 'subfields': [{'b': '2'},
{'c': '940803'}, {'d': 'm'}, {'e': 'a'}, {'f': '-'}, {'g': '4'}]}},
              {'994': {'ind2': ' ', 'ind1': ' ', 'subfields': [{'a':
'tbp'}]}},
              {'945': {'ind2': ' ', 'ind1': ' ', 'subfields': [{'a':
'PR2825.A2 B7 1967'}, {'g': '1'}, {'i': '33027001268287'}, {'j': '0'},
{'l': 'tbp '}, {'h': '0'}, {'o': '-'}, {'p': '$0.00'}, {'r': '-'}, {'s':
'-'}, {'t': '1'}, {'u': '10'}, {'v': '0'}, {'w': '0'}, {'x': '1'}, {'y':
'.i10024165'}, {'z': '940804'}]}}],
            'leader': '01144nam  2200313   4500'}
```

Before inserting our `marc_json` into our Mongo database, we'll need to import the `pymongo` Python module for MongoDB and instantiate a Mongo client:

```
>>> from pymongo import MongoClient
>>> client = MongoClient()
```

To insert our `marc_json` as a MongoDB document, we'll first create a Mongo database and collection and then call the `insert_one` method to insert our `marc_json` into our MongoDB datastore and store the resulting ID:

```
>>> marc_db = client.marc_db
>>> marc_collection = marc_db.marc_collection
>>> sample_record_id = marc_collection.insert_one(marc_json).inserted_id
>>> sample_record_id
ObjectId('55e9958f0f55c501f6802edf')
```

Before implementing both a usage counter and population count in Redis, we'll instantiate a Python Redis client and connect to a single Redis instance running on the default `localhost:6379`:

```
>>> import redis
>>> marc_redis = redis.StrictRedis()
```

We'll start by inserting the `ObjectId` into a Redis sorted set with the weight being an incremented insertion offset that we'll use later to record usage of MARC record:

```
>>> offset = marc_redis.incr("insertion-offset")
>>> marc_redis.zadd("marc-insertion", offset, str(sample_record_id))
1
```

Now, we will populate both our MongoDBs with the JSON versions of our MARC records, while also incrementing our `insertion-offset` counter and adding the MongoDB `ObjectId` to the sorted set `marc-insertion` using the `insertion-offset` as the score. The preceding logic is available as the Python function `process_records` in the `marc_example.py` Python code file, available under the Apache2 license, which accompanies this chapter and is available as a download for this book's website or GitHub repository. We'll import the `process_records` from the `marc_example` and run our sample MARC records through it:

```
>>> import marc_example
>>> marc_example.process_records(marc_records)
```

After running our test record set, we should be able to get a population count from two sources, our Redis instance and our MongoDB datastore:

```
>>> marc_collection.count()
17145
>>> marc_redis.get('insertion-offset')
b'17145'
```

So, to test our hypothesis that using Redis as a real-time analytics technology is faster in retrieving the count; we will use the Python `timeit` code module for measuring execution time of small code snippets. In this test, the retrieval of a count from a MongoDB collection of MARC JSON records and the current value of the `insertion-offset` from the `marc_redis` instance will run with the default number of runs set to 1 million:

```
>>> marc_collection_timeit = timeit.timeit(stmt=marc_collection.count)
>>> marc_collection_timeit
167.59296235199963
```

For the Redis test, we'll need to run a setup statement that creates our Redis Python client, `marc_redis`, and then run a GET command on the `insertion-offset` integer sting:

```
>>> redis_get_timeit = timeit.timeit(stmt='marc_redis.get("insertion-offset")',
    setup="import redis; marc_redis=redis.StrictRedis()")
>>> redis_get_timeit
66.52741511400018
```

This crude testing example does not account for any latencies from either Python code clients for Redis or MongoDB; the difference between the two in running this GET command and the MongoDB collection's count method call is that our Redis analytics returns a population count over 2 times faster than MongoDB. The GET command has a *O(1)* time complexity and performs this well against our MongoDB test, we can also test a different Redis command, ZCARD, to retrieve a population count in *O(1)* time complexity:

```
>>> redis_zcard_timeit = timeit.timeit(stmt='marc_redis.zcard("marc-
insertion")',

    setup="import redis; marc_redis=redis.StrictRedis()")
>>> redis_zcard_timeit
66.67229959900033
```

As we would expect, both ZCARD and GET take approximately the same time to retrieve 1,000,000 count calls of 66 seconds. With this outcome, we could adjust our Redis analytics key schema and instead of having both an increment for the offset, we could use a single sorted set to meet this requirement.

 An interesting exercise for the reader would be to benchmark MongoDB and Redis client performances by repeating this experiment using Ruby, Node.js, and Java MongoDB, and Redis clients.

With even this small sample size of fewer than 20,000 MARC21 records, we can move to the next experiment of tracking daily usage of MARC records in our MongoDB/Redis catalog. To track this usage using MongoDB requires creating a new collection, marc_usage where we'll store a JSON object containing a BSON time-stamp and the MARC21object ID. We'll use a MongoDB query to retrieve all usage in a 24-hour period. Our Redis solution will use the MongoDB ID offset by first retrieving the score with the ZRANK command in the marc-insertion sorted set and then flipping the bit at that offset in a bit-string for the day. In our example, we will define usage if a MARC record was used in a checkout event, which only occurs once a day.

In the marc_example code file, another function named add_mongo_daily_usage, creates and writes a usage document made up of a time-stamp and a reference to the object ID:

```
def add_mongo_daily_usage(object_id, date):
    usage_collection = MARC_USAGE.usage_collection
    usage_document = { "datetime": date.isoformat(),
                        "marc-id": str(object_id) }
    return usage_collection.insert_one(usage_document).inserted_id
```

A similar function for the bit-string flip based on the object ID is called
add_redis_daily_usage:

```
def add_redis_daily_usage(offset, date):
    usage_key = date.strftime("%Y-%m-%d")
    MARC_REDIS.setbit(usage_key, offset, 1)
```

To simulate usage traffic for 90 days, a daily run of between 500 to 1,000 random
offsets that generate both a MongoDB usage document using the add_mongo_daily_
usage function as well as a bitstring flipped in the Redis analytics instance with
a call to the add_redis_daily_usage function. We will execute the run_usage_
simulation function found in marc_example to generate test data from which we
will run performance testing to retrieve daily usage from both our MongoDB as well
as our Redis analytics instance:

```
def run_usage_simulation(seed_seconds, runs=90):
    seconds_in_day = 60*60*24
    max_records = int(MARC_REDIS.get('insertion-offset'))
    for day in range(runs):
        timestamp = datetime.datetime.utcfromtimestamp(
            seconds_in_day*day + seed_seconds)
        daily_usage = random.randint(500, 1000)
        for use in range(daily_usage):
            offset = random.randint(1, max_records)
            result = MARC_REDIS.zrange('marc-insertion', offset, offset)
            if len(result) < 1:
                continue
            object_id = result[0]
            add_mongo_daily_usage(object_id, timestamp)
            add_redis_daily_usage(offset, timestamp)
```

Running this simulation result gives us two ways to determine the total usage
count during the 90-day time period. Storing the usage document in the usage_
collection means we can get a rough count by executing the usage_collection.
count method in our Python terminal session:

```
>>> usage_collection.count()
66712
```

After populating a simulated 90-day usage period and storing the results in MongoDB and in Redis, we will now compare the performance of doing a daily query against both MongoDB and Redis by comparing the performance by first retrieving the count using the following MongoDB query:

```
>>> usage_collection.count({ "datetime": { '$lt': '2015-11-
06T00:00:00.0', "$gt": "2015-11-05T00:00:00.000Z"}})
681
```

Computing the same daily usage count using Redis involves using the `BITCOUNT` Redis command on a single day:

```
>>> marc_redis.bitcount("2015-11-05")
671
```

Why is there a 10 unit difference between the MongoDB and our Redis bitcount for the date November 5th? One possible reason is that a single MARC document may have been used multiple times in a single day with corresponding usage documents for each occurrence. We can investigate this discrepancy further by running our query again but this time iterating through all of the results and check to see if there are ten duplicates:

```
>>> nov5_ids = {}
>>> duplicates = 0
>>> for doc in daily_usage:
        marc_id = doc.get('marc-id')
        if marc_id in nov5_ids:
            duplicates += 1
        else:
            nov5_ids[marc_id] = 1
>>> duplicates
10
```

This simple test confirms that our problem is with handling multiple checkouts during a single day in our simulation. We can address this data issue through a number of different ways in our current implementation. Improving our MongoDB query to filter out duplicates could be one solution but it introduces additional code complexity to the solution that now needs to be maintained by operations in a production environment. A better solution is to improve `run_usage_simulation` by replacing the `random.randint` function call with the following code:

```
        daily_usage = random.randint(500, 1000)
        offsets = random.sample(range(1, max_records), daily_usage)
```

```
    for offset in offsets:
        result = MARC_REDIS.zrange(
            'marc-insertion',
            offset,
            offset)
```

To retest, we'll start with an empty MongoDB and Redis instance, and executing `run_usage_simulation` again results in the same number when we repeat our daily count for both the MongoDB and Redis test for November 5th:

```
>>> usage_collection.count({ "datetime": { '$lt': '2015-11-
06T00:00:00.0', "$gt": "2015-11-05T00:00:00.000Z"}})
577

>>> marc_redis.bitcount("2015-11-05")
577
```

Now, we'll run a `timeit` comparison again and run 10,000 trials to average the performance for retrieving a daily count first with a test Redis test:

```
>>> redis_setup = """import redis
marc_redis = redis.StrictRedis()"""
redis_daily_count_test = timeit.timeit(stmt= """marc_redis.
bitcount("2015-11-05")""",
    setup=redis_setup,
    number=10000)
>>> redis_daily_count_test
0.6927584460008802
```

Now, we will do the same for a MongoDB test:

```
>>> mongodb_setup = """from pymongo import MongoClient
client = MongoClient()
usage_collection = client.marc_usage.usage_collection"""
>>> mongo_stmt = """usage_collection.count({ "datetime": { '$lt': '2015-
11-06T00:00:00.0', "$gt": "2015-11-05T00:00:00.000Z"}})"""
>>> mongodb_daily_count_test = timeit.timeit(
        stmt=mongo_stmt,
        setup=mongodb_setup,
        number=10000)
>>> mongodb_daily_count_test
274.93577796200043
```

Even at the relatively low number of trials, the difference in time between our Redis and MongoDB daily usage is stark, under a second for retrieving 10,000 usages with Redis verses over 274 seconds for running the MongoDB query. Again the usual caveats apply, your test results will vary depending on your hardware and software setup and that for the MongoDB there may be optimizations in constructing the document and the query that could improve MongoDB's performance for this example.

Using the `BITOP` Redis command, we further calculate the total record usage during that time span by running the following command in a Redis-cli session connected to our Redis analytics instance:

```
127.0.0.1:6379> BITOP OR "2015:christmas-week" "2015-12-19" "2015-12-20"
"2015-12-21" "2015-12-22" "2015-12-23" "2015-12-24" "2015-12-25"

(integer) 2143

127.0.0.1:6379> BITCOUNT "2015:christmas-week"

(integer) 4710
```

Running the same query from our Python MongoDB client results in:

```
>>> usage_collection.count({ "datetime": { "$gt":
"2015-12-19T00:00:00.000Z", '$lt': '2015-12-26T00:00:00.0', }})
5371
```

Why aren't these retrieved values the same? This is because of the nature of the BITOP OR operation does not actually do a bitcount, but instead is the union of all of the bitmaps, any bit that is set to 1 is only counted once, even if it appears multiple times in other days. In other words, the Redis key 2015 `:christmas-week` stores all of the **unique** usage during the time-span, not the **total** number of visits. We can confirm this by looping through each day, retrieving the `BITCOUNT` for each day, and adding it to our total:

```
>>> christmas_count = 0
>>> for day in range(19, 26):
        key = "2015-12-{}".format(day)
        count = marc_redis.bitcount(key)
        christmas_count += count
        print(key, count, christmas_count)


2015-12-19 656 656
2015-12-20 784 1440
2015-12-21 745 2185
2015-12-22 891 3076
```

```
2015-12-23 825 3901
2015-12-24 616 4517
2015-12-25 854 5371
```

From this simple example, we can see how Redis complements a MongoDB datastore by being more efficient at tasks that are time-consuming and expensive in MongoDB. Not all data is well suited as a JSON document and that was tested using the Python `timeit` module. Allowing Redis to handle your analytics in an application that uses MongoDB as the primary data-storage will improve the speed for counting and other reporting tasks while simplifying the data persistence in MongoDB with a properly structured BSON format.

Redis as a preprocessor complement to ElasticSearch

ElasticSearch started off as a JSON-based frontend to Lucene. Lucene is an open source enterprise search index sponsored by the Apache Foundation that is also the core search technology for another popular search-based technology called Solr. ElasticSearch indexes JSON documents into a Lucene index and uses a custom JSON-base DSL (domain specific language) for querying the search index. ElasticSearch uses sharding and clustering techniques for scaling search to include large data sets. ElasticSearch powers searching for a number of well known websites including Netflix, The New York Times, Cisco, eBay, and Goldman Sachs.

The main sponsor of ElasticSearch, the for-profit company Elastic.co, also supports a number of other technologies that complement or build upon the ElasticSearch search index including Logstash, a log harvester that indexes logs into ElasticSearch, and Kibana, a visualization tool for ElasticSearch. Using all three together with Redis will be highlighted later in this chapter.

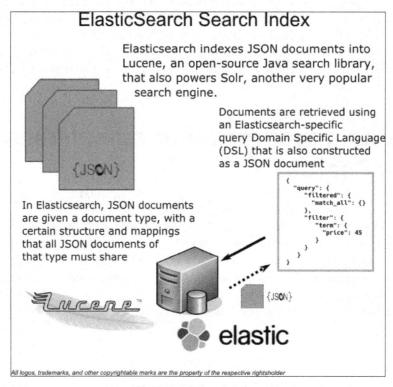

ElasticSearch Search Index

Using Redis and ElasticSearch in BIBCAT

During the design and development of a linked-data bibliographic search and display system for the Library of Congress (shortened to BIBCAT for bibliographic catalog) uses Redis as a initial deduplication method for preprocessing BIBFRAME 1.0 RDF graphs. Although ElasticSearch could easily be used for deduplication using an ElasticSearch term query against the BIBFRAME `authorizedAccessPoint` triples, using Redis instead, we can more closely match the triple patterns through the Linked Data Fragments Server that is faster as well as simplifying the matching logic.

Using the Linked Data Fragments Server also allows for alternative testing of matching algorithms and approaches such as one used by OCLC at https://viaf.org, a website that aggregates official national libraries assertions (called authorities) about people such as authors, composers, artists, photographers, illustrators, organizations, subjects, and other entities that have an identifiable roles or relationships with creative works.

To start, we will retrieve the latest ElasticSearch TAR file from https://www.elastic.com/, extract ElasticSearch, and run an instance:

```
$ wget https://download.elastic.co/elasticsearch/elasticsearch/
elasticsearch-1.7.1.tar.gz

$ tar xvf elasticsearch-1.7.1.tar.gz

$ mv elasticsearch-1.7.1

$ ./elasticsearch/bin/elasticsearch
```

In our example, we will just use the default mappings and configuration for ElasticSearch although in the actual BIBFRAME datastore, we load custom mappings and configuration specific to the BIBFRAME vocabulary. For this example, we'll start by creating BIBFRAME RDF graphs from two MARC21 samples files, the first made of MARC21 records related to Jane Austen's *Pride and Prejudice* and the second sample made up of MARC21 records related to Hermin Meville's *Moby Dick*:

```
>>> import pymarc
>>> pride_and_prejudice = [r for r in pymarc.MARCReader(open("/var/tmp/
automatic-bibframe-classification/ColoradoCollege/pride-and-prejudice.
mrc", "br+"), to_unicode=True)]
>>> moby_dick = [r for r in pymarc.MARCReader(open("/var/tmp/automatic-
bibframe-classification/ColoradoCollege/moby-dick.mrc", "br+"), to_
unicode=True)]
>>> len(pride_and_prejudice)
30
>>> len(moby_dick)
22
```

Next, we'll run the 52 MARC records through the convert2bibframe function that uses the marc2bibframe project from the Library of Congress and a socket server function xquery_socket that wraps the converter with a lightweight socket server using Jython, the Python project for running Python code on a JVM:

```
>>> def convert2bibframe(record):
return xquery_socket(pymarc.record_to_xml(record, namespace=True))
>>> pp_bibframe = [convert2bibframe(r) for r in pride_and_prejudice]
```

When running the conversion on the Moby Dick MARC records, we receive an error with one of the records, record 9, from the `convert2bibframe` XQuery function. Looking at the problematic record, we discover that it is missing the MARC 001 field required by the BIBFRAME conversion process. When we add a stub 001 field, the conversion works correctly:

```
>>> moby_dick[9].add_field(pymarc.Field('001', data='1415005'))
>>> md_bibframe = [convert2bibframe(r) for r in moby_dick]
>>> len(md_bibframe), len(pp_bibframe)
(22, 30)
```

Our total number of triples can be calculated using the Python sum method that applies a summation function to each graph, returning the total number triples in each of the graphs for both the *Pride and Prejudice* and the *Moby Dick* lists of BIBFRAME RDF graphs:

```
>>> (sum(len(g) for g in pp_bibframe), sum(len(g) for g in md_bibframe))
(7116, 3113)
```

The 52 MARC21 records in our graph produce 10,229 triples. Each triple will be the input to our Redis preprocessor that will deduplicate the subjects, and add the triple to the Redis Cache before creating a JSON body for indexing into ElasticSearch. For example, in our *Pride and Prejudice* sample set, we would expect to see Jane Austen as an author and as a subject and our catalog should be able to converge all of the separate Jane Austen BIBFRAME Person entities into a single entity before being indexed into ElasticSearch. To confirm, we will first create a SPARQL query to run on each of our *Pride and Prejudice* BIBFRAME graphs:

```
>>> sparql_query = """PREFIX bf: <http://bibframe.org/vocab/>
PREFIX rdf: <http://www.w3.org/1999/02/22-rdf-syntax-ns#>
SELECT DISTINCT ?sub ?pt
WHERE {
  ?sub rdf:type bf:Person .
  ?sub bf:authorizedAccessPoint ?pt
}"""
```

If we just want to see what RDF subjects are BIBFRAME Persons, we will just display the Person in our first BIBFRAME graph:

```
>>> for row in pp_bibframe[0].query(sparql_query):
    print(row[1])
```

```
Ehle, Jennifer, 1969-
Chancellor, Anna.
Bamber, David.
Steadman, Alison, 1946-
Sawalha, Julia, 1968-
Whitrow, Benjamin.
Langton, Simon.
Bonham-Carter, Crispin.
Harker, Susannah.
Firth, Colin, 1960-
Austen, Jane, 1775-1817.
Austen, Jane, 1775-1817--Film adaptations.
```

If we perform the same query on our last graph, we would expect to see at least one other subject with the bf:authorizedAccessPoint to be Austen, Jane, 1775-1817:

```
>>> for row in pp_bibframe[-1].query(sparql_query):
    print(row[1])
```

```
Cronin, Richard, 1949-
McMillan, Dorothy, 1943-
Austen, Jane, 1775-1817.
```

As we add each RDF graph to our Redis Cache, we will go through and check to see whether the subject has a BIBFRAME authorized AccessPoint and if this property matches a preexisting subject. If a match exists, the original subject is substituted for the incoming subject and any triples that do not already exist for the original subject are added to the Linked Data Fragments Server as additional triples with the pre-existing subject and the new predicates and objects:

```
def dedup_bibframe(graph, cache_datastore):
    query = graph.query(SPARQL_PERSON_QUERY)
    for row in query:
        subject = row[0]
        access_point = row[1]
        access_point_digest=hashlib.sha1(
            str(access_point).encode()).hexdigest()
        pattern = "*:{}:{}".format(
            BF_AUTH_PT_DIGEST,
```

```
                    access_point_digest)
        existing_subjects = cache_datastore.keys(pattern)
        if len(existing_subjects) > 0:
            subject_digest = existing_subjects[0].split(":")[0]
            new_subject=rdflib.URIRef(
                cache_datastore.get(subject_digest))
            for pred, obj in graph.predicate_objects(
                subject=subject):
                graph.add((new_subject, pred, obj))
                graph.remove((subject, pred, obj))
    return graph
```

Our second Python function goes through the list of BIBFRAME graphs and runs our deduplication function dedup_bibframe on each graph and then adds each of the graph's triples into our Redis Cache using the Linked Data Fragments server's add_triple function before calling our third function index_graph that then indexes the graph's JSON serialization as the body for our ElasticSearch index:

```
def process_graphs(graphs):
    for graph in graphs:
        graph = dedup_bibframe(graph)
        for s,p,o in graph:
            add_triple(cache_datastore, str(s), str(p), str(o))
        index_graph(graph)
```

After all of the RDF graphs have been ingested into the Linked Data Fragments Server, we can then query Redis to see if there are any duplicate BIBFRAME People in our cache by first calculating the SHA1 hash digest of the authorized access points for Jane Austen and Herman Melville as well as the digest for BIBFRAME authorizedAccessPoint:

```
>>> jane_sha1_digest = hashlib.sha1('Austen, Jane, 1775-1817.'.encode()).
hexdigest()
>>> jane_sha1_digest
'4c4da79455d1cee81d7d8737026f0607835f4e77'
>>> herman_sha1_digest = hashlib.sha1('Melville, Herman,
1819-1891.'.encode()).hexdigest()
>>> herman_sha1_digest
'04d0ae092106877146b59ef161409ae25f43df92'
```

```
>>> auth_access_pt_digest = hashlib.sha1(str(BF.authorizedAccessPoint).
encode()).hexdigest()
>>> auth_access_pt_digest
'a548a25005963f85daa1215ad90f7f1a97fbe749'
```

Next, we'll see if there are duplicate subjects by using the SHA1 for each access point and construct a Redis pattern that we will use to retrieve any keys that match our pattern. If our deduplication algorithm is correct, we should only see one triple when we evaluate the pattern using the Redis KEYS command against our Redis cache:

```
>>> jane_pattern = "*:{}:{}".format(auth_access_pt_digest, jane_sha1_
digest)
>>> jane_pattern
'*:a548a25005963f85daa1215ad90f7f1a97fbe749:4c4da79455d1cee81d7d8737026f0
607835f4e77'
>>> bibcat_redis.keys(jane_pattern)
[b'2b6f885ab822be23947c5a822b928554cf25d4cd:a548a25005963f85daa1215ad90f7
f1a97fbe749:4c4da79455d1cee81d7d8737026f0607835f4e77']
>>> herman_pattern = "*:{}:{}".format(auth_access_pt_digest, herman_sha1_
digest)
>>> herman_pattern
'*:a548a25005963f85daa1215ad90f7f1a97fbe749:04d0ae092106877146b59ef161409
ae25f43df92'
>>> bibcat_redis.keys(herman_pattern)
[b'9cf06cced925d745e8bd6ce74ea28950d9a41c64:a548a25005963f85daa1215ad90f7
f1a97fbe749:04d0ae092106877146b59ef161409ae25f43df92']
```

In this example, we are using Redis and the Linked Data Platform Fragments server to preprocess incoming RDF graphs before the graphs are serialized and indexed into our ElasticSearch search index. We are avoiding indexing any transitory or needless duplicate information that is part of the cache but should not be indexed as an ElasticSearch document before we have a graph that has all of the persons deduplicated.

ElasticSearch, Logstash, and Redis

Logstash is an open source program that takes operating and error logs from a wide range of programs and indexes these logs into ElasticSearch for better analysis and searching of logs while also offering a rich visualization and reporting through the Kibana project. The three technologies, ElasticSearch, Logstash, and Kibana are often referred to as the "ELK Stack" and is a popular data log visualization combination. Logstash accepts different input data sources that are configured and run through input plugins. A Redis input plugin is available that takes incoming Redis messages and Logstash indexes the message into ElasticSearch.

In some of the more complex ELK configurations, Redis is used as a message queue (a topic we will be exploring in more detail in a later chapter) that as logged events are captured by input plugins, the event notification is pushed to a message queue and then a Logstash message input plugin takes and indexes the event into ElasticSearch. Redis is one of the options for the message queue and it is relatively easy to configure and activate both the message output and input plugins when configuring and then deploying Logstash and ElasticSearch.

Using Redis with Logstash

Logstash is a data pipeline that specialized in processing logs and saving the results to an Elasticsearch instance. Typically, Logstash and Elasticsearch are used in conjunction with Kibana, an HTML web visualization tool that together form the popular ELK stack.

Redis can be used with Logstash in two parts; as a Data Source Input Plugin or Redis can be used as a Message Broker between the Logstash shipping Instance and a separate Logstash Indexing instance into a Elasticsearch

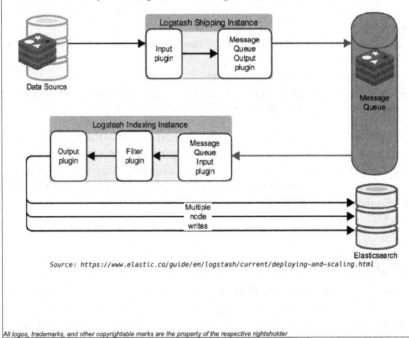

Source: https://www.elastic.co/guide/en/logstash/current/deploying-and-scaling.html

Redis Message Queue with Logstash

Redis as a smart cache complement to Fedora Commons

One of a more specialized NoSQL data storage technology used in the digital library and archival fields is an open source project called Fedora Commons, a Java-based linked data platform, for storing and preserving digital objects. This platform stores the metadata describing an object as an RDF graph; however, to fully leverage the capabilities of the Fedora Commons, commonly shortened to just Fedora (although this does introduce some confusion especially between the Fedora, the digital repository, and Fedora the Linux distribution), you need an attached SPARQL triple-store with the most popular being Apache's Fuseki and Blazegraph. Most libraries and other cultural heritage institutions that use Fedora as their digital repository also use a web presentation frontend with the two most popular choices being a Drupal-based open source project called Islandora (`http://islandora.ca`) and a Ruby-on-Rails open source project called Hydra (`http://projecthydra.org/`). Both of these projects also provide a Fedora interface to a Solr search index in their applications for full-text searching of ingested digital objects that have textual content like born-digital documents or through a workflow that takes the raw images from a scanned text, like a book or article, performs **optical character recognition (OCR)**, and indexes the resulting text in the associated Solr instance:

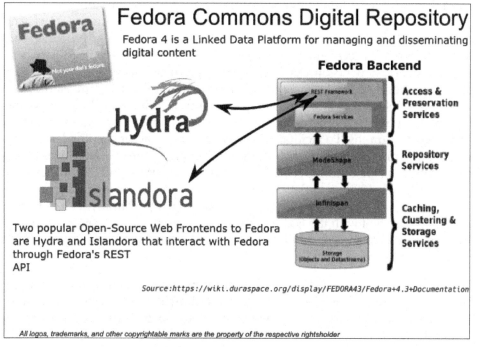

Typical Fedora Repository

Prior to version 4, the Fedora digital repository had limited support for storing RDF triples and required a relational database (typically MySQL or Postgre) for storage and management of the metadata necessary for describing and manipulating the digital objects stored in the repository. As interest grew into looking for new ways to describe these digital objects, the community surrounding Fedora Commons made a bold departure from the previous architecture by moving towards a fully functioning linked-data solution.

Linked Data started with an article, please refer bullet point 5 in *Appendix, Sources, Chapter 7: Redis and Complementary NoSQL Technologies*, in 2006 by Sir Tim Berners-Lee where he lists four rules for exposing data on the Web in a way that is machine actionable. They are:

- Use URIs as names for things
- Use HTTP URIs so people can look up those names
- When someone looks up a URI, provide useful information using RDF and/or SPARQL
- Include links to other URIs so they discover more things

Using these rules, the **World Web Consortium (W3C)** released in 2015 a recommendation available at `http://www.w3.org/TR/ldp/` for a Linked Data Platform that was then adopted by the Fedora development community as a requirements source for Fedora 4. The Fedora 4 component stack stores objects and datastreams to disk using two Java-based datastorage technologies ModeShape and Infinispan to provide access and preservation REST services. These REST services allow you to create new Resources that can be containers that are described as RDF graphs or binaries that also have associated metadata. Fedora also request the use of an external triplestore with the most popular options being Apache's Fuseki and Blazegraph both of which provide an HTTP SPARQL endpoint for running queries and updating the graphs. To facilitate and ease the overhead of keeping Fedora in sync with the triplestore, Fedora publishes notification events on a **Java Messaging Service (JMS)** topic that through JMS broker offers OpenWire and STOMP protocols that can be interacted with a variety of programming languages including Java, Python, Ruby, and PHP. For more complex messaging applications, such as keeping a triplestore consistent with the Fedora repository, Apache Camel routes are used that respond to create, update, or delete events that occur from users or processes interacting with the repository.

In the Linked Data Fragments Server, if an incoming pattern is not matched in the Redis cache, a SPARQL query is sent to the triplestore SPARQL endpoint and the query is run. If a triplestore returns a value, the Redis cache is updated with the new triple and the result is returned to the requesting client. If the SPARQL query fails to retrieve any information matching the query, an HTTP error is returned to the client.

To illustrate how the interaction between a Blazegraph SPARQL endpoint that mirrors the RDF graphs contained in a Fedora repository and the Redis-based Linked Data Fragments Server, we will model a portion of Nelson Mandela's genealogy using persistent RDF containers in Fedora that represent a person using the RDF-based vocabulary from `http://schema.org/`.

We will start with a simple RDF graph in the Turtle format that uses a `schema.org` person node for Nelson Mandela, his father, and mother that is saved as the file `nelson-mandela.ttl`:

```
@prefix rdf: <http://www.w3.org/1999/02/22-rdf-syntax-ns#> .

@prefix rdfs: <http://www.w3.org/2000/01/rdf-schema#> .

@prefix schema: <http://schema.org/> .

@prefix xml: <http://www.w3.org/XML/1998/namespace> .

@prefix xsd: <http://www.w3.org/2001/XMLSchema#> .


<https://en.wikipedia.org/wiki/Nelson_Mandela> a schema:Person ;

    schema:name "Nelson Rolihlahla Mandela" ;

    schema:parent <http://personuid.info/3eaa6bd7-cfa0-4ded-a8f9-
b745618bb4d2>,

        <http://personuid.info/e8205b68-0af8-4faa-947d-0f22f3a3a77d> .


<http://personuid.info/3eaa6bd7-cfa0-4ded-a8f9-b745618bb4d2> a
schema:Person ;

    schema:name "Nonqaphi Fanny Nosekeni" .
<http://personuid.info/e8205b68-0af8-4faa-947d-0f22f3a3a77d> a
schema:Person ;

    schema:name "Nkosi Mphakanyiswa Gadla Henry" .
```

With this simple graph loaded into our Python shell as `mandela_graph` that relates Nelson Mandela's parents to him, we will create a subgraph for each subject, and POST each of the subject's graph to Fedora Commons, which will automatically add the RDF graph to Blazegraph:

```
>>> sparql = """SELECT DISTINCT ?subject WHERE { ?subject ?pred ?obj .
}"""
>>> for row in mandela_graph.query(sparql):
        subject = row[0]
        result = requests.post("http://localhost:8080/fedora/rest")
        new_subject = rdflib.URIRef(result.text)
        subject_graph = rdflib.Graph()
```

```
    subject_graph.parse(str(new_subject))
    subject_graph.namespace_manager.bind(
        'schema',
        'http://schema.org/')
    subject_graph.add((new_subject, rdflib.OWL.sameAs, subject))
    for pred, obj in mandela_graph.predicate_objects(
        subject=subject):
        subject_graph.add((new_subject, pred, obj))
    update_result = requests.put(str(new_subject),
    data=subject_graph.serialize(format='turtle'),
    headers={"Content-Type": "text/turtle"})
```

After launching an instance of the Linked Data Fragments server, we first query
Blazegraph for all of the triples in our genealogy application, displaying an example
triple, and then ingesting each triple into the Redis cache using our previous defined
`add_triple` function from a Python shell:

```
>>> result = requests.post(
        "http://localhost:8080/bigdata/sparql",
        data={"query": "SELECT ?s ?p ?o WHERE { ?s ?p ?o .}",
            "format": "json"})
>>> bindings = result.json().get('results').get('bindings')
>>> len(bindings)
122
>>> print(bindings[8])
{'s': {'value': 'http://localhost:8080/fedora/rest/7f/61/e3/d0/7f61e3d0-
7e53-4d4f-809f-8158631b1608',
        'type': 'uri'},
'p': {'value': 'http://fedora.info/definitions/v4/repository#mixinTypes',
'type': 'uri'},
 'o': {'value': 'schema:Person', 'type': 'literal', 'datatype': 'http://
www.w3.org/2001/XMLSchema#string'}}
>>> for row in bindings:
        add_triple(redis_cache,
                row.get('s').get('value'),
                row.get('p').get('value'),
                row.get('o').get('value'))
```

We'll use node.js for our web application and query the Linked Data Fragments
Server using the N3 (https://www.npmjs.com/package/n3) RDF Node.js library
developed by the Ruben Verborgh who is also the originator of the linked data
fragments approach to accessing RDF triples. First, we'll install this Node.js library:

```
$ npm install n3
n3@0.4.3 node_modules/n3
```

To experiment using this library to parse and add triples to the Linked Data
Fragments, we will run a Node.js shell session and then load the n3 library:

```
$ node
> var N3 = require('n3');
```

We will now load the core fs Node.js library to read the nelson-mandela.ttl file
into a string:

```
> var fs = require('fs');
> var mandela_ttl = '';

> fs.readFile('nelson-mandela.ttl', 'utf8', function(error, data) {
      if (error) {
        return console.log(error);
      }
        mandela_ttl = data;
  });
```

Next, we'll create an n3 RDF parser, and parse mandela_ttl and print each RDF
triple to the console (we'll only display the first two triples to illustrate how N3
represents triples in JavaScript):

```
> var parser = N3.Parser();
> parser.parse(mandela_ttl, function(error, triple, prefixes) {
... if (triple) {
..... console.log(triple);
..... } else {
..... console.log("Finished");
..... }
... });
> { subject: 'https://en.wikipedia.org/wiki/Nelson_Mandela',
    predicate: 'http://www.w3.org/1999/02/22-rdf-syntax-ns#type',
```

```
    object: 'http://schema.org/Person',
    graph: '' }
{ subject: 'https://en.wikipedia.org/wiki/Nelson_Mandela',
    predicate: 'http://schema.org/name',
    object: '"Nelson Rolihlahla Mandela"',
    graph: '' }
```

Now, to set up the example, we will go back to our Python shell and remove the triple pattern for Nelson Mandela's father's name:

```
>>> redis_cache.exists(
"56b5bce1875a80f1975edadf3316dc1d0caa1733:30cd0bd17373373839fb3a0ffaa6bba
51a17ba6c:543718498c1fb0ee1fe75744728f22ea25e8d47f")
True
>>>redis_cache.delete("56b5bce1875a80f1975edadf3316dc1d0caa1733:30cd0bd1
7373373839fb3a0ffaa6bba51a17ba6c:543718498c1fb0ee1fe75744728f22ea25e8d4
7f")
1
```

The logic flow for the Linked Data Fragments server is to query the SPARQL datastore if no results are found from an initial query. If the triple is found in the triplestore, the triple is added to the cache and returned back to the calling function. Since we removed the Redis key for the father's name, if we connect to the running REST API for the Linked Data Fragments Server with the subject being the father's URI and the predicate being the `http://schema.org/name` from our Node.js session, the Linked Data Fragments server should query our Blazegraph SPARQL endpoint, add the triple back to the cache, and return the completed answer in JSON.

Summary

This chapter started with a survey of data storage technologies, starting with the most popular, a relational database system supporting SQL. From the relational databases, we examined document datastores focusing on MongoDB with BSON documents. Following document datastores, graph databases were briefly examined finishing with full-text search and key-value data-storage, highlighting Redis. We finished the survey by examining wide column datastores.

Four detailed examples of using Redis as a complement were demonstrated with an experiment using MongoDB to store usage data verses Redis and the performance and reduction in complexity of the application using Redis for analytics in a hypothetical MARC21 catalog. The second example explored using Redis as preprocessor for deduplicating BIBFRAME RDF graphs using the Linked Data Fragments Server as a transitory datastore. The third example showed Redis and the Linked Data Fragments Server complement the Graph Linked Data Platform combination of Fedora Commons and Blazegraph.

Continuing on the DevOps track to *Mastering Redis*, the next chapter delves into how Docker containers and Redis open up new and better methods for IT operations and development.

8

Docker Containers and Cloud Deployments

Are you puzzled by the exploding popularity of Docker and the growing interest in building and running applications with Linux containers in the past few years? Using Docker in your organization offers real efficiency improvements in how applications are developed but more importantly, how applications are deployed, secured, and restored in a production environment. Docker is based on the container, basically a Linux "operating-system virtualization" approach that allows multiple applications to run in isolated environments within a single Linux host instance. Running Redis within Docker allows for configuration and other setup options to be defined in a Linux environment that can be replicated and isolated from other processes and applications. While Docker offers much in the way of improving operational efficiencies, hosting your Redis databases on public or private clouds is another option and, in fact, most of the popular cloud providers support running Docker containers on their platforms thereby reducing and shifting the work load from your organization to a third-party. This chapter finishes by examining the cloud hosting options for Redis from three providers; Amazon, Redis Labs, and DigitalOcean as examples of how to use Redis in the cloud.

Linux containers

Docker containers are based on already existing functionality, such as **cgroups** and **namespaces**, that was in the Linux kernel prior to the first Docker release in 2013. In the Linux kernel, cgroups is a feature that isolates and limits CPU, memory, disk I/O, and network access processes that are all bound by the same criteria. cgroups also capture all STDOUT, STDERR, and STDIN output from a container and store the results in accessible logs from outside the container itself. Related to cgroups, kernel namespaces allow groups of processes to cluster together such that these processes are isolated and cannot access other resources in the OS. Specific Linux subsystems that have their own namespaces include the PID namespace, network namespace, mount namespace, IPC namespace, and user namespace, that all contain the processes to a single "virtual" view of the OS without have even knowledge of, other system or user processes that may be also running in the Linux machine. While other Linux container implementations such as LXC (https://linuxcontainers. org/) exist, by far, the most popular Linux container project has been Docker, although Docker can use LXC as the backend. Docker's native container is called libcontainer that has been in use since Docker version 0.9, and supports many commands that LXC does not.

A container is a lightweight Linux environment that encapsulates an application and all of its dependencies into a single package that is runnable and can be deployed in a consistent and reliable manner. Particularly for server-side applications that may use Redis and other technologies such as web and application servers, a container approach means all of these subsystems are wrapped into a single object that can be launched, stopped, and restarted like a single application. Docker, the company, has developed a suite of supporting open source software now bundled in Docker Toolbox that includes the Docker engine that manages containers. Docker Inc also provides the largest source for pre-build containers, called images at https://hub. docker.com, where Docker images can be found and downloaded for launching containers. One reason for the explosive growth in popularity of Docker is because of the ease of use of the platform surrounding containers that Docker Inc. has cultivated and built out to support this technology.

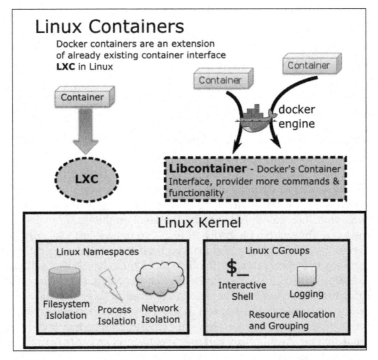

Linux Containers

What Docker containers really provide to your application is a static runtime environment that can then be replicated and run in different contexts. Running containers share the underlying host's Linux kernel but then the container supplies its own environment. For example, if a programmer is using Ubuntu to develop an application but in production the application needs to run in a SELinux environment, Docker allows for Ubuntu to run in the container with the host running SELinux. Containers eliminate a whole class of complex operational issues that can arise when different distributions are used in development versus deployment. Containers encapsulate such aspects of your application as the data, code, libraries, and systems dependencies. All of the requirements and external dependencies can be packaged and run inside a container that does not then interact with or mutate any of host's environmental variables or processes. The environment packaging removes an entire set of problems and debugging nightmares when running multiple applications in the same operational environment.

Docker containers are copy-on-write by default so that changes made to the container are local to that container and not to any other containers being run by the host computer. This also means that any new containers made from an image do not have any of the programs or changes propagate from a prior running container of the same Docker image. In this manner, we are assured that every container that is generated from a Docker image starts from a predictable and repeatable initial state.

Virtual Machines versus containers

A common reaction to first hearing about Linux containers is how are containers different from virtual machines? The basic difference between the two is where virtualization occurs in the software stack. A virtual machine abstracts the hardware that an operating system requires to run, while a container runs at a higher level on the stack by abstracting the operating system for applications. A container supplies only the executables and library interfaces required to mimic the operating system for the application taking advantage that Linux distributions all use the same underlying Linux kernel. When virtual machines are used in infrastructural roles, such as web or application servers, database servers, and so on, applications that run in these systems often have complex interactions that may interfere with each other when run in the same environment. Another key difference between Docker containers and VMs is the speed in launching and shutting down a container versus the starting or stopping of a VM. Depending on the application, container start up in a matter of milliseconds while a Virtual Machine can take seconds or minutes to fully start up. Docker containers are effectively applications that do not require a full boot-up as required for a Virtual Machine. Likewise, containers can shut down almost instantaneously while a Virtual Machine can take seconds to do a full-shutdown. It is because of this speed that containers can operate make them attractive for scaling out when traffic or usage dramatically increases.

Most Docker solutions are usually a combination of virtual machines and containers and together they provide flexibility and usability for application development and eventual deployment in production for the end users of the application. The advantages of using virtual machine is that new machines can be easily created and deployed in minutes versus the prior months that were needed in the past to purchase, load, and configure a physical server in a datacenter. VMs can be easily created, moved, and removed rapidly as operational circumstances change and allow for better hardware utilization by allowing multiple machines to be hosted on a single, physical computer instead of needing multiple servers for different roles.

The growth of VMs has also enabled the growth of computing clouds (public, private, or hybrid) where a single VM image can be run or deployed on multiple vendor clouds such as Amazon EC2, Rackspace, DigitalOcean, Google Cloud, and Microsoft Azure. VMs also enable different pricing and cloud computing models such as **Infrastructure as a Service (IaaS)**, **Platform as a Service (PaaS)**, or **Software as a Service (SaaS)**. Later in this chapter we introduce a couple of Redis-specific cloud options that operate at the higher level PaaS or SaaS options.

Containers also better support and align more closely with **service-oriented architecture (SOA)** or microservices design patterns for application development and support. In SOA, many small services that typically communicate over network or some other communication protocol are aggregated into an application. This approach allows the problem or application to be decomposed into smaller units that interoperate over a set of well-defined interfaces with each and with external services. If the service can be isolated enough so that it is more atomic, then the easier it is to encapsulate the logic and dependencies for the service, and the more likely the service will be reused by other components or applications in the future. As containers and services are likely to have the same cardinality, that is, services and containers that run a single process are equivalent in their requirements and so containers are a natural fit for supporting SOA and microservices. This matching also enables operation groups to better support these discrete services, with each service having its own environment and dependencies that can be isolated and restarted if the service fails. Docker containers are also well-suited for other operational roles such as a **Continuous Integration (CI)** platform, partner distribution, running either as a cloud deployment, or as a local executing program.

Another aspect of containers that is worth mentioning is the ability to fine-tune inter-service communication between different containers. With containers, communication can occur over a localhost IP loopback, directories can be shared between containers thereby supporting UNIX sockets, memory mapped files, or named `pipes`, and shared memory or over kernel semaphores and messages queues. Containers can also be run in complete isolation from each other based on Linux namespaces.

Docker containers can be broken down into types of container based on their usage. The most common container type is an application container that is further broken down into executable containers and service containers. Executable containers are designed to be run binaries from the command-line and allow the binary to run on different host operating systems than the original OS that the binary was compiled on. Service containers encapsulate application services and typically run in the background as a daemon. Machine containers house the nonkernel elements of a Linux distribution and are usually used as a base image for more complex containers as well as providing a mechanism to run and test different Linux distributions from a single host OS. The final type of Docker container is a volume container that does not run or execute any programs but provides a wrapper around persistent volumes for use by other containers.

The Docker architecture is made up a Linux daemon (called the Docker engine) and one or more Docker clients that connect to the Docker engine through a REST API. The Docker daemon listens on a Unix socket located on the host machine at `/var/run/docker.sock` and is owned by the *docker* group. Communication between the Docker client and server is not encrypted by default so opening up access to the daemon from outside your trusted network could result in a security risk as outside clients can run processes with elevated privileges. Depending on whether you are running Docker on an Ubuntu host, the configuration for the Docker daemon is in a settings file at `/etc/default/docker` while the settings file on Red Hat Enterprise is at `/usr/lib/systemd/system/docker.service`. Logs for the Docker daemon are stored on a Ubuntu host at `/var/log/upstart/docker/log`. In addition, the Docker engine uses the `/var/lib/docker` directory as the Docker's primary working directory:

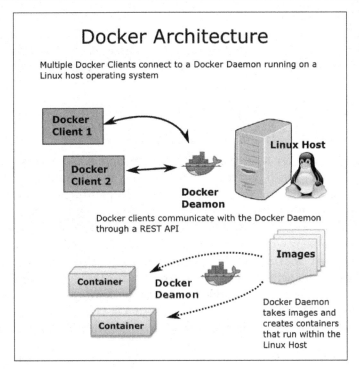

Docker Architecture

Docker clients can connect to local or remote Docker daemons using either the -H switch when running client commands or the DOCKER_HOST environmental variable can be set for host and port by running the following Bash command export DOCKER_HOST="tcp://0.0.0.0:4646" that changes the default port that the client connects and sends messages to the REST API. Using a proxy server with Docker client is accomplished by setting on the following environmental variables: HTTP_PROXY, HTTPS_PROXY, or NO_PROXY.

Docker images are container templates that are either created locally or can be downloaded from either a local or enterprise registry of Docker images, or can be download from a public Docker image repository. The most active and large repository of Docker images is available from Docker at http://hub.docker.com/. A Docker container is a running instance of a Docker image. Included in the thousands of images available on Docker Hub, are base images for all of the most popular Linux distributions such as Ubuntu, Fedora, Debian, CirrOS, CentOS, and CoreOS as well as prepackaged images for the most applications including nginx, WordPress, MongoDB, MySQL, and Redis. When launching a Docker container from an image, if the image isn't found locally, Docker looks next at Docker Hub for a matching image and if the image is found, downloads the image and creates the container.

Docker initially started off being written in Python but over the years Docker, Inc has reimplemented and improved Docker by writing Docker in Go, the programming language developed and supported by Google. As an open source technology released under the Apache 2 License, Docker can be forked or downloaded at `https://github.com/docker/docker`.

Docker basics with Redis

If you are already a Docker user, please skip this section as we will explain the steps to getting starting with Docker by running the official Redis Docker image available at `https://hub.docker.com/_/redis/`. Depending on your operating system, directions for installing Docker are available at `https://docs.docker.com/installation/`. For Macintosh and Windows host operating systems, installation of Docker involves the use of the Docker Toolbox lightweight Linux system that has been designed to run Docker container execution on these platforms. Alternatively, you can use a VM manager such as VirtualBox to run a Linux distribution to install and run Docker. To run the Docker daemon on Linux requires a Linux kernel that is newer than version 3.10 and is 64-bits. Docker's goal is to eventually run on a wide range of processors and operating systems with including Window Server 2016.

After you have installed Docker on Linux, you can make your life easier by adding your current user to a new Docker group with the following command after we open a new terminal window:

```
$ sudo usermod -aG docker {your-username}
```

Be sure to log out and log back in to ensure that the current user is an active member of the new Docker group. Using Docker on Windows or Macintosh with Docker Toolbox will set up and load the necessary environment variables for use on those platforms. Next, we will see what version of Docker is active before launching our first container, the Docker hello-world image:

```
$ docker --version
Docker version 1.8.2, build 0a8c2e3
$ docker run hello-world
Unable to find image 'hello-world:latest' locally
latest: Pulling from library/hello-world
535020c3e8ad: Pull complete
af340544ed62: Pull complete
library/hello-world:latest: The image you are pulling has been verified.
Important: image verification is a tech preview feature and should not be
relied on to provide security.
```

```
Digest: sha256:02fee8c3220ba806531f606525eceb83f4feb654f62b207191b1c92091
88dedd
Status: Downloaded newer image for hello-world:latest

Hello from Docker.
This message shows that your installation appears to be working
correctly.
```

If you have Docker running correctly, a daemon will be running in the background that is used to coordinate and run the pulled containers or any newly constructed containers. Next, we will pull the official Redis Docker container with the Docker PULL command:

```
$ docker pull redis
Using default tag: latest
latest: Pulling from library/redis
ba249489d0b6: Pull complete
19de96c112fc: Pull complete
d990a769a35e: Pull complete

    .

    .

    .

library/redis:latest: The image you are pulling has been verified.
Important:
image verification is a tech preview feature and should not be relied on
to provide security.
Digest: sha256:3c3e4a25690f9f82a2a1ec6d4f577dc2c81563c1ccd52efdf4903ccdd2
6cada3
Status: Downloaded newer image for redis:latest
```

We can see if there are any running Docker containers by using the Docker ps command:

```
$ docker ps

CONTAINER ID        IMAGE               COMMAND             CREATED
STATUS              PORTS
```

So far, we haven't launched any running Docker containers. We can see if there are any existing containers being managed by the Docker engine by running the same command but with the -a parameter to see all existing containers:

```
$ docker ps -a

CONTAINER ID        IMAGE          COMMAND           CREATED
STATUS              PORTS          NAMES
```

```
822c7c12672f       hello-world   "/hello"        34 minutes ago    Exited
(0) 34 minutes ago                      pensive_pasteur
```

Docker containers are assigned a unique UUID with a shortened version being displayed under the `CONTAINER ID` column, for our `hello_world` container, the shortened UUID is `822c7c12672f`. If you don't specify a name of your container, the Docker engine will create a random name, in this case, `pensive_pasteur`. Your own containers will most likely be a different random name. Using the `--name` switch allows your to set the name of the container explicitly; however, container names must be unique within the scope of the Docker daemon running on the host. We will now launch a container by using the `run` command based upon the official Redis image we downloaded earlier.

We will pass the `--detach=true` parameter to run in the background, the `--name=redis` to name our container `redis` instead of a random name, and we will also pass a parameter to map the container's default Redis port of `6379` to the Docker host port of `6379` with the `-p 6379:6379` parameter that returns a container `sha1` ID:

```
$ docker run --detach=true --name=redis -p 6379:6379 redis

51fde4c2100f64fbc720fb395e2857be8b98a78e50ba75d0dbaed89ded4c1b18
```

Now, by rerunning the `ps` command we should see our new active `redis` container:

```
$ docker ps
CONTAINER ID       IMAGE              COMMAND                CREATED
STATUS             PORTS                NAMES
51fde4c2100f       redis                  "/entrypoint.sh redis"   About a
minute ago    Up About a minute   0.0.0.0:6379->6379/tcp    redis
```

Opening a new terminal window, we will launch a Redis-cli instance and see if we can connect to the Redis instance running in our Docker container:

```
~/redis/src/redis-cli

127.0.0.1:6379> DBSIZE

(integer) 0
```

To halt our `redis` Docker container, we use the Docker `stop` command and confirm that our container is no longer active by issuing the `ps` command:

```
$ docker stop redis

redid

$ docker ps
CONTAINER ID       IMAGE              COMMAND                CREATED
STATUS             PORTS
```

Docker containers can also be run in the interactive mode with a pseudo `tty` by passing the `-it` parameters to the Docker `run` command and dropping `--detach=true` to run the container in the foreground. For now, we will go ahead and remove our `redis` Docker container from our local environment before creating a new Redis container in the `interactive` mode:

```
$ docker rm redis

redis

$ docker run -it -p 6379:6379 redis
```

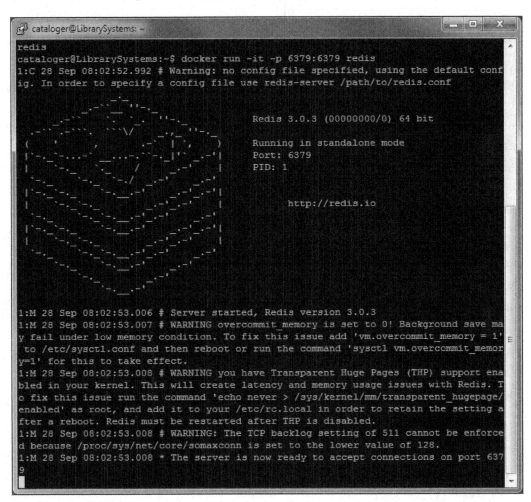

Our Redis container's default execution path is to run Redis without any configuration file on port 6379 with STDERR and STDOUT being redirected to your screen. In production, you would run your Redis container in the background. To assist in troubleshooting or debugging, running your container in the foreground in a pseudo terminal session can be helpful to track down Redis- and Docker-related issues. To close and stop your container, select *Ctrl + C* from your keyboard to the active window where Redis container is running. We can bypass this default execution path when running our Redis container by providing a path to an executable as a parameter after specifying the image:

```
$ docker run -it -p 6379:6379 redis /bin/bash
root@55ec569c1ded:/data#
```

By passing in the path to bash, running this command drops you into a root session in your container. From this Command Prompt, we can explore our Redis container by displaying the contents of the /etc/os-release file:

```
root@55ec569c1ded:/data# cat /etc/os-release
PRETTY_NAME="Debian GNU/Linux 7 (wheezy)"
NAME="Debian GNU/Linux"
VERSION_ID="7"
VERSION="7 (wheezy)"
ID=debian
ANSI_COLOR="1;31"
HOME_URL="http://www.debian.org/"
SUPPORT_URL="http://www.debian.org/support/"
BUG_REPORT_URL="http://bugs.debian.org/"
```

From this display, we see our Redis image is based upon the Debian Linux distribution. From our root terminal session in our running container, we can check to see that the container is running its own network interfaces by:

```
root@55ec569c1ded:/data# ip a
1: lo: <LOOPBACK,UP,LOWER_UP> mtu 65536 qdisc noqueue state UNKNOWN
    link/loopback 00:00:00:00:00:00 brd 00:00:00:00:00:00
    inet 127.0.0.1/8 scope host lo
       valid_lft forever preferred_lft forever
    inet6 ::1/128 scope host
       valid_lft forever preferred_lft forever
```

```
8: eth0: <BROADCAST,MULTICAST,UP,LOWER_UP> mtu 1500 qdisc noqueue state
UP
    link/ether 02:42:ac:11:00:03 brd ff:ff:ff:ff:ff:ff
    inet 172.17.0.3/16 scope global eth0
       valid_lft forever preferred_lft forever
    inet6 fe80::42:acff:fe11:3/64 scope link
       valid_lft forever preferred_lft forever
```

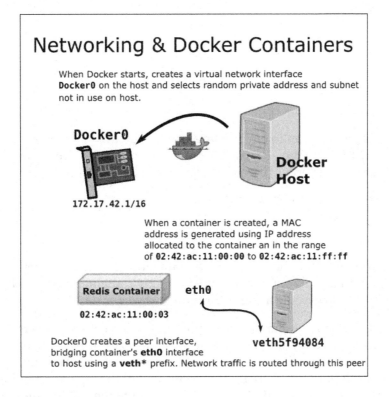

Finally, we will check the contents of the current /data directory and exit our running container:

```
root@55ec569c1ded:/data# ls
root@55ec569c1ded:/data# exit
```

Because we did not launch Redis in our container, the /data directory was empty and did not contain a dump.rdb file. We'll now run a new Redis container, naming it redis, and running it in the background making the container available on port 6379 by mapping it to the host port 6379:

```
$ docker run --detach=true --name=redis -p 6379:6379 redis
```

In a second terminal window, we will run our Redis-cli and add a new key:

```
127.0.0.1:6379> dbsize
(integer) 0
127.0.0.1:6379> set book 1
OK
127.0.0.1:6379> BGSAVE
Background saving started
```

Now, if we want to connect to our running redis container, we can use the Docker exec command to - with the -i switch to run the session interactively and the -t flag to run a pseudo tty session to check the contents of the /data directory:

```
$ docker exec -it redis /bin/bash
root@e4629ca31026:/data# ls
dump.rdb
```

Two other arguments that the exec Docker command accepts are -d or --detach=true to run the command on the running container in the background and -u or --user= to execute a command under a specific username or UID.

Another useful Docker command for examining running containers is the logs command. The logs command displays the container's captured STDOUT/STDERR output and the log command accepts a --tail parameter similar to the UNIX tail program for displaying 1 or more lines from the end of the log file. Running the command on our container and restricting the output to the last five lines in the log file results in the following output when selecting our redis container:

```
$ docker logs --tail 5 redis
1:M 22 Sep 13:44:20.510 * The server is now ready to accept connections
on port 6379
1:M 22 Sep 13:47:22.755 * Background saving started by pid 18
18:C 22 Sep 13:47:22.817 * DB saved on disk
18:C 22 Sep 13:47:22.818 * RDB: 6 MB of memory used by copy-on-write
1:M 22 Sep 13:47:22.849 * Background saving terminated with success
```

Two other Docker commands `top` and `stats` allow you to examine additional runtime and environmental variables and processes in a running container. The `top` command shows the running process in the `redis` container:

```
$ docker top redis
UID                    PID                    PPID                   C
STIME                  TTY                    TIME                   CMD

999                    15553                  696                    0
06:38                  ?                      00:00:00               redis-server
*:6379
```

`stats` displays a live status view of the `redis` container, which we can test by running Redis CLI session to issue a couple of commands and then seeing the results:

```
CONTAINER              CPU %                  MEM USAGE/LIMIT        MEM %
NET I/O

redis                  0.20%                  6.619 MB/1.579 GB      0.42%
1.296 kB/5.044 kB
```

The Docker commands `start`, `restart`, and `attach` along with `stop`, allow for greater control of the Docker containers that may reside in your local Docker repository. First, we will stop our running `redis` container:

```
$ docker stop redis
redis
```

Second, we will start our Redis container and confirm that `redis` is still active with the `ps` command:

```
$ docker start redis
redis
$ docker ps
CONTAINER ID           IMAGE                  COMMAND                CREATED
STATUS                 PORTS                    NAMES
e4629ca31026           redis                    "/entrypoint.sh redis" 46 hours
ago        Up 3 seconds      0.0.0.0:6379->6379/tcp   redis
```

Using the `attach` Docker command brings the container up to the foreground and displays its STDOUT/STDERR output. Be careful, because if you send a *Ctrl + C* to the now active window, it will send a kill signal (SIGINT) to the container, stopping it:

```
$ docker attach redis
^C1:signal-handler (1443097862) Received SIGINT scheduling shutdown...
```

```
1:M 24 Sep 12:31:02.861 # User requested shutdown...
1:M 24 Sep 12:31:02.861 * Saving the final RDB snapshot before exiting.
1:M 24 Sep 12:31:02.864 * DB saved on disk
1:M 24 Sep 12:31:02.864 # Redis is now ready to exit, bye bye...
$ docker ps
CONTAINER ID        IMAGE               COMMAND             CREATED
STATUS              PORTS               NAMES
```

To avoid shutting down your container after you have attached to the container, you can instead use the *Ctrl + P* and *Ctrl + Q* key combination to detach from the running container. *Ctrl + C* will work if you initially started your container with the `--sig-proxy` flag set to `false`. Now that that we stopped our Redis container, we can issue a `restart` command to activate and run our `redis` container:

```
$ docker restart redis
redis
$ docker ps
CONTAINER ID        IMAGE               COMMAND                 CREATED
STATUS              PORTS               NAMES
e4629ca31026        redis               "/entrypoint.sh redis"  46 hours
ago         Up 4 seconds        0.0.0.0:6379->6379/tcp   redis
```

With these core set of commands to manage your Docker containers, we shift to the next important component of Docker, understanding and creating images that provide the runtime template for our containers.

Layers in Docker images

While being able to run your application within a Docker container is, in of itself, a great feature, it is only in combination with a Docker image—a template for container creation—that the advantages of Docker start to become apparent. Docker images are constructed by adding new file system layers on top of preexisting file system layers. Each layer is made up of a static feature, such as the executables, libraries, and other configuration for an application, program, or utility. Upper level layers file paths that match preexisting files in lower layers mask the file from executing code.

For example, say you start with the existing official Redis layer, adding a new layer with its own `redis.conf` configuration file will mask any existing `redis.conf` file that is located at the same filepath or location:

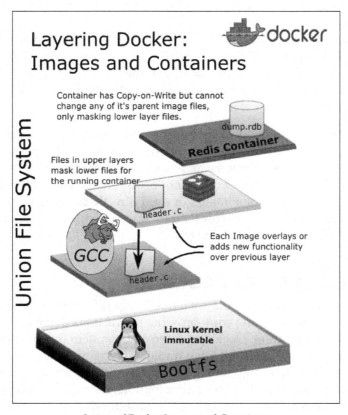

Layers of Docker Images and Containers

A Docker Base image is an image that does not have a parent and are typically made up of the operating system, such as Ubuntu or CentOS, and the root filesystem. For security-operations reasons, you can also create an empty Docker Base image and then add only the necessary files to run an application as separate and distinct layers. The filesystem within an image layer is read-only and a running container cannot change the file in a lower image layer although the file can be changed and saved that masks the lower image layer's file. Immutable files in an image file system allows one image to provide a consistent and repeatable environment to run multiple containers with the same results while also reducing the disk and memory footprint of containers that share the same parent images within a running instance of the Docker host.

When a container is first started, its filesystem is initially empty. Any writes from running processes in the new running container are saved in the container's filesystem, and as mentioned before, any files that match existing files in any of the lower-level image layers are masked. Container filesystems contain only the changes between the file and any underlying file system states in the container's image layers. Starting from the top, all of the changes made by the container and all of the existing image layer filesystems are collectively called the union filesystem. The lowest layer in the stack is called `bootfs` and supplies the in-memory filesystem interface to the Linux kernel, and `bootfs` also supplies the kernel library interface as well to upper image layer processes.

Each Docker container and image has a parent image except for Docker's base images. Docker images are built from intermediate images and these intermediate layer images do not have a repository name or tag and are used together to provide source layers for the parent images of a container or image. These intermediate layers are not used as standalone images or used directly by the container but can be shared by multiple descendant images thereby saving disk and resource space for use directly by containers and final images.

Docker filesystem backends

Depending on the Docker host, there are a number of different filesystem backends used by images and the resulting copy-on-write interactions that a running container may execute during operation. Docker's preferred filesystem type is **advanced multi-layered unification filesystem (aufs)** that implements a union mount where file level information is stored with shared storage with other filesystems in a single mount point. Ubuntu, Debian, and other Linux distributions use aufs as the default. Red Hat and CentOS are two very popular Linux distributions that do not enable aufs as a default. The number of layers in a Docker images is limited by aufs default number of layers at `127`. Docker also supports `btrfs` for filesystem snapshot where block level scheme with shared storage requires the Docker host files located at `/var/lib/docker` use `btrfs` filesystem with each image and container layers are stored as subvolumes at `/var/lib/docker/btrfs/subvolumes`. Docker hosts running Red Hat and CentOS systems use the `devicemapper` filesystem as a default where like `btrfs`, block level scheme are used to support layers and shared storage. Other filesystems that Docker supports are **vfs** for universal support on the Docker host but is inefficient because vfs do not support snapshotting of layers but create separate directories for each layer with a deep copy of the parent layer. Finally, Docker also supports the **OverlayFS** union mount for other file systems.

The `docker images` command displays all of the images present in the Docker host and snippet of this display for an example environment is demonstrated here:

```
$ docker images
REPOSITORY                      TAG                          IMAGE ID
CREATED            VIRTUAL SIZE
<none>                          <none>
1bbc3672404f       2 weeks ago         521.9 MB
java                            8-jre
81f1a5272622       2 weeks ago         487.9 MB
redis                           latest
2f2578ff984f       2 weeks ago         109.2 MB
```

Docker images are stored on a Linux host in the default location at `/var/lib/docker/aufs/layers` and in our example environment can be displayed by switching to root, changing directories, and displaying the contents:

```
$ sudo su
# cd /var/lib/docker/aufs/layers
# ls
00db3659acd05f0a98a41d69cab0791055844fcee84f7f53ab2b0cbfd27cb9ae
017d6be562b544d03de624546b63ba8e9c0b21ce3bfd05a32058e9b39efc8672
0225617d4328e423e5e98ad28efd6e10063242aafeaad9a9758865f026b0a732
038233a03eefb40279ac0eb3a2a87b2961ce819c8ca9c6f938e456d68bde6297
04ac98492065dc05dac0d5da333afcdad50b4e886b9efc3599ea48ea39683ea0
```

The Docker containers directory located at `/var/lib/docker/containers` has a separate directory for each container and holds the container's metadata and log files. Each container directory is the unique ID and we can retrieve the first part of the container's ID for our `redis` container by running the `docker ps -a` command:

```
# docker ps -a
CONTAINER ID       IMAGE                  COMMAND
CREATED            STATUS                 PORTS              NAMES

e4629ca31026       redis                  "/entrypoint.sh redis"   5
days ago           Exited (0) 3 days ago                     redis
```

Now, we change directories to our container and display the contents of the directory:

```
# cd /var/lib/docker/containers/
e4629ca310264f7f4a930dcdaf5f8a91710b8a2fe5109996dffdf9adbfd5c5a8/
# ls
config.json
e4629ca310264f7f4a930dcdaf5f8a91710b8a2fe5109996dffdf9adbfd5c5a8-json.log
hostconfig.json
hostname
hosts
resolv.conf
resolv.conf.hash
```

The `config.json` files contain runtime and environmental variables for running the Redis container. The `json` log file is what is displayed when running the Docker command `docker logs redis` as well as storing the activity in the container.

A running container in Docker generates deltas — stored on the Docker host — of **copy on write (COW)** data that is either existing files from parent layers that have been modified or any new files that have been created by processes in the container. These diffs are stored in the `/var/lib/docker/aufs/diff/` directory. To view these changes, using the `docker diff` command displays the changes in the container's filesystem layer. *Add (A)*, *Delete (D)*, and *Change (C)* are the three types of deltas that are captured and displayed when running the container. First, we will run the diff command on our new `redis` container and we see nothing has changed:

```
$ docker diff redis
$
```

Next, we'll open a Redis CLI session, add a key, and issue a BGSAVE command to persist RDB snapshot to the container's file system layer:

```
$ redis/src/redis-cli
127.0.0.1:6379> SET person:1 "Lucy van Pelt"
127.0.0.1:6379> GET person:1
"Lucy van Pelt"
127.0.0.1:6379> BGSAVE
Background saving started
```

Creating a Docker image is accomplished one of two ways; taking a snapshot of a modified running container or building a new Docker image from a Dockerfile, a simple text format containing a list of Dockerfile specific commands. The first method of image creation, taking a snapshot of a running container, is the simplest method. For example, if we wanted to create a custom image based on the official Redis image, load some data, and then save the result as a new image, we would go through these steps:

First, we'll stop and remove our `redis` container:

```
$ docker stop redis
redis
$ docker rm redis
redis
```

Second, we'll launch a fresh Redis container instance in the background and then connect to the container with the `docker exec` command:

```
$ docker run --detach=true -p 6379:6379 --name=redis redis
2f0b562fe09c4b9663cf3e122d3256ecaf96773c459536dcb9674fd0d347ce26
$ docker exec -it redis /bin/bash
root@2f0b562fe09c:/data#
```

The running Docker container does not have any data yet, so we'll open up a second command line, launch a Redis CLI instance, confirm we have an empty Redis database, and then load some data into our custom Redis image:

```
$ redis/src/redis-cli
127.0.0.1:6379> DBSIZE
(integer) 0
127.0.0.1:6379> MSET ichi one ni two san three shi four go five roku six shichi seven hachi eight kyuu nine ju ten
OK
```

After we saved our ten keys (a count of Japanese one through ten with the English translation as the string value), we go back to our first terminal window and confirm that there is a now a `dump.rdb` file in our data directory:

```
root@2f0b562fe09c:/data# ls
dump.rdb
```

A less desirable method for creating an image that contains the `dump.rdb` file of our persisted data we'll first exit our running *redis* container and then issue a `docker commit` command, passing in the author and message parameters that create a custom Redis image to a `redis-japanese-numbers` repository and then confirming that our new image is available by displaying a list of images:

```
root@2f0b562fe09c:/data# exit
exit
$ docker commit --author="Jeremy Nelson" --message="Japanese Numbers"
redis jermnelson/redis-japanese-numbers
6ef38a2d2efb5253db128d4fbaad6379679c2dc5d533e0b54750e1653e038cae
$ docker images
REPOSITORY                          TAG           IMAGE ID
CREATED              VIRTUAL SIZE
jermnelson/redis-japanese-numbers   latest        6ef38a2d2efb     2
minutes ago          109.2 MB
redis                               latest        2f2578ff984f     3
weeks ago            109.2 MB
```

Now, we will stop our `redis` container and launch a new Docker container based on the new `redis-japanese-numbers` image:

```
$ docker run --detach=true -p 6379:6379 jermnelson/redis-japanese-numbers
6537f3e95269439aa976d8220a4c7f6b7c1815ba19fd04814d7c9415f3ae6571
```

To check to see whether our new image contains the saved data, we'll connect with a Redis CLI and check whether there is any data available:

```
$ redis/src/redis-cli
127.0.0.1:6379> dbsize
(integer) 0
```

So what happened, where is our data? This is a common "gotcha" because the base redis image mounts its data at the `/data` directory as a data volume. Any volumes in a container are not saved when launching containers because of the way Docker persists and shards data through its volume syntax. Committing a running container as a new image does NOT persist any mounted volumes.

This is a feature of Docker and it means that if we want to persist our `rdb` files, we have a couple of options, including restarting Redis with a file path different from the `/data` directory for our `dump.rdb` file or we can use the second method for creating a Docker image by using a Dockerfile.

Building images with a Dockerfile

As we saw in the previous section, creating a Docker image through a snapshot of a running container is a very manual process requiring you to connect to, install, and then later commit your changes in order to create a working image. Fortunately, the second and preferred method for creating a new Docker image is to use a text-based Dockerfile instead of committing changes on a running container to create an image. A Dockerfile is composed of a series of instructions that create an image in the order the commands are written in the file. Each command creates a separate layer in the Docker image so care should be taken to minimize the number of commands. Having too many layers will create a bloated image that takes longer to build, download, or upload to your Docker host. The first command of all Dockerfiles is the FROM command that specifies the parent image from which the new image will be built upon which most of the time will be a Operating System image. The current recommendation for the operating system base image is to use the Alpine Linux Image as it provides a full OS and has been optimized for use as a base container in Docker at less than 100 megabytes:

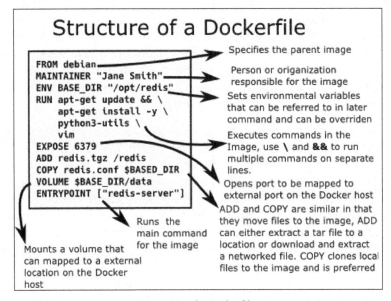

Structure of a Dockerfile

The RUN, ADD, and COPY Dockerfile commands perform most of the real work in a Dockerfile. The RUN instruction executes one or more Linux commands in the image and is useful for installing packages and other dependencies in your application. Multiple commands can be concatenated into a single RUN instruction by separating each Linux command with double ampersands (&&). Another suggestion is to put each of these command on separate lines using the backslash (\ ) character. The ADD and COPY commands are similar in that they transfer files to the image; however, ADD offers additional functionality in that TAR file are automatically extracted to the local file system and ADD can also download a file from a URL. The COPY command clones any local files relative to the Dockerfile location on the host and saves those files to the image. If there are files that you want to exclude from the COPY command, create a .dockerfile in the root directory where your Dockerfile is located and similar to the .gitignore file, the COPY command will not clone any files that match the patterns in the .dockerfile to the image.

The VOLUME and EXPOSE commands provide outside access between the Docker host and the image and the subsequent containers that are run off the image. The VOLUME command provides a mount-point between the image's filesystem and the Docker host and can be a directory or file located on the host that is then available for saving and persisting data between container sessions. The EXPOSE instruction specifies an internal port number in the image that can then be mapped to a Docker host port number when the container is launched with the -p parameter and its use is seen in the previous examples when we ran the redis image with port number 6379 on the host is mapped to the same port within the image.

The ENTRYPOINT and the CMD instructions are also related but provide different functionality within the image. The ENTRYPOINT instruction specifies the default executable to be run when the image is instantiated into a running container. Script files can also be the target with the ENTRYPOINT instruction where configuration and set-up instructions are part of the bash script that then calls the main executable to be run. Alternatively, the CMD instruction allows you to specify the software to run in the image along with any parameters to be passed into the software's executable. The official Redis Dockerfile used the CMD instead of the ENTRYPOINT instruction and is CMD ["redis-server", "/etc/redis/redis.conf"] where the location of the redis.conf file is passed to the redis-server executable. Regardless, if you use CMD or ENTRYPOINT in your Dockerfile, you'll want to specify the directory location in the image where the executable or script is located by using the WORKDIR instruction to set the location to run the command in your image.

Hosting and publishing Docker images

After creating custom Docker images through either a committing a snapshot of a running Docker container or by writing a Dockerfile and building a new image, Docker provides a way number of ways to allow you to share your image. Docker, the company, sponsors a service for hosting your image at `https://hub.docker.com/` where you can upload your image after creating an account by using the `docker push {repository}/{image-name}:{tag}` command that then is available for use. With the free account level on Docker Hub, you have one free private repository and an unlimited number of public images. A paid membership on Docker Hub provides you multiple private repositories on Docker Hub depending on your level of membership.

If you do not wish to use Docker Hub but you would like to provide your image for use by others in your organization, a part of the Docker Corporations affiliated project Docker Toolkit available at `https://github.com/docker/distribution` allows you to host your own repository. It should be no surprise that the mechanism that this project employs is a Docker image that you run locally by running the following command on your Docker host:

```
$ docker run --detach=true -p 5000:5000 --restart=always --name registry registry:2
```

From this Docker command, we are running a container instance of the *registry* image in the background and is available on port `5000`. A new parameter `--restart` is set to `always` so that if the container fails, the Docker host will automatically restart the container. With the registry running on port `5000`, if you want to push your custom Redis image to your local container, you'll need to tag it to point to the registry, in this case `localhost:5000`. If you intend to share your private registry with others in your organization, you'll likely want to have a dedicated server with its own network name. Here are the steps to first push the official Redis image to your registry by tagging it:

```
$ docker tag redis localhost:5000/redis
```

With the `redis` image now tagged, we can push this image to our locally running repository on port `5000`:

```
$ docker push localhost:5000/redis
The push refers to a repository [localhost:5000/redis] (len: 1)
2f2578ff984f: Image successfully pushed
```

```
54647d88bc19: Image already exists
ed09b32b8ab1: Image already exists
.

.

.

ba249489d0b6: Image successfully pushed \nlatest: digest: sha256:1b47e11f
b5d6395aa1631f60e61cc92d21308d55485e1316c8c8421fc4c07385 size: 34407
```

The registry image uses a Docker volume container to store all related registry information about the images saved in your locally hosted Docker repository.

Docker and Redis issues

In the chapter on Redis Cluster and Sentinel we didn't cover some major issues that can occur when trying to deploy Redis's high availability solution when using Docker. Docker performs a dynamic port reallocation when using the –p directive when launching a new Docker container. Sentinel's auto discovery of other running Sentinel process as well as discovering a list of slaves from a master assumes a fixed port numbers, this Sentinel feature will break if the internally running Sentinel on a Docker container is mapped to a different port.

To use Sentinel with Docker you have two options: the first is to update the `sentinel announce-ip` and `sentinel announce-port` for each of Docker container running Sentinel so that the Docker Sentinel is broadcasting (or announcing) the correct IP address and port number to other running Sentinel instances in your Redis operation. The second option (and likely the easiest to implement if you are starting your Sentinel setup and Redis configuration from scratch) is to either map the same ports on the host as on the container with the –p parameter (that is, `-p 26379:26379` when running any container that has Redis Sentinel running), or you can pass in the `--net=host` parameter that does this mapping automatically. Using this option is somewhat limiting because you then cannot run multiple Docker containers on the same port with each container having a Sentinel running because only one container can be mapped to the Docker host port at a time.

Packaging your application with Docker Compose

Decomposing application to effectively use Docker often requires multiple running containers of different Docker images. If your application has multiple containers that are linked to each other, manually coordinating the management of application's Docker containers (starting, stopping, and so on) can be time consuming and prone to errors, especially if you forget any of the necessary parameters for specific containers (that is, you may have a volume container that is linked to your application container, with your application container requiring different port mappings). Fortunately, there is an open source project, Docker Compose, sponsored by Docker, Inc. that alleviates a lot of these problems.

Docker Compose is automatically included if you installed Docker Toolbox. Docker Compose can also be installed by following the directions at http://docs.docker.com/compose/. To illustrate the use of Docker Compose in an application, we'll create a very simple Flask web application that just displays the current output of the Redis INFO command in an HTML document. We will also demonstrate Docker's nice inter-container communication by linking our application container with our previously created Redis container using Docker Compose.

To start, here is the Python source code for our simple Flask application, called info.py that, after importing Flask, the render_template function, and the Python Redis client, creates an application and a Redis client instance. Note that the Redis client's host name is *redis*, the name of our Redis container that we'll link to in our Docker Compose YAML configuration file. This application has a single function, default, that returns HTML template (not shown) that displays the results of executing the info command in a formatted table to the requesting web browser:

```python
from flask import Flask, render_template
import redis

    app = Flask(__name__)

    redis_db = redis.StrictRedis(host='redis')


@app.route("/")
def default():
    return render_template(
        'index.html',
        info=redis_db.info())
if __name__ == '__main__':
    app.run(host='0.0.0.0', port=5001, debug=True)
```

In the same root directory where we have our info application, we'll create a minimum Dockerfile that extends the Python 3.4 base image, exposes port 5001, and finally executes our code file with the Dockerfile CMD command:

```
FROM python:3.4.3
RUN pip3 install flask redis
COPY . /info_app
WORKDIR /info_app
EXPOSE 5001
CMD ["python", "info.py"]
```

The next stage in creating our Docker Compose project is to create a YAML configuration file called docker-compose.yml. The first section in our configuration file will define a new container for our application that we call info. In the info section, a build directive refers to the Dockerfile we created and the links directive lists the name of our Redis container. In the ports directive, we'll map the internal port that the app is running 5000, to port 8080 on the Docker host. Finally, we'll define our Redis container that is based on the official Redis image on Docker Hub. Our docker-compose.yml file is displayed here:

```
info:
  build: .
  links:
    - redis
  ports:
    - "8080:5001"
redis:
  image: redis
```

Now that we have the necessary pieces are in place, we can attempt to build our application with docker-compose:

```
$ docker-compose build .
redis uses an image, skipping
Building info...
Step 0 : FROM python:3.4.3
 ---> 575cb3ad9b67
Step 1 : RUN pip3 install flask redis
 ---> Running in 5342e1c49874
Collecting flask
  Downloading Flask-0.10.1.tar.gz (544kB)
```

```
Collecting redis
  Downloading redis-2.10.3.tar.gz (86kB)
Collecting Werkzeug>=0.7 (from flask)
  Downloading Werkzeug-0.10.4-py2.py3-none-any.whl (293kB)
Collecting Jinja2>=2.4 (from flask)
  Downloading Jinja2-2.8-py2.py3-none-any.whl (263kB)
Collecting itsdangerous>=0.21 (from flask)
  Downloading itsdangerous-0.24.tar.gz (46kB)
Collecting MarkupSafe (from Jinja2>=2.4->flask)
  Downloading MarkupSafe-0.23.tar.gz
Installing collected packages: Werkzeug, MarkupSafe, Jinja2,
itsdangerous, flask, redis
  Running setup.py install for MarkupSafe
  Running setup.py install for itsdangerous
  Running setup.py install for flask
  Running setup.py install for redis
Successfully installed Jinja2-2.8 MarkupSafe-0.23 Werkzeug-0.10.4
flask-0.10.1 itsdangerous-0.24 redis-2.10.3
 ---> 21d5378d91b3
Removing intermediate container 5342e1c49874
Step 2 : COPY . /info_app
 ---> b65c476ad781
Removing intermediate container 001debb1ff52
Step 3 : WORKDIR /info_app
 ---> Running in 59a5a7f29c4a
 ---> 5a7557640f84
Removing intermediate container 59a5a7f29c4a
Step 4 : EXPOSE 5001
 ---> Running in 8ccd0b16a8a7
 ---> 9451da0dc4ba
Removing intermediate container 8ccd0b16a8a7
Step 5 : CMD python info.py
 ---> Running in 59e66bc7787c

 ---> 8e165172aa53\nRemoving intermediate container 59e66bc7787c
Successfully built 8e165172aa53
```

This launches and builds our application's image and we can then launch our
application from the command line with the `docker-compose up` command and
pass in the `-d` parameter to run in the background:

```
$ docker-compose up -d
Starting infoapp_redis_1...
Starting infoapp_info_1...
```

We can now check if our application is being displayed by opening up our web browser and pointing it to `http://localhost:8080/` as shown in the following screenshot:

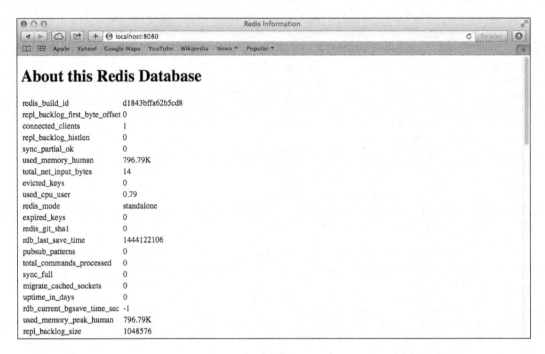

To check to see what containers are running, we see there are two containers running on our Docker host:

```
$ docker ps
CONTAINER ID          IMAGE                COMMAND                CREATED
STATUS                PORTS                   NAMES
b4ac9d5a18dc          infoapp_info          "python info.py"          7
minutes ago      Up 2 minutes       0.0.0.0:8080->5001/tcp    infoapp_
info_1

6662e75f3ffc          redis               "/entrypoint.sh redis"    37
minutes ago      Up 2 minutes       6379/tcp                  infoapp_
redis_1
```

We see our two containers running in the background and Docker-compose conveniently named both containers using the `infoapp_info_1` and `infoapp_redis_1`.

Now, we'll open a second terminal window and connect to our Redis database using our Redis-cli:

```
$ redis/src/redis-cli
127.0.0.1:6379> INFO
Error: Server closed the connection
```

So what happened? One of the great features of Docker is that we isolate our services in containers from external processes but the services can still connect and use services by linking from our application container. Docker Compose handles all of the underlying container linkages and would be equivalent to us running our info container by manually linking our Redis container that doesn't expose any ports.

Besides easing the burden of building and running our application with multiple containers, Docker Compose also allows you to gracefully and easily shutdown your application's services with a `docker-compose stop` command:

```
$ docker-compose stop
Stopping infoapp_info_1... done
Stopping infoapp_redis_1... done
```

As we can see even with this simple example of a web application, Docker Compose simplifies the management and provisioning of our containers and bypassing all of the error-prone manual steps for running multiple containers. In either case, Docker Compose is an essential companion when using Docker in your workflow.

Redis and AWS

Amazon Web Services (AWS), through its ElastiCache service available at `https://aws.amazon.com/elasticache/`, offers a Redis protocol in-memory cache that provides you with the Redis command set but using Amazon's own backend. This includes functionality for automating common virtual machine tasks such as patch management and failure detection and recovery. Scaling with ElastiCache is also easier than other options because you can configure and add more Cache nodes through the AWS Management Console as your application's operational demands increase due to greater demands from your customers or internal clients in your organization. Pricing for ElastiCache varies depending on your usage where you pay only for the resources your ElastiCache nodes consumes while operating your application. Because ElasticCache is only Redis protocol compliant and does not use Redis server in the backend, there are some limitations that should be considered when using ElastiCache with your Redis clients.

For starters, ElastiCache is currently restricted to Redis 2.8 and earlier commands and functionality, so all of the Redis Cluster commands are not available. If your application does require sharding across multiple Redis masters, when using ElastiCache means you'll need to use a fully client-based sharding approach for your data and not use Redis Cluster. ElastiCache does offer types of nodes that are equivalent to Redis master and slave instances:

Running Redis on AWS
You have a couple of options of running Redis or Redis-like service with Amazon Web Services.

ElastiCache is Amazon's own caching service that provides a Redis 2.8 Protocal that will appears as a live Redis instance for applications. But the internals of this service is **NOT** Redis and you cannot adjust the configurations specific to your application and you cannot upgrade to the latest versions of Redis

The other option is to launch a EC2 virtual machine and manually install, configure, and manage Redis on your own.

All copyright and logos are property of Amazon

Running Redis on AWS

Another option for running Redis on AWS, and one that many take advantage of, is to spin-up **hardware virtual machine (HVM)** instance on Amazon's **Elastic Compute Cloud (EC2)**. To run Redis on an EC2 virtual machine, you'll want to minimize latency when Redis forks its process to save to disk by selecting an EC2 instance with multiple cores so that the workload per CPU core is minimized. You'll also want to disable OS swapping because if your Redis instance exceeds the available RAM, with OS swapping enabled, your Redis instance will become very slow as Redis attempts to access and write data to disk through the swap. Many organizations and individuals are running their development and operational Redis databases on AWS through dedicated EC2 VMs and with Amazon's aggressive pricing, getting up and running with Redis on AWS is an attractive and compelling reason to use Redis on AWS.

Dedicated cloud hosting options

There are a number of companies that offer dedicated Redis hosting where you do not have to worry about the operational specifics of the operating system and environment that is running Redis. Instead you can quickly launch and use Redis without worrying about hosting a virtual machine or other system management tasks. Instead of providing a review for all of these Redis service providers, we will look at two of the most popular options for dedicated Redis hosting, the first from Redis Labs at `https://redislabs.com/`, and the second is using DigitalOcean's Redis hosting service.

Redis Labs

In 2015, Salvatore Sanfilippo creator and principal developer of Redis, accepted a position at Redis Labs as the lead for open source development and Redis Labs also became the principal sponsor of Redis as well. Redis Labs is headquartered in Mountain View, California with their Research and Development offices located in Tel Aviv, Israel. Redis Labs offers two Redis products (as well as a Memecached hosting service) **Redis Labs Enterprise Cluster** (**RLEC**) and Redis Cloud. RLEC is an enterprise cluster product that encapsulates multiple Redis databases into a highly scalable and available environment running in a Docker container. RLEC supports multiple types of configuration including a single Redis instance with one Master node, highly available Redis master instance with one or more Redis slave instances, a Redis cluster database with multiple master shards, and finally a setup similar to Redis Cluster with multiple master shards instances with each master being replicated to one or more Redis slave instances. RLEC can be downloaded and used within your own environment or you can purchase a commercial subscription to use RLEC in production in your environment or through any of the most popular cloud providers such as AWS, Google, Microsoft, Heroku, and others.

Redis Labs also offers a fully-managed Redis hosting option for organizations through their Redis Cloud that can run on the customer's choice of public or private clouds. Pricing for Redis Cloud at the time of writing ranged from a free level at 30 MB to $36 a month for 500 MB, to $71 for GB, to $338 for 5 GB all fully supported and hosted by Redis Labs. Additional space is available as a pay-as-you-go service of 10 percent per 15 GB increments over the maximum price. If your needs include complex setups for master-slave replication, high availability, and cluster-support, part of the services provided by Redis Labs is to manage all of the configuration and operational support as part of their premium services. The downside, of course, is that these services are not cheap but the extra support may be well worth it to you or your organization.

DigitalOcean Redis

While other cloud providers offer Redis specific hosting, DigitalOcean is one of the least expensive and provides a Redis-specific virtual machine used in their naming schema—a "droplet", a virtual machine running Ubuntu 14.04 with Redis preinstalled that can be launched in minutes from their easy-to-use web console. Depending on how the droplet is configured, the monthly costs for running a minimum droplet with 512 MB RAM and 1 CPU core with 1 GB SSD hard disk is 5 dollars per month ranging up to $640 a month for 64 GB RAM and 20 CPU cores with 640 GB hard disk size.

Digital Ocean recommends securing your Redis application (not bad advice for any Redis cloud server) by either enabling the `requirepass` Redis configuration directive in the `redis.conf` file located at `/etc/redis/` in the Redis droplet or you could issue the `CONFIG SET requirepass {your-redis-password}` to the running Redis instance on your droplet. In the same article, they also recommend updating the `/etc/init.d/redis` system startup script by changing the `CLIEXEC` directive to:

```
CLIEXEC="/usr/local/bin/redis-cli -a your_redis_password"
```

In this droplet, remote access to the Redis instance is disabled by the `bind` directive set to `127.0.0.1`. You'll need to either comment-out or delete the bind directive from the running Redis instance and then restart the Redis service by issuing this command after you connect to your droplet through an `ssh` session:

```
$ sudo service redis restart
```

While DigitalOcean is just one of many options to run Redis on a public cloud, compared to other options, Digital Ocean's Redis droplet is a simple option for quickly getting a small-to-medium Redis database up and running.

Summary

This chapter introduced Docker, a container technology for Linux, that can ease the difficulties of managing Redis-based applications by providing isolated, replicated, and fast application virtualization without the need to launch a new virtual machine. We went through the steps to download and launch a container instance of the official Redis Docker image and showed how to send in various command-line options for running Redis in a Redis container. We then looked at how Docker compose can be used to automate and simplify the deployment of multiple containers in a typical application. Finally, we examined three-cloud hosting options for running your Redis application and some of the advantages and disadvantages of each option. In *Chapter 9, Task Management and Messaging Queuing* we will turn back to more application design and development and look in much more depth on how to use Redis Pub/Sub functionality for messaging and other types of functionality between applications that can be implemented and optimized in Redis.

9
Task Management and Messaging Queuing

While the uses of Redis in enterprise are many, Redis's support for the publication/ subscription (Pub/Sub) messaging design pattern allows for a fast and easy way to use Redis as a messaging broker. Redis's role in richer and more feature complete messaging frameworks also gives the application designer added flexibility if Redis's own Pub/Sub is insufficient for the requirements of the application or the project.

Overview of Redis Pub/Sub

Redis Publisher/Subscriber - Pub/Sub for short - is a messaging model that is fast and stable. Instead of processes sending messages directly to each other, a publisher or sender submits messages to one or more channels and the receivers or subscribers that have subscribed to a channel receive all messages posted to the specific channels. If you design your application being mindful of race conditions and the possibility of delivery failure, Pub/Sub offers fast messaging solutions.

Conceptually, Redis Pub/Sub is similar to **Really Simple Syndication (RSS)**, or the atom formats used by websites to publish feeds for consumption by clients or readers. In either case, neither the website publisher nor the consuming client are directly sending messages to each other. The client connects and consumes the content from feeds from those websites' publications – either blogs, data, podcasts, or other media. Like RSS, Redis Pub/Sub, and other publish/subscribe systems, the advantage of this messaging pattern is better scalability for the systems for more dynamic networks.

Instead of having to build management and coordinating code for routing messages between specific senders and receivers, large numbers of senders and receivers just need to post and receive messages from a channel. The downside of publication/subscription message pattern is that the publisher syntax is not easy to modify or change. For Redis, the Pub/Sub publisher message and commands are stable and not likely to change, and Pub/Sub messages formats are also stable and broken up into three or four parts that we will examine in the next section:

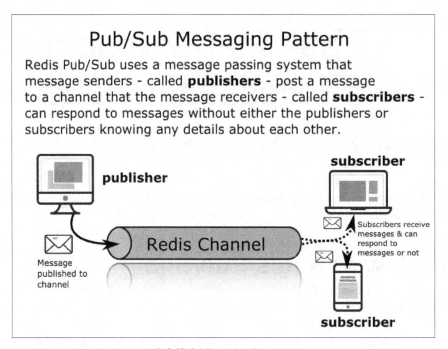

Pub/Sub Messaging Patterns

More specifically, Redis implementation of Pub/Sub is a type of topic-based messaging pattern that are called channels in Redis's nomenclature. Other alternatives to topic-based messaging systems are Pub/Sub systems that route messages based on the characteristics or metadata of the message. An example of a topic-based messaging system might be error-handling logging code in an application where a message is sent that includes levels, such as INFO, DEBUG, ALERT, or SEVERE that depend on the type of logic, I/O, or network failure in an application. A responding subscriber may send an e-mail if a message is marked or tagged as ALERT or SEVERE level. This type of functionality, while not directly supported by Redis, can be implemented by having separate INFO, DEBUG, ALERT, or SEVERE channels that subscribing processes would send emails to if a message is received in the ALERT or SEVERE channels.

Pub/Sub RESP replies

In Redis Pub/Sub, the messaging format is in RESP Array reply with three or four elements. The first element in the Pub/Sub messaging format determines the type of message and can be one of these four Redis commands, SUBSCRIBE, UNSCRIBE, PSUBSCRIBE, and PUNSUBSCRIBE.

SUBSCRIBE and UNSUBSCRIBE RESP Arrays

Connecting to a Redis instance with two connections, the first with a standard Redis CLI client and the second with telnet, we will illustrate the RESP reply for three element commands SUBSCRIBE and UNSUBSCRIBE:

```
$ telnet localhost 6379
Trying ::1...
Connected to localhost.
Escape character is '^]'.
SUBSCRIBE info
*3
$9
subscribe
$4
info
:1
```

In this SUBSCRIBE command, the first element is $9 followed by carriage-return line feed. The second element is the channel, info, that the client is subscribing to, with the third element in a subscribe message being the number of channels that the client is currently subscribed to receive messages. In our Redis CLI, we'll send a message with the PUBLISH command to the info channel:

```
127.0.0.1:6379> PUBLISH info "Sending a message"
(integer) 1
```

The resulting RESP message array for our subscribing telnet client with the message is as follows:

```
*3
$7
message
$4
```

```
info
$17
Sending a message
```

This three-element array, with the first element being the `message` keyword, followed by the second element being the channel `info`, followed finally with the text string of the actual message, `"Sending a message"` is RESP for most channels when a client uses the `SUBSCRIBE` command.

Now, we'll issue an `UNSUBSCRIBE` command with the channel info:

```
UNSUBSCRIBE info
*3
$11
unsubscribe
$4
info
:0
```

In this `UNSUBSCRIBE` message, the second element in the message array is set if the client successfully unsubscribed from the channel, with the last element in the array indicating the number of channels the client is still subscribed to, if the number is zero, then the client is no longer in pub/sub mode and can send any normal Redis command to the server.

PSUBSCRIBE and UNSUBSCRIBE arrays

The `PSUBSCRIBE` command is a four element array command and includes all of the fields as `SUBSCRIBE` with an additional field for the pattern being matched. In our telnet session, we'll issue a `PSUBSCRIBE` command using an asterisk * to subscribe to all of the channels that start with info:

```
PSUBSCRIBE info*
*3
$10
psubscribe
$5
info*
:1
```

For the PSUBSCRIBE command, the second element in the RESP Array is info* being the pattern that matched, the third element being the original channel, and the fourth element being the message body. The psubscribe format is for the special case when the client subscribes to a channel through a pattern matching, which we'll discuss in more detail in the next section of this chapter. Sending a second message from our Redis-cli session:

For the PUNSUBSCRIBE command, the RESP Array that is returned from the Redis server includes three elements with the pattern for all the channels that match the pattern:

```
PUNSUBSCRIBE info*
*3
$12
punsubscribe
$5
info*
:0
```

Pub/Sub with Redis CLI

The basic publish/subscribe commands with Redis start with a client issuing a SUBSCRIBE command followed by the name of a channel, in this case a generic status channel in a Redis CLI session:

```
$ redis/src/redis-cli
127.0.0.1:6379> SUBSCRIBE status
Reading messages... (press Ctrl-C to quit)
1) "subscribe"
2) "status"
3) (integer) 1
```

Now, in a different terminal window (either using the screen utility or opening up a separate tab in your terminal client), start a second Redis CLI client and submit a message from client to the status channel with the PUBLISH command:

```
$ redis/src/redis-cli
127.0.0.1:6379> PUBLISH status "Ok, everything working"
(integer) 1
```

Switching back to our original Redis-cli window, we can see the results as follows:

```
1) "message"
2) "status"
3) "Ok, everything working"
```

Unlike other clients, exiting the subscribe mode with our first Redis CLI session requires a *Ctrl + C* key combination that quits the Redis CLI session and drops you back to the bash shell. We'll relaunch Redis CLI and start monitoring all channels that start with status using the PSUBSCRIBE command:

```
^C
$ redis/src/redis-cli
127.0.0.1:6379> PSUBSCRIBE status*
Reading messages... (press Ctrl-C to quit)
1) "psubscribe"
2) "status*"
3) (integer) 1
```

Returning to our second Redis CLI session where we submitted our first message, we'll go ahead and send a few messages to a status-error, status-alert, and stats channels:

```
127.0.0.1:6379> PUBLISH status-error "Program failed to run"
(integer) 1
127.0.0.1:6379> PUBLISH status-alert "Program approaching maximum memory"
(integer) 1
127.0.0.1:6379> PUBLISH stats "100 Clicks"
(integer) 0
```

The results of sending these PUBLISH commands to our first client that is subscribed to these channels using the PSUBSCRIBE are as follows:

```
1) "pmessage"
2) "status*"
3) "status-error"
4) "Program failed to run"
1) "pmessage"
2) "status*"
3) "status-alert"
4) "Program approaching maximum memory"
```

So, using the PSUBSCRIBE pattern, the monitoring Redis-cli session received messages from both the status-error and status-alert channels, but didn't receive any messages from the stats channel because the glob-pattern didn't match that channel. You'll also notice that there are four elements in the PMESSAGE response, which now includes what channel is matched with the original glob-pattern.

An important limitation of Pub/Sub that should be noted is that Redis's Pub/Sub implementation does NOT provide reliable delivery of messages, that is, Redis Pub/Sub is *fire and forget*. Messages published to a channel are not guaranteed to be delivered to the client monitoring the channel by subscription. For example, if a Pub/Sub client monitoring a channel fails and later reconnects and subscribes to the channel, the client will not receive the messages that were posted to the channel during the interim.

Redis Pub/Sub in action

To see how Redis Pub/Sub may be used within an application context, we'll look at modeling a simple Kanban manufacturing setup that involves three stations in the construction of a toy airplane in an imaginary factory at the North Pole: Elves Mfg. Inc. Kanban is a management philosophy and a set of techniques that was first developed and popularized by Toyota Manufacturing in the construction of automobiles that showed drastic improvement in quality and reliability over the past fifty years. Based on Toyota's success with lean manufacturing, the practices and philosophy surround Kanban spread to other manufacturers in Japan – particularly suppliers and other companies supporting Toyota – and spread across the world. By the early 2000s, lean manufacturing has become accepted and used in a wide range of manufacturing, service, governmental, and non-profit organizations to improve the quality of their products and services under tight budget constraints.

 Use the PUNSUBSCRIBE * command to stop monitoring all channels and return your Redis client to normal Redis mode.

In a traditional manufacturing line at a factory, each workstation takes the result of the previous manufacturing station and adds and assembles material, before sending the partially completed product to the next station in the manufacturing line. The overall goal of the traditional manufacturing system is continual throughput for all workstations, with the most products manufactured in the least amount of time, resulting in more profits as costs per unit decline with higher total volumes. This type of manufacturing tends to result in very top-down, centralized command-and-control structures that are tightly coupled across the enterprise. If a step fails, the entire operations grinds to halt with the excess work-in-process inventory accumulating at the stations behind the station with the error, and the work slowing, or even stopping, for work stations further down stream in the manufacturing line. This process is identified as a "push process" in the lean start-up and lean manufacturing literature and is contrasted by a "pull process" used in Kanban, and is the heart of "just-in-time" manufacturing and increasingly service-oriented processes.

In the more realistic and manual Kanban implementation, each manufacturing step has physical color-coordinated cards with relevant product details attached and associated with a bin of materials at each step in the production of a product. Each bin has a level of partially completed product that is consumed in the process of manufacturing in that step. When the level of inventory is depleted in a bin, a Kanban card and the empty bin is sent to the previous step and replaced with a full-bin that also contains a Kanban card. The first step in the process signals that an order for supplies needs to be sent to the supplier.

To simulate three different workstations, we'll create three applications in different programming languages both as a way to illustrate how heterogeneously messaging with Redis Pub/Sub works and as an example of a Kanban work-flow. The product our manufacturing factory will construct is a child's "Jack-in-the-Box", where a child turns a lever and at a random moment, the lid pops open and a clown head pops out:

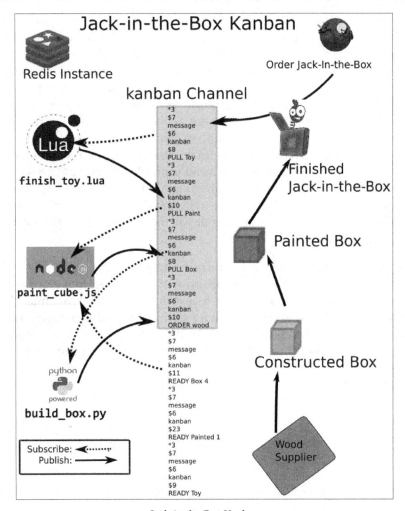

Jack-in-the-Box Kanban

First workstation using Python Pub/Sub

The first workstation in our hypothetical North Pole product takes a raw piece of wood, constructs a five-sided cube with a lid, and passes the resulting box to the second step in the manufacturing line. We will create a Python class that monitors a Kanban channel, requests the raw material from the supplier if the bin drops below a threshold, builds the box, and then sends the bin, with an accompanying Kanban message, to our second workstation.

The second manufacturing station in our Elves Mfg factory has a bin of completed, painted cubes, and sends the bin when it receives a message while monitoring the Kanban channel for a `"PULL Paint"` message. At the second workstation, when a message is received, the completed bin is forwarded on to the last step along with a `"PULL Box"` message to the kanban channel for a bin of roughly constructed wooden boxes. After the bin is received from the previous station, the second workstation paints, installs hinges on the lid, and now has a work-in-progress bin ready to send when a `"PULL Paint"` message in the Kanban channel is received from the final workstation on our assembly line. At the final workstation, a bin of painted boxes from the second workstation is available as an input. When an `"ORDER Jack-in-the-box"` message is received on the kanban channel, a painted box is taken from the bin, a pop-up mechanism and the doll are assembled, and the resulting completed Jack-in-the-Box toy is sent to the shipping department to a bag for the North Pole Sleigh Shipping Company.

The Python code for step one in the manufacturing assembly line is a `BuildBoxWorkstation` class that is initialized with a Redis instance, sets a bin and threshold when a kanban message is sent to a supplier for more raw material, and the class monitors the **kanban** channel for a message indicating a completed bin of boxes is ready for the second workstation. An instance of the `BuildBoxWorkstation` class also monitors an **operations** channel for starting and stopping work on the assembly line:

```
class BuildBoxWorkstation(object):

    def __init__(self,
                 database = redis.StrictRedis()):
        self.database = database
        self.messages = self.database.pubsub()
        self.messages.subscribe("kanban")
        self.messages.subscribe("operations")
        self.input_bin, self.output_bin = 0, 0
        self.threshold = 5
```

In this class, a `run` method creates an event-loop where messages are polled and responded to depending on the channel and the message. Just as a shortcut and not to respond to SUBSCRIBE, UNSUBSCRIBE, PSUBSCRIBE, and PUNSUBSCRIBE (to build a more robust system, we would want to create handlers for all of these types of messages), we'll ignore any messages that is an integer, as seen here:

```
def run(self):
    while 1:
        for item in self.messages.listen():
            channel = item.get('channel')
            message = item.get('data')
```

```
                    type_of = item.get('type')
                    if type(message) == int:
                        continue
                    message = message.decode()

                    if channel == b"kanban":
                        if message.startswith("PULL Box"):
                            self.__construct_box__()
                    if channel == b"operations":
                        if message.startswith("STOP"):
                            return
```

When a message comes through one of the channels that the `BuildBoxWorkstation` instance is monitoring, either ordering raw materials or creating a bin of boxes and lids as an input bin for the Jack-in-the-box paint step. The internal method `__construct_box__` first checks to see if there is any raw wood material in the `input_bin` and if the amount is below the threshold, an `"ORDER wood"` message is sent in the `__pull_material__` method, as seen here:

```
    def __pull_material__(self):
        # Sends message to supplier to order wood
        message = "ORDER wood"
        self.database.publish("kanban", message)
        print("{}, input_bin={}".format(message, self.input_bin))
        # For convenience we'll just add an order of 5
        # to our input bin in a real operation, an order
        # would be placed, hopefully with a kind supplier API
        self.input_bin += 5
```

Next, the `output_bin` is filled with assembled wooden boxes from the `input_bin` and a `"READY box"` message is published to the **kanban** channel for processing by the second step in the manufacturing process, and then both input and output bins are set to `0`. The `__construct_box__` is as follows:

```
def __construct_box__(self):
    if len(self.input_bin) > 0:
        self.input_bin -= 1
    if len(self.input_bin) <= self.threshold:
        self.__pull_material__()
    # Cuts and assembles box with a lid
    self.output_bin = [i for i in range(1, len(self.input_bin))]
    # Sends Kanban Message to next station
    self.database.publish(
        "kanban",
        "READY Box {}".format(len(self.output_bin)))
    # Bins are now empty
    self.input_bin, self.output_bin = 0, 0
```

Second workstation Node.js Pub/Sub

The second workstation's code is implemented with Node.js and is available in the `paint_cube.js` source file at the book's website and GitHub repository. In the `paint_cube.js` file, the first lines import the `node_redis` module to create two Node.js Redis clients:

```
var redis = require("redis"),
  client = redis.createClient(),
  client_subscriber = redis.createClient();
```

After creating two Redis instances, the first function in `paint_cube.js` of the second workstation creates a Javascript object containing a Redis client as the object's database and two Javascript integer variables for both the input and output bins that are set to `0`:

```
function PaintCubeWorkstation(redis) {
  var self = this;
  self.database = redis;
  self.input_bins = 0;
  self.output_bins = 0;
```

After setting these initial variables, the `PaintCubeWorkstation` instance then creates a log message for subscribing to any channels:

```
self.database.on("subscribe", function(channel) { console.
log("Subscribed to "+channel); } self.database.subscribe("kanban");
self.database.subscribe("operations");
```

The function callback in our `PaintCubeWorkstation` instance responds to Redis messages that come through the operations and Kanban Pub/Sub channels:

```
self.database.on("message", function(channel, message) {
  if(channel === "operations") {
    if(message === "STOP") {
      self.database.unsubscribe();
      self.database.end();
      console.log("Stopping PaintCubeWorkstation");
      process.exit(1);
    }
  }
  if(channel === "kanban") {
    if(message === "PULL Paint") {
      console.log("Output bins " + self.output_bins);
      if(self.output_bins > 0) {
        client.publish("kanban", "READY Painted " +
self.output_bins);
        self.output_bins -= 1;
```

```
      } else {
        client.publish("kanban", "PULL Box");

      }
    }
    if(message.indexOf("READY Box") === 0){
      self.input_bins += 1;
      console.log("Input bin size " + self.input_bins)
      for(i = 0; i<=self.input_bins; i++) {
        // adds hinges and paints each box and adds to output bin
        console.log("\tAdds hinges and paints " + i);
        self.output_bins += 1;
      }
      client.publish("kanban", "READY Painted " +
self.output_bins);

    }
  }

}
```

The final lines in the `paint_cube.js` file instantiate a `PaintCubeWorkstation` object with the callback function to handle any messages sent to the channels that are being monitored by the object.

Third workstation Lua Client Pub/Sub

The software code we'll be using for the final work station that assembles the Jack-in-the-Box for the customer are a couple of server-side Lua scripts that we'll call from our Redis CLI and a client-side Lua script for subscribing and responding to messages. Like the `BuildBoxWorkstation` Python code and the `PaintCubeWorkstation`
Node.js code, the client-side Lua script responds to a toy order by first using any existing Jack-in-the-Box toys in its current output bin and then publishing a message to the kanban message channel requesting new partially completed toys from the second workstation when the third workstation is running low.

To set up the local environment to support Redis client-side Lua scripts, we'll need to first install the LuaRocks package manager for Lua at `https://luarocks.org/` after you have installed the latest version of Lua (if you haven't already) from `http://www.lua.org/`. With LuaRocks installed, we'll next need to install the `redis-lua` client located at `https://github.com/nrk/redis-lua` with the following command (assuming you are using Linux or Mac):

```
$ sudo luarocks install redis-lua
```

After the Lua Redis client is installed, we can then create a subscription service for handling and responding to messages on the kanban and operations channels. The lua script, `finish_toy.lua`, contains the functions that listen to these channels and calls the appropriate server-side Lua scripts for publishing messages to the kanban channel based on receiving an "ORDER Toy" message. Unlike the code for the previous two workstations, the final workstation has a single bin that has a Lua table type in the `finish_toy.lua`.

At the beginning of the Lua client script `finish_toy.lua` we import and set up two Redis clients for use later in the script and we create a Lua variable `toys` for finished Jack-in-boxes that are ready for delivery, and a Lua table `channels`:

```
local redis = require 'redis'
local client = redis.connect('127.0.0.1', 6379)
local publisher = redis.connect('127.0.0.1', 6379)
local toys = 0
local channels = {"kanban", "operations" }
```

Next, we define two functions – `build` and `deliver` – that are called in a main function when either a "PULL toy" or "READY Painted" Jack-in the-Box messages come when monitoring the kanban channel.

The `build` function prints a message and increments the global `toys` variable by one:

```
function build ()
  print("Building Toy "..toys)
  toys = toys + 1
end
```

The `deliver` function sends a "READY Toy" message to the kanban, prints some text, and decrements the toys variable:

```
function deliver ()
  publisher:publish("kanban", "READY Toy")
  print("Toy delivered")
  toys = toys - 1
end
```

The `main` function creates a `pubsub` loop, checks the value of the message and determines what step to follow in the workstation based on the message's channel and payload. When a STOP message comes through the operations channel, the `pubsub` mode is aborted and this workstation ceases operation by returning a Boolean. Depending on the message's payload in the kanban channel, either a toy is delivered and/or a "PULL Paint" message is published to the kanban channel.

Finally, when the `PaintCubeWorkstation` posts a `"READY Painted"` message to the kanban, the Lua script's `build` and then the `deliver` functions are called as a result, as seen here:

```
for msg, abort in client:pubsub({ subscribe = channels}) do
    if msg.kind == 'message' then
      if msg.channel == "operations" then
          if msg.payload == "STOP" then
            print("Stopping Finish Toy")
            abort()
          end
      elseif msg.channel == "kanban" then
        if msg.payload == "PULL Toy" then
        if toys > 0 then
          deliver()
        else
          publisher:publish("kanban", "PULL Paint")
    end
        elseif msg.payload == "READY Painted" then
          build()
          deliver()
        end
      end
    end
  end
```

With the code in place for these three workstations, we can run a simulation of a Jack-in-the-Box Kanban run by starting a command-line terminal session and launching all three of the workstations' code using the UNIX screen utility. We will start by launching a Redis CLI session:

```
127.0.0.1:6379> PUBLISH kanban "PULL Toy"
(integer) 3
```

The `"PULL Toy"` message initiates an action in the Lua and prints out the following to the command line:

```
$ lua finish_toy.lua
Final Assemble Toy Workstation
Pull Paint box
Building Toy 0
Toy delivered
```

Monitoring the second, we can see the result of the Node.js `PaintCubeWorkstation` object:

```
$ node paint_cube.js
In Paint Cube Application
Subscribed to kanban
Subscribed to operations
Output bins 0
Input bin size 1
        Adds hinges and paints 0
        Adds hinges and paints 1
```

The first workstation responds to the `"PULL Box"` message sent by the Paint Cube workstation, which results in the following display in the terminal window for the `build_box` Python module:

```
$ python3 build_box.py
Running BuildBoxWorstation
ORDER wood, input_bin=0
READY Box 4
READY Box 3
READY Box 2
```

Now, we'll post a `STOP` message to the operations channel that each workstation is also subscribed to, which should stop each workstation from our Redis CLI session:

```
127.0.0.1:6379> PUBLISH operations "STOP"
(integer) 3
```

The `build_box.BuildBoxWorkstation` instance outputs the following after responding to the `STOP` message:

```
Stopping
$
```

The Node.js `PaintCubeWorkstation` logs a message to the console and sends a 1 integer to the `process.exit` call to terminate script execution to the bash shell when responding to the `STOP` message on the operations channel:

```
Stopping PaintCubeWorkstation
$
```

The `finish_toy.lua` script `main` function prints a text string and returns control back to the bash shell:

```
Stopping Finish Toy
$
```

In this simple implementation of a Kanban signaling manufacturing assembly-line for Jack-in-the-Box toys, a pull demand process builds each toy instead of a push manufacturing process. To simulate how Redis Pub/Sub messaging uses different programming systems, we created three different scripts in Python, Node.js, and Lua, and showed how using each respective programming language's Redis client could interoperate using just a Redis Pub/Sub messaging framework and associated commands.

Redis keyspace notifications

A common use case when using Redis is the ability for an application to respond to changes that may occur to the value stored at a particular key or keys. Fortunately, since version 2.8, Redis provides a mechanism for client code to subscribe to a Pub/Sub channel that monitors events related to data. Called keyspace notification, functionality for monitoring events like all the commands that change a given key, all keys receiving specific commands such as `HSET`, or all keys that are about to be deleted because of an `EXPIRE` command. Using Redis Pub/Sub allows existing Redis clients that already implement Pub/Sub to use keyspace notification to respond to changes in the Redis data.

When a command is issued that triggers a Redis keyspace notification, two events occur that monitoring clients can respond to; the first is called a **Key-space notification** and the second is called a **Key-event notification**. In a **Key-space notification** event, a message is sent to a channel, `__keyspace@0__:your_key hset`, when a field value is changed at the Redis hash `your_key` key.

At the same time, another message is sent as a **Key-event notification** to the __ keyevent@0_:hset your_key channel for clients monitoring any HSET commands in the Redis instance:

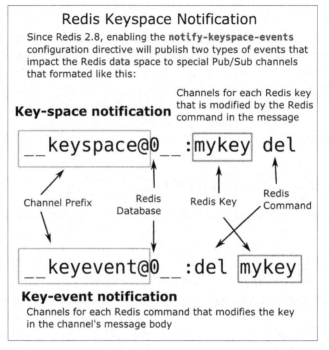

Redis Keyspace notification

Redis keyspace notification is disabled by default, because although this functionality is not an intensive operation in terms of memory, it still requires additional CPU resources. To enable keyspace notification, either enable and modify the notify-keyspace-events configuration directive in redis.conf or through the CONFIG SET Redis command. The notify-keyspace-events directive takes a number of parameters in order to determine which type of channel (keyspace or keyevent) and what will be posted to these channels:

- K parameter is for all keyspace events.

- E parameter is for all keyevent events. One or both must be present for these notifications to be enabled, otherwise no channels will be enabled.

The type of commands to monitor is determined by the following:

- $ for strings

- l for lists

- s for sets

- h for hashes

- z for sorted sets

Finally, the x parameter is for a message when a key has expired and the e parameter is for a message when a key has been evicted because a maxmemory condition has been triggered in the running Redis instance.

Going back to the Linked Data Fragments server project, Redis keyspace notifications are used in the latest iteration of the project. Instead of using KEYS or SCAN with string-matching globs for matching triple patterns, the latest version of the Linked Data Fragments server uses hashes for representing triples, but there is not a way to automatically delete fields from these hashes when an element has expired and been evicted from the Redis instance due to the LRU policy set in the Redis cache. Although people have requested the feature of setting an expiration on individual fields in a hash, this currently doesn't exist in Redis without any plans to do so in the future. Instead, we can replicate this functionality through the use of Lua scripting and keyspace notifications.

To enable keyspace notifications, we'll edit the main redis.conf file for the project and change the notify-keyspace-events configuration directive to include the following parameters AE to monitor all key events for expiration.

In the main cache module cache/__init__.py for the linked data fragments server, a new function remove_expired monitors the key event channel __keyevent@_: for expired keys. As a cache backend, the Linked Data Fragments server sets an expiration time limit for each individual subject, predicate, and object SHA1 hash that is stored in Redis. When a particular key expires, we'll first check for any associated predicate-object, subject-predicate, and subject-object hashes, iterate through these hashes, and remove the expired hash digest from any associated hashes for other keys.

The remove_expired function calls three functions: remove_subject, remove_object, and remove_predicate that all remove the secondary keys for the expired digest as well as any members or fields (depending on what Redis data structure strategy is being used to represent triples in the Redis cache) that may in other secondary keys in the cache. Here is the remove_expired Python function:

```
def remove_expired(**kwargs):
    datastore = kwargs.get("datastore", redis.StrictRedis())
    strategy= kwargs.get("strategy", "string")
    database = kwargs.get('db', 0)
    if strategy.startswith('string'):
        return
    expired_key_notification = "__keyevent@{}__:expired"
    expired_pubsub = datastore.pubsub()
    expired_pubsub.subscribe(expired_key_notification)
```

```
for item in expired_pubsub.listen():
    sha1 = item.get("data")
    transaction = datastore.pipeline(transaction=True)
    remove_subject(sha1, transaction, datastore)
    remove_predicate(sha1, transaction, datastore)
    remove_object(sha1, transaction, datastore)
    transaction.execute()
```

While the remove_subject, remove_object, and remove_predicate functions are similar in structure and purpose, the following remove_subject function illustrates the general approach of removing any members or fields of related keys that are either subjects, predicates, or objects in the represented triples in the Linked Data Fragments server's Redis cache:

```
def remove_subject(
    digest,
    transaction,
    datastore=redis.StrictRedis()):
    subject_key = "{}:pred-obj".format(digest)
    if not datastore.exists(subject_key):
        return
    for row in datastore.smembers(subject_key):
        predicate, object_ = row.split(":")
        pred_subj_obj = "{}:subj-obj".format(predicate)
        if datastore.exists(pred_subj_obj):
            transaction.srem(pred_subj_obj,
                        "{}:{}".format(digest, object_))
        obj_subj_pred = "{}:subj-pred".format(object_)
        if datastore.exists(obj_subj_pred):
            transaction.srem(
                obj_subj_pred,
                "{}:{}".format(digest, predicate))
    transaction.delete(subject_key)
```

For example, say the URL http://catalog.coloradocollege.edu/abde34 SHA1 hash 1dac26e30da98f3b64ce7e0e6de9704e18deefd1 has the following Redis hash 1dac26e30da98f3b64ce7e0e6de9704e18deefd1:pred-obj that stores all of the predicates and objects SHA1 hashes that together make-up the complete triple. When 1dac26e30da98f3b64ce7e0e6de9704e18deefd1 expires, a message is sent to the channel and the remove_expired function then goes through the fields for the attached hash and removes all references of 1dac26e30da98f3b64ce7e0e6de9704e18deefd1 from any of the sets or hashes that are stored in the Redis cache.

Task management with Redis and Celery

Celery, an asynchronous task queue project available at http://www.celeryproject.org, is based on distributed message passing and allows execution of individual tasks. With Celery, you can specify different message broker backends, with Redis being one of the supported message brokers. In a basic use case for Celery, a Celery application or instance is created for handling such operations as creating tasks and managing workers that respond to those tasks.

To show how Celery can be used in a simple application, we'll implement an application based on the following scenario: a small school district with a single high school wants a class room reservation system for after-school activities. While there are many approaches you could take to create a simple room reservation system, we'll go ahead and build a Python-based system that uses Celery and Redis to manage the room reservations in this high school. Each room that is available for reservation will switch its state from any of these states:

- Cancelled
- Confirmed
- Denied
- Mediated
- Tentative

When a reservation task is sent to the room reservation system from other applications, the returned state depends on a number of factors. If the room is available to book, a Tentative or Confirmed status will automatically be returned depending on the user or application's permissions. If the room cannot be booked because the room is already booked, a Denied status will be returned to the user. If the user or application does not have permissions to reserve a particular room a Mediated status is returned. In a typical school setup, teachers would automatically be able to reserve rooms and students can tentatively reserve rooms from the school's website:

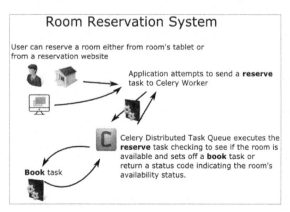

A tablet is attached to the door for each of these rooms that should display the status of the reservation while also showing upcoming reservations for the room. The purpose of this architecture, using a task and messaging framework like Celery, is that we can easily add more rooms that respond to reserve requests as well as displaying their current state.

To start, we will create a new directory for our project and create three files, __ init__.py, backend.py, and tasks.py. The __init__.py can be blank and is present in this directory to be able to use our application as a Python module. In the backend.py code file, we'll import the celery module and create a Celery application using a Redis broker:

```
from celery import Celery

app = Celery("room_reservation",
             broker="redis://localhost",
             backend="redis://localhost/1")
```

The Celery app uses our Redis instance as both a messenger broker and the backend result store. In the tasks.py code file, the Celery application app will be imported and a task decorator used to indicate that the availability, reserve and book, cancel, search, and room functions are Celery tasks:

```
from celery import app

STATUS = ['Cancelled',
          'Confirmed',
          'Denied',
          'Mediated',
          'Tentative']

@app.task
def availability(room):
    .
    .
    .


@app.task
def book(status):
    .
    .
    .
```

```
@app.task
def reserve(room, start, duration):
    .
    .
    .


@app.task
def search(text):
    .
    .
    .


@app.task
def room(name):
    .
    .
```

The basic task flow for our room reservation system starts with a `reserve` function that takes an instance of a Room object, `room`, the event's start time, and the total duration of the event. The `reserve` task does two things; first it checks to see if the room can be reserved by checking the state of the room with an `availability` function call with the start time, and a second `availability` call with the total time made up of the start time plus the duration. If the room is available, the `reserve` task issues a lock on the room's availability that begins at the start time and lasts until with a delay equal to the start time plus the duration. The room lock is a simple implementation and not at all robust for a multi-instance Redis setup with multiple masters and slaves, with risks of a race condition developing if the Redis instance fails and the lock is not released. Incoming reserve tasks will attempt to lock a non-existent room key for this application. A more robust distribute lock manager – like the Redlock implementation linked from the official Redis documentation at `http://redis.io/topics/distlock` – would be implemented for production-level use in a room reservation situation.

When a room is no longer being used, the lock expires and the `availability` task function will return `True` for further reserve tasks. The cancel task function is for situations where a meeting room becomes available earlier before the room key has expired or if a room was reserved for a future time and the meeting or event is canceled. The cancel function acquires the lock and deletes it from the Redis result datastore so the room is now available for use. The `availability` task function checks for an existing room key and if it is found, returns `False` to the calling client and `True` if the room's key is not found.

To run the Celery worker for the `room_reservation` module from the command-line, the following command will run Celery:

```
$ celery -A room_reservation worker -l info
```

The following screenshot of running this command shows the results:

```
[2015-10-24 11:52:14,647: WARNING/MainProcess]
/usr/local/lib/python3.4/dist-packages/celery/apps/worker.py:161: CDeprecationWarning:
Starting from version 3.2 Celery will refuse to accept pickle by default.

The pickle serializer is a security concern as it may give attackers
the ability to execute any command.  It's important to secure
your broker from unauthorized access when using pickle, so we think
that enabling pickle should require a deliberate action and not be
the default choice.

If you depend on pickle then you should set a setting to disable this
warning and to be sure that everything will continue working
when you upgrade to Celery 3.2::

    CELERY_ACCEPT_CONTENT = ['pickle', 'json', 'msgpack', 'yaml']

You must only enable the serializers that you will actually use.


  warnings.warn(CDeprecationWarning(W_PICKLE_DEPRECATED))

 -------------- celery@LibrarySystems v3.1.19 (Cipater)
---- **** -----
--- * ***  * -- Linux-3.13.0-66-generic-x86_64-with-Ubuntu-14.04-trusty
-- * - **** ---
- ** ---------- [config]
- ** ---------- .> app:         room_reservation:0x7fe97203eeb8
- ** ---------- .> transport:   redis://localhost:6379//
- ** ---------- .> results:     redis://localhost
- *** --- * --- .> concurrency: 1 (prefork)
-- ******* ----
--- ***** ----- [queues]
 -------------- .> celery           exchange=celery(direct) key=celery


[tasks]


[2015-10-24 11:52:14,684: INFO/MainProcess] Connected to redis://localhost:6379//
[2015-10-24 11:52:14,694: INFO/MainProcess] mingle: searching for neighbors
[2015-10-24 11:52:15,700: INFO/MainProcess] mingle: all alone
[2015-10-24 11:52:15,715: WARNING/MainProcess] celery@LibrarySystems ready.
```

For example, to check the availability of room 101, we'll start a Python shell, import our `availability` task and run the task immediately:

```
$ python3
Python 3.4.3 (default, Oct 14 2015, 20:28:29)
[GCC 4.8.4] on linux
Type "help", "copyright", "credits" or "license" for more information.
>>> from room_reservation.tasks import availability
>>> result = availability.delay("room-101")
```

The `availability` task is executed immediately with the Celery worker displaying the following:

[2015-10-24 12:41:18,637: INFO/MainProcess] Received task: room_reservation. tasks.availability[abc10c51-beb3-4e8b-abc5-21dda4dd7ddf]

[2015-10-24 12:41:18,641: INFO/MainProcess] Task room_reservation. tasks.availability[abc10c51-beb3-4e8b-abc5-21dda4dd7ddf] succeeded in 0.0029513250046875328s: -1

A client application sends a `reserve` task in similar fashion that then uses the `availability` and `book` tasks to accomplish a distributed and asynchronous room booking using Celery and Redis.

GIS and RestMQ

Geographical data structures and commands have been added to Redis's 3.2 branch and offer new opportunities to add GIS capabilities to Redis-based projects. Before we examine how a GIS-based messaging system can be built with Redis, we'll explore the basic operations of these newer geographical-based commands.

 Currently, the geographical commands and functionality is only available in the Redis 3.2 version. To use these commands, you'll need to download the 3.2 release of Redis and compile it for use.

The geographical-based commands operate by using a technique called geohashing that is a latitude/longitude encoding system which constructs a hierarchical spatial structure dividing space into buckets on a grid. The geohash algorithm was created by Gustavo Niemeyer for the `http://geohash.org` web service. The construction of geohash allows for nearby geographical locations to share the same initial characters that, as the hash's characters are defined, the precision of the location becomes progressively restricted to a point. Because nearby locations share prefixes, geohashing allows the user to gradually broaden the scope of their search by removing characters from the right-hand side of the geohash.

The first Redis commands to support geographical applications we will look at are GEOADD and GEODIST. The GEOADD command takes a key and one or more triples made up of a latitude, longitude, and member name. The geohashes of locations are stored in Redis as sorted sets, hence the need for a member. To use GEOADD, first launch a Redis 3.2 instance and then in either a separate terminal window or using screen, a different session, launch Redis CLI program to connect to the datastore. We will build a ski weather messaging application that sends a task with the current slope conditions to a skier's or snowboarder's cellphone. We'll use GEOADD to create a Colorado Ski Mountain that contains the longitude and latitude for four Ski resorts in Colorado, USA:

```
127.0.0.1:6379> GEOADD colorado_ski_mountains -106.926982 38.905476
"Crested Butte"

(integer) 1

127.0.0.1:6379> GEOADD colorado_ski_mountains -106.3381 38.502855
"Monarch Mountain"

(integer) 1

127.0.0.1:6379> GEOADD colorado_ski_mountains -106.822146 39.165098
"Aspen Mountain"

(integer) 1

127.0.0.1:6379> GEOADD colorado_ski_mountains -106.355999 39.605234 "Vail
Mountain"

(integer) 1
```

To use the colorado_ski_mountains Redis key, we can use the GEODIST command to calculate the distance in meters between the Crested Butte Ski Mountain and Aspen Mountain with the following command:

```
127.0.0.1:6379> GEODIST colorado_ski_mountains "Crested Butte" "Aspen
Mountain"

"30263.881549595"
```

We can also return the distance in kilometers or miles by using the following command switches:

```
127.0.0.1:6379> GEODIST colorado_ski_mountains "Crested Butte" "Aspen
Mountain" km

"30.263881549595002"

127.0.0.1:6379> GEODIST colorado_ski_mountains "Crested Butte, Colorado"
"Aspen Mountain" mi

"18.80515090011744
```

The GEOHASH command returns the geohashes of one or more elements. With Crested Butte and Aspen Mountain relatively close to each other, as seen with this result of GEOHASH, notice that the two left-most characters, "9w", are the same:

```
127.0.0.1:6379> GEOHASH colorado_ski_mountains "Crested Butte" "Aspen
Mountain"
1) "9wgvqfd0ud0"
2) "9wuncly3px0"
```

The GEOPOS command returns the longitude and latitude of a member of a GEO sorted set. Here is the longitude and latitude for Vail and Monarch Mountains:

```
127.0.0.1:6379> GEOPOS colorado_ski_mountains "Vail Mountain"
1) 1) "-106.35600060224533"
   2) "39.605234833330236"
127.0.0.1:6379> GEOPOS colorado_ski_mountains "Monarch Mountain"
1) 1) "-106.33809953927994"
   2) "38.502854184479808"
```

With the GEORADIUS command, you pass in the geohash key, a center location in longitude and latitude, and a radius in either meters, kilometers, feet, or miles will return the nearest locations from the center. The GEORADIUS includes these additional options with the WITHCOORD option to get each location's longitude and latitude, the WITHDIST option provides the distance between the location and the center radius, and the WITHHASH option provides the raw geohash-encoded set score. Taking the longitude and latitude of the center of the state of Colorado in the United States, we can then demonstrate these various options of the GEORADIUS command from our Redis-cli session:

```
127.0.0.1:6379> GEORADIUS colorado_ski_mountains -105.692242 38.875350
100 km
1) "Vail Mountain"
2) "Monarch Moutain"
127.0.0.1:6379> GEORADIUS colorado_ski_mountains -105.692242 38.875350
100 km WITHCOORD
1) 1) "Vail Mountain"
   2) 1) "-106.35600060224533"
      2) "39.605234833330236"
2) 1) "Monarch Moutain"
   2) 1) "-106.33809953927994"
      2) "38.502854184479808"
```

```
127.0.0.1:6379> GEORADIUS colorado_ski_mountains -105.692242 38.875350
100 km WITHHASH
1) 1) "Vail Mountain"
   2) (integer) 1396750187740657
2) 1) "Monarch Moutain"
   2) (integer) 1396482048060275
```

Adding task management with RestMQ

With these Redis geographic commands available, we'll now add task management functionality by using RestMQ. RestMQ is an open source project that implements a message queue in Python and can be downloaded and installed from `https://github.com/gleicon/restmq`. RestMQ can be run as a Docker container and instead of installing and running RestMQ with Redis, we'll first clone the repository:

```
$ git clone https://github.com/gleicon/restmq.git
Cloning into 'restmq'...
remote: Counting objects: 796, done.
remote: Total 796 (delta 0), reused 0 (delta 0), pack-reused 796
Receiving objects: 100% (796/796), 241.22 KiB | 0 bytes/s, done.
Resolving deltas: 100% (426/426), done.
Checking connectivity... done.
```

Because we want to run the 3.2 branch of Redis in order to use the GIS commands, we'll modify the `restmq` Dockerfile to download and extract the `redis-` TAR file, compile `redis-server`, and copy it to `/usr/bin/redis-serve` with this RUN line as the Dockerfile:

```
RUN apt-get install -y wget && \ wget http://download.redis.io/releases/
redis-3.2.0.tar.gz && \
    tar xzvf redis-3.2.0.tar.gz &&\
    cd redis-3.2.0 && \
    make && \
    cp src/redis-server /usr/bin/redis-server
```

Because Redis 3.2 runs in protected mode as a default, we'll need to modify the `restmq/dockerfiles/supervisor/redis.conf` and add the following at the line 2:

```
command=/usr/bin/redis-server --protected-mode no
```

We'll then issue the following Docker commands to build the RestMQ image and then run RestMQ on port 8888 and a Redis instance on the default port of 6379:

```
$ docker build -t restmq .
```

```
$ docker run --rm -p 6379:6379 -p 8888:8888 restmq
```

The RestMQ server running on port 8888 accepts HTTP GET, POST, and DELETE methods as verbs in a simple REST service at http://localhost:8888/q/<queue-name> where:

- GET requests remove an object from a RestMQ queue
- POST requests insert an object into a RestMQ queue
- DELETE requests purge the queue

To illustrate a weather application with a function for monitoring weather events and alerts of all the ski resorts when an event is within a 100 km radius, the following Python function monitor_weather is an application that polls a RestMQ queue for events, extracts the latitude and longitude for the weather event, runs a GEORADIUS Redis command, and then posts an alert to a RestMQ queue specific to each resort:

```python
def monitor_weather(
        base_url,
        datastore=redis.StrictRedis()):
    channel_url = "{}/c/monitor".format(base_url)
    monitor_resp = requests.get(channel_url, stream=True)
    line_buffer = str()
    for char in monitor_resp.iter_content():
        line_buffer += char.decode()
        if line_buffer.endswith('\r\n'):
            line = line_buffer[0:-2]
            if line.startswith('null'):
                break
            message = json.loads(line)
            result = json.loads(message.get('value'))
            if 'location' in result:
                location = result.get('location')
                alert = result.get('event')
                in_ski_area = datastore.execute_command(
                    "GEORADIUS",
                    "colorado_ski_mountains",
                    location.get('longitude'),
                    location.get('latitude'),
                    100,
                    "km",
                    "WITHHASH")
                # Goes through each resort and add a weather alert
                # to a queue resort's hash value
```

```
for row in in_ski_area:
    queue_url = "{}/q/{}".format(base_url, row[1])
    alert_result = requests.post(queue_url,
        data={"value": alert}
```

From this function we can see how a GIS application using Redis for both GIS calculations and as a message queue backend can be developed and used in a fairly simple fashion. To see the all of the steps in using monitor_weather, please check-out the app.py module documentation. In the next section we'll examine another messaging alternative that doesn't use Redis server but is built using RESP and Redis design patterns.

Messaging with Redis technologies

In distributed systems design, a popular usage pattern is to implement a message queue where producers and consumers communicate across a middleware platform. The producers and consumers are not necessarily running on the same machine with the messaging backend that may not use Redis's own Pub/Sub commands.

Messaging with Disque

In early 2015, Salvatore Sanfilippo announced and then released the first alpha release of a new distributed message broker project called Disque, with the source code available at https://github.com/antirez/disque. Disque is based on the Redis protocol, but does not actually use the Redis server. Redis clients can communicate and use Disque; however, a number of language-specific Disque clients for many of the most popular programming languages have been released and are available from the Disque's GitHub main page.

To get Disque running is similar to Redis. First, open a terminal window and either clone the Disque repository with Git or download the code repository as a ZIP file at https://github.com/antirez/disque/archive/master.zip:

```
$ git clone https://github.com/antirez/disque.git
Cloning into 'disque'...
remote: Counting objects: 2565, done.
remote: Total 2565 (delta 0), reused 0 (delta 0), pack-reused 2565
Receiving objects: 100% (2565/2565), 1.38 MiB | 441.00 KiB/s, done.
Resolving deltas: 100% (1617/1617), done.
Checking connectivity... done.
```

Next, we change directories to Disque and then run the make command:

```
$ cd disque
$ make
```

After Disque has been compiled, we'll start-up Disque and start investigating its capabilities as a distributed job or task queue for a hypothetical situation where an intra-solar communication system between Earth, the moon, Mars, and an asteroid and comet is desired. The design pattern for Disque is similar to Redis in that we'll create a cluster of nodes running on different ports using copies of the `disque.conf` file for each running node. To begin our experiment with using Disque, we'll create a project directory and copy our `disque.conf` four times:

```
$ mkdir solar-com
$ cd solar-com
$ cp ~/disque/disque.conf .
```

To run a simple Disque instance (if you're interested in running Disque in cluster mode, see the documentation on the Disque website), run `disque-server`:

```
$ ~/disque/src/disque-server disque.conf
```

Now, we'll create two messages and send it to the Earth queue using the Disque client with the ADDJOB command that takes as its first parameter a text string for the queue name and as its second parameter the name of the job, with a final parameter being a timeout in milliseconds:

```
$ ~/disque/src/disque
127.0.0.1:7711> ADDJOB Earth "Get latest news" 0
DI11e16675a292b568ad0e7a01ecc51aeeeb53bd9105a0SQ
```

With the GETJOB Disque command with the FROM keyword, we retrieve any jobs from the Earth queue, once for each message that is in the queue we call:

```
127.0.0.1:7711> GETJOB FROM Earth
1) 1) "Earth"
   2) "DI11e16675a292b568ad0e7a01ecc51aeeeb53bd9105a0SQ"
   3) "Get latest news"
```

Now, we'll send a second message with ADDJOB to the Moon queue and retrieve the message from the Moon queue with GETJOB:

```
127.0.0.1:7711> ADDJOB Moon "Get moon rock sample" 0
DI11e166757cd789784008299f7a393dbcdd36e14d05a0SQ127.0.0.1:7711> GETJOB
FROM Moon
1) 1) "Moon"
   2) "DI11e166757cd789784008299f7a393dbcdd36e14d05a0SQ"
   3) "Get moon rock sample"
```

We can see that the output is similar to a Redis-cli session, with Disque offering a richer set of messaging options than Redis but built using the Redis nomenclature and the successful execution model of Redis.

Summary

In this chapter, we covered in detail Redis support for the Publish/Subscribe messaging model with Redis's special Pub/Sub mode that clients enter when issuing either a SUBSCRIBE or with glob-style pattern matching variant PSUBSCRIBE Redis commands. When in Pub/Sub mode, other Redis commands cannot be used with the client and the client will monitor one or more channels for any incoming messages. Other clients can push messages to a channel using the PUBLISH Redis command, and all clients subscribing to that channel, either directly or through pattern matching, will receive those messages. To illustrate how to use Redis Pub/Sub with three different programming languages and clients, we constructed a simplified Kanban manufacturing process for constructing Jack-in-the-Box toys for a fictional North Pole company. We then examined two task and messaging frameworks – Celery and RestMQ – that use Redis to implement richer and more robust messaging for client applications, in this case a school room reservation example and a geographic-app that uses Redis's new GIS commands with RestMQ. Finally, we examined a relatively new project from Redis creator Salvatore Sanfilippo called Disque, that uses RESP (so Redis standard clients can connect and use) to manage a distributed, in-memory, message broker as a C-based non-blocking networked server.

Our final chapter takes and builds upon the knowledge and skills from other chapters in *Mastering Redis* and shows how Redis can be used in many ETL workflows as a critical component in many "big data" analytics and management in modern enterprises.

10
Measuring and Managing Information Streams

This chapter focuses on Redis's role in capturing information and data analytics leading to actionable knowledge for organizations. We'll start with a detailed description and examples of how to extract, transform, and load large volumes of data into Redis through mass insertion and other techniques. Next, we will examine how security considerations can impact management, along with a web-based dashboard to display runtime statistics with Redis. Finally, we'll experiment with using Redis with machine learning techniques such as Naïve Bayes and linear regression.

Extracting, transforming, and loading information with Redis

Redis's flexibility and speed make it an ideal candidate for many **extract, transform, and load** (ETL) processes for both homogeneous data as well as complex and heterogeneous data sources that are becoming increasingly common in the modern organization.

Unlike expensive and proprietary ETL systems, Redis's open source model offers capabilities that even these commercial systems lack, while giving the small and medium-sized enterprise opportunities to improve the flow of their own, constantly growing, and increasingly complex data:

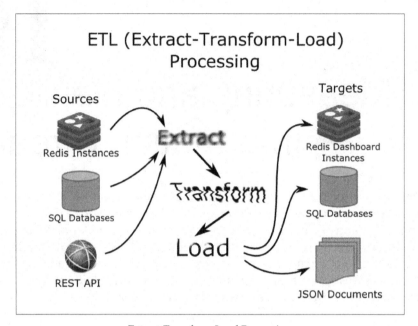

Extract-Transform-Load Processing

Importing data through most Redis clients, even using Redis clients that support transactions and command pipelining, is slow and inefficient due to the penalty of round-trip write and reply from the Redis server to the Redis client. Most clients do not support non-blocking I/O mode and often cannot parse the replies back from the Redis server in a manner that maximizes throughput between the client and the server. We have, through most of the examples in this book, ignored these performance hits when importing large amounts of data into a running Redis instance. As mentioned in the official Redis documentation on mass insertion of data refer bullet point number 1 in *Appendix, Sources, Chapter 10: Measuring and Managing Information Streams*, the preferred method for feeding data into Redis by the fastest means possible is by generating a text file containing raw Redis protocol (RESP). This RESP text file can then be fed into either Netcat, or into the Redis-cli program, using a special pipeline mode.

Illustrating the differences between using a Redis client to send multiple commands in a transaction versus the pipeline method of inserting raw RESP into Redis by modifying the existing ingestion code taken from the Linked Data Fragments Server project. Our first step is to create a simple script that uses the Linked Data Fragments Server Lua script, called `add_get_triple`, to create and store SHA1 digest of elements into a Redis instance. Depending on which option is passed into the script when ingesting a triple into a Redis instance, a triple representation in the Linked Data Server will either be a single string, three hashes, or three sets, depending on the strategy. For our testing purposes, we'll use the set strategy so that for each triple we will either create a new set or add to an existing set for each subject, predicate, and object in a triple.

For a triple made up a subject with a SHA1 hash of `440bd91cb8b77850e5ca4cc648adaa3769b5a7ab` for the URL `http://dp.la/api/items/971d73fd2dfd6376f258dd6a533697a5#sourceResource`, a predicate SHA1 hash of `2298d2f28daae5f02504a5b048d0c036ea73e3bd` for the URL `http://purl.org/dc/elements/1.1/description`, the Dublin Core Description element, and a SHA1 hash of `fe8fb512487c2a945f03e0efcfe8c670ea861f60` of a string literal for the object. We can explore these Redis keys and data structures using a Redis-cli session to a get a general feel of what we want the end data to look like:

```
127.0.0.1:6379> GET 440bd91cb8b77850e5ca4cc648adaa3769b5a7ab
"http://dp.la/api/items/971d73fd2dfd6376f258dd6a533697a5#sourceResource"
127.0.0.1:6379> GET 2298d2f28daae5f02504a5b048d0c036ea73e3bd
"http://purl.org/dc/elements/1.1/description"
127.0.0.1:6379> GET fe8fb512487c2a945f03e0efcfe8c670ea861f60
"Relief shown by hachures. Includes 1 inset map in 2 sections: Mission du
Docteur Bayol a Timbo en 1881."
```

To represent this triple, we also have three sets:

- `440bd91cb8b77850e5ca4cc648adaa3769b5a7ab:pred-obj` for all of the subject's predicates and objects
- `2298d2f28daae5f02504a5b048d0c036ea73e3bd:subj-obj` for all of the predicate's subjects and objects
- `fe8fb512487c2a945f03e0efcfe8c670ea861f60:subj-pred` for all of the object's subjects and predicates

The size of each of these sets is easily retrieved using the SCARD command:

```
127.0.0.1:6379> SCARD 440bd91cb8b77850e5ca4cc648adaa3769b5a7ab:pred-obj
(integer) 25
127.0.0.1:6379> SCARD 2298d2f28daae5f02504a5b048d0c036ea73e3bd:subj-obj
(integer) 62473
127.0.0.1:6379> SCARD fe8fb512487c2a945f03e0efcfe8c670ea861f60:subj-pred
(integer) 1
```

Conceptually, the size of these sets is within reason, as a subject graph for a digital item is 25, while the common Dublin Core description metadata element is much larger at 62,473, and finally, the literal string object only has one subject and predicate. The contents of each of these sets is just the SHA1 hash digests of the corresponding triple fragment, which can be retrieved in various ways using the SMEMBERS or SSCAN Redis commands; we can test if the remaining elements are present in the set with the SISMEMBER command. We'll start first with the subject:

```
127.0.0.1:6379> SSCAN 440bd91cb8b77850e5ca4cc648adaa3769b5a7ab:pred-obj 0
1) "28"
2)  1) "490fd4e5ac1e267bbd873e6df9f79f6e21bb39a4:a7efd7cea070322c1f9e0b34
641afdea7e9eed09"
    2) "d82a0c98602164078281e22c3d2096c214887d4e:5972d70a66a4f74a915ffd29
a6afe09c89353986"
    3) "490fd4e5ac1e267bbd873e6df9f79f6e21bb39a4:601230576f399ca97b523372
1ce327e0bbd4f206"
    4) "490fd4e5ac1e267bbd873e6df9f79f6e21bb39a4:5b15ed3dd0b60e11d575d29c
640cea554cf91d82"
    5) "2298d2f28daae5f02504a5b048d0c036ea73e3bd:fe8fb512487c2a945f03e0ef
cfe8c670ea861f60"
    6) "54aed229df691a2f772c19d4396852b26f960827:1586bf7cee37fa79f91d94d2
210591205365432a"
    7) "2298d2f28daae5f02504a5b048d0c036ea73e3bd:6a645f0ef32ac10c04201498
242bd6fa7bf7dc91"
    8) "d9e34bac9b6f5b13a338df39bf61ec1965bab39d:15073464d418bafe273534b3
30ebf3a4cba5cae1"
    9) "490fd4e5ac1e267bbd873e6df9f79f6e21bb39a4:c4aae22fdbf6c4799741377f
4054d2efcaa247a3"
   10) "2298d2f28daae5f02504a5b048d0c036ea73e3bd:68b04fe437611ca606c29aa9
e96a7e3f8f31d707"
127.0.0.1:6379> SISMEMBER 440bd91cb8b77850e5ca4cc648adaa3769b5a7ab:pred-
obj 2298d2f28daae5f02504a5b048d0c036ea73e3bd:fe8fb512487c2a945f03e0efcfe8
c670ea861f60
(integer) 1
```

Next, we'll retrieve values from the large number of members in the object's set by using the SSCAN command with a MATCH parameter to restrict to just those members that match the subject SHA1 that we're interested in:

```
127.0.0.1:6379> SSCAN 2298d2f28daae5f02504a5b048d0c036ea73e3bd:subj-obj 0
MATCH 440bd91cb8b77850e5ca4cc648adaa3769b5a7ab:* COUNT 100000

1) "0"

2) 1) "440bd91cb8b77850e5ca4cc648adaa3769b5a7ab:68b04fe437611ca606c29aa9e
96a7e3f8f31d707"

   2) "440bd91cb8b77850e5ca4cc648adaa3769b5a7ab:6a645f0ef32ac10c042014982
42bd6fa7bf7dc91"

   3) "440bd91cb8b77850e5ca4cc648adaa3769b5a7ab:fe8fb512487c2a945f03e0efc
fe8c670ea861f60"

   4) "440bd91cb8b77850e5ca4cc648adaa3769b5a7ab:7581c0c2d4d7e33db91e689dc
a8b84e1f449ac24"

   5) "440bd91cb8b77850e5ca4cc648adaa3769b5a7ab:19bc513b98fa411e352f7f10d
4ee59c1c49c036c"

127.0.0.1:6379> SISMEMBER 2298d2f28daae5f02504a5b048d0c036ea73e3bd:subj-
obj 440bd91cb8b77850e5ca4cc648adaa3769b5a7ab:fe8fb512487c2a945f03e0efcfe8
c670ea861f60

(integer) 1
```

We will use the SMEMBERS to retrieve all of the subjects and predicates for the object:

```
127.0.0.1:6379> SMEMBERS fe8fb512487c2a945f03e0efcfe8c670ea861f60:subj-
pred

1) "440bd91cb8b77850e5ca4cc648adaa3769b5a7ab:2298d2f28daae5f02504a5b048d0
c036ea73e3bd"
```

Using the University of Illinois data set, refer bullet point number 2 in *Appendix, Sources, Chapter 10: Measuring and Managing Information Streams* from the Dp.la website as the raw RDF graph input, the JSON linked data (JSON-LD) file is parsed with the Python rdflib module into a RDF graph. The new RDF graph has the following characteristics:

Size of raw JSON-LD file	101 MB
Number of triples	605,150
Unique subjects	132,671
Unique predicates	34
Unique objects	227,302

Using the Lua script `add_get_triple` in the Linked Data Fragments Server, ingesting on average 5,000 triples took about 2.53 minutes on a 4-core 16 GB of RAM workstation, that took approximately five hours to ingest the complete data set using this Python function:

```python
def ingest_graph(graph, lua_script_digest, datastore):
    start = datetime.datetime.now()
    counter = 0
    print("Started ingesting {} triples at {}".format(len(graph),
start.isoformat()))
    for subject, predicate, object_ in graph:
        datastore.evalsha(lau_script_digest, 3, subject, predicate,
object_)
        if not counter%10 and counter > 0:
            print(".", end="")
        if not counter%100:
            print(counter, end="")
        if not counter%100 and counter > 0:
            print(":{} mins".format((datetime.datetime.now()-start).
seconds / 60.0))
        counter += 1
    end = datetime.datetime.now()
    print("Finished at {} total time {}".format(end, (end-start).
seconds / 60.0))
```

The resulting Redis `dump.rdb` file for this data set is 181 megabytes, with a total number of Redis keys at 605,150.

If you already have your data extracted and loaded into Redis, using the rdb tool from `https://github.com/sripathikrishnan/redis-rdb-tools` project allows you to transform a Redis `dump.rdb` (or any Redis `rdb` file) to RESP format that can then be loaded into Redis using the bulk ingestion process. After installing this project either using `pip install rdbtools` or cloning the project and then running sudo Python `setup.py` install will enable us to use the `rdb` executable. Executing the following command generates the RESP file and pipes the output to `dpal_resp.txt`:

```
$ rdb --command protocol dump.rdb > dpla_resp.txt
```

We can then use the UNIX `time` command to get an estimate of how long it takes to mass insert the `dpla_resp.txt` file into an empty Redis instance using the `netcat` UNIX utility:

```
$ time (cat dpla_resp.txt; sleep 10) | nc localhost 6379 > /dev/null

real    0m14.265s
user    0m0.127s
sys     0m1.459s
```

Retrieving the total size and then flushing the Redis instance in a separate terminal window:

```
127.0.0.1:6379> DBSIZE
(integer) 605150
127.0.0.1:6379> FLUSHALL
OK
(1.71s)
```

Finally, we'll perform a second test using the Redis-cli program in pipeline mode:

```
$ time cat dpla_resp.txt | ~/redis/src/redis-cli --pipe
All data transferred. Waiting for the last reply...
Last reply received from server.
errors: 0, replies: 2025798


real    0m3.750s
user    0m0.259s
sys     0m0.411s
```

Now, back in our interactive Redis-cli session, we confirm that all data has been loaded by running the DBSIZE command again:

```
127.0.0.1:6379> DBSIZE
(integer) 605150
```

Ingesting the RESP file using both Netcat and Redis-cli takes significantly less time to load then our initial Python script took to ingest the original JSON-LD file. Take this into consideration when looking at the various data and information flows in your application, especially applications that perform common ETL workflows, like ingesting large quantities of data into a Redis datastore.

Knowing the incoming JSON data structure for each of these records, we can create a function to output the SHA1 for each subject, predicate, and object that generates the RESP file instead of using the Redis client and sending commands directly to the running Redis instance. This bulk uploading is somewhat easier and definitely orders of magnitude faster, although we will need to do some manipulation and JSON filtering in order to transform the JSON linked data into the RESP format before we can load the data set into Redis. To transform this JSON linked data into RESP requires a way to filter out the structural metadata of the RDF record as well as expanding individual fields to a full URL before calculating the SHA1 hash digest of either the predicate or object elements.

Extracting JSON to transform into RESP

Like many ETL workflows, before extracting and transforming the data, we need additional structural information about the record before the information can be transformed into a format for loading. Fortunately, dp.la provides a comprehensive description of their record format, what they call their **Metadata Application Profile** (**MAP**), available at http://dp.la/info/developers/map/. The dp.la MAP uses a combination of Dublin Core metadata standard and the **Europeana Data Model** (**EDM**) for their records, each with their own namespace that is used in the JSON-LD.

This code performance is poor and an alternative approach to speed up the ingestion to the Linked Data Fragment server is to parse the JSON Linked Data file, calculate the SHA1 hashes for the subject, predicate, and objects, and then generate the RESP text file. To assist in outputting the RESP, a generate_redis_protocol function will be used:

```
def generate_redis_protocol(cmd):
    proto = ""
    proto += "*" + str(len(cmd)) + "\r\n"
    for arg in cmd:
        proto += "$" + str(len(arg)) + "\r\n"
        proto += arg + "\r\n"
    return proto
```

Before using the generate_redis_protocol function, the loading of the raw JSON-LD file is accomplished by first loading the file object into a Python list containing the records – the record is a Python dictionary – using the standard JSON Python module that is imported next:

```
>>> import json
>>> dpla_ui = json.load(
    open("/tmp/university_of_illinois_at_urbana-champaign"))
>>> len(dpla_ui)
18103
```

Displaying a section of a random record's JSON dictionary gives the structure and a sense of what information is available with the following abbreviated annotation of this DP.LA record that was harvested from the University of Illinois's digital repository:

```
>>> record = dpla_ui[5678]
```

Using this sample record, we will first get a feel for the structure and content of this JSON-LD object to determine the subjects, predicates, and objects we want to extract, so we can be build our extraction and transformation script. To begin, we take a look at what are the top-level keys in this Python dictionary:

```
>>> record.keys()
dict_keys(['ingestionSequence', '_id', 'ingestType', 'admin', 'object',
'isShownAt', 'aggregatedCHO', '_rev', 'dataProvider', 'originalRecord',
'sourceResource', 'id', 'ingestDate', '@type', '@context', '@id',
'provider'])
```

The `@context` section of this JSON-LD record defines the default namespace for all of the properties:

```
>>> record.get('@context')
'http://dp.la/api/items/context'
```

Part of the JSON-to-RESP script `dpla2resp.py` output will need to expand all of the properties based on the `http://dp.la/api/items/context` and `http://www.europeana.eu/schemas/edm/` URLs:

```
>>> record.get('@id')
'http://dp.la/api/items/b85d182ccb7d800c8c13b65743ef9ac7'
```

The `@id` key in this record dictionary is the subject with an URI of `http://dp.la/api/items/b85d182ccb7d800c8c13b65743ef9ac7` will need to set to the key SHA1 of `d7210e2eca59b8c25086dbef406b2a41720f079c`:

```
>>> item_hash = hashlib.sha1(record.get('@id').encode())
>>> item_hash.hexdigest()
'd7210e2eca59b8c25086dbef406b2a41720f079c'
```

With this `item_hash` and `@id`, we generate our first RESP by calling the `generate_redis_protocol` function with a list made up of three items:

```
>>> resp = generate_redis_protocol(["SETNX", item_hash.hexdigest(),
record.get('@id')])
>>> print(resp.encode())
*3\r\n
$5\r\n
SETNX\r\n
$40\r\n
d7210e2eca59b8c25086dbef406b2a41720f079c\r\n
$55\r\n
http://dp.la/api/items/b85d182ccb7d800c8c13b65743ef9ac7\r\n'
```

Going back to our original Redis instance called `dpla_redis` with the loaded DPLA University of Illinois triplestore, we can now retrieve all of the predicates and objects of this record to see what fields we need to extract from the record JSON to create our RESP file:

```
>>> dpla_redis = redis.StrictRedis()
>>> for row in dpla_redis.smembers("d7210e2eca59b8c25086dbef406b2a41720f0
79c:pred-obj"):
    print(dpla_redis.get(row.decode().split(":")[0]))
```

```
b'http://www.europeana.eu/schemas/edm/isShownAt'
b'http://www.europeana.eu/schemas/edm/provider'
b'http://www.europeana.eu/schemas/edm/dataProvider'
b'http://www.europeana.eu/schemas/edm/object'
b'http://purl.org/dc/elements/1.1/_rev'
b'http://www.europeana.eu/schemas/edm/aggregatedCHO'
b'http://www.w3.org/1999/02/22-rdf-syntax-ns#type'
b'http://dp.la/terms/SourceResource'
```

The RDF `@type` for this record will need to be expanded to the full URL of `http://www.openarchives.org/ore/terms/Aggregation`, but is stored in the JSON record with a namespace, as follows:

```
>>> record.get('@type')
'ore:Aggregation'
```

For this subject we will extract predicate and object values from the other fields in the record dictionary, including the `isShownAt dataProvider`, `object`, `aggregateCHO`, `SourceResource`, and the `_rev` key in in JSON-to-RESP script's `aggregation2resp` function. The `aggregation2resp` function starts by getting this aggregation record's RDF ID, creating a SHA1 hash of the aggregation record's IRI, generating the RESP for the new record using a Redis `MSETNX` command for the RDF class IRI, and its value, and then creating a Redis set key for storing all of the predicate and objects of this use later in the function, starting with the RDF class value:

```
    def aggregation2resp(record):
        raw_protocol = ''
        record_iri = record.pop("@id")
        record_hash = hashlib.sha1(record_iri.encode())
        record_type = record.pop("@type")
        rdf_type_hash = hashslib.sha1(str(rdflib.RDF.type).encode())
```

```
record_type_hash = hashlib.sha1(record_type.encode())
raw_protocol += generate_redis_protocol(
    ["MSETNX",
    record_hash.hexdigest(),
    record_iri,
    rdf_type_hash,
    str(rdflib.RDF.type),
    rdf_type_value_hash.hexdigest(),
    record_type])
record_pred_obj = "{}:pred-obj".format(record_hash)
raw_protocol += generate_redis_protocol(
    ["SADD",
    record_pred_obj,
    "{}:{}".format(rdf_type_hash, record_type_hash)])
```

For the record keys, the aggregation2resp function goes through the Europeana vocabulary's isShownAt, dataProvider, object, aggregateCHO properties and adds the full IRI of each property and corresponding SHA1 hash if it doesn't exist within RESP, using the Redis MSETNX command:

```
for key in record.keys():
    # EDM simple triples
    if key in ['isShownAt',
                'dataProvider',
                'aggregatedCHO',
                'object']:
        key_iri = getattr(EDM, key)
        key_hash = hashlib.sha1(key_iri.encode())
        key_value = record.get(key)
        key_value_hash = hashlib.sha1(key_value.encode())
        raw_protocol += generate_redis_protocol(
            ["MSETNX",
            key_hash.hexdigest(),
            key_iri,
            key_value_hash.hexdigest(),
            key_value])
```

After these EDM properties are added to RESP string, the corresponding Redis set RESP for the subject, predicate, and objects from the individual EDM properties are generated for the `subj_pred_key`, `edm_subj_obj`, and the `edm_subj_pred` Redis keys:

```
raw_protocol += generate_redis_protocol(
    ["SADD",
     record_pred_key.hexdigest(),
     "{}:{}".format(
         key_hash.hexdigest(),
         key_value_hash.hexdigest())])
edm_subj_obj = "{}:subj-obj".format(key_hash.hexdigest()
raw_protocol += generate_redis_protocol(
    ["SADD",
     edm_subj_obj,
     "{}:{}".format(record_hash.hexdigest(,
                    key_value_hash.hexdigest())])
edm_subj_pred = "{}:subj-pred".format(
    key_value_hash.hexdigest())
raw_protocol += generate_redis_protocol(
    ["SADD",
     edm_subj_pred,
     "{}:{}".format(record_hash, key_hash)])
```

The `aggregation2resp` function creates and adds a Dublin-core `_rev` value to the protocol:

```
if '_rev' in record:
    dc_rev_hash = hashlib.sha1(getattr(DC, '_rev').encode())
    dc_rev_value = record.get('_rev')
    dc_rev_value_hash = hashlib.sha1(dc_rev_hash.encode())
    raw_protocol += generate_redis_protocol(
        ["MSETNX",
         dc_rev_hash.hexdigest(),
         getattr(DC, '_rev'),
         dc_rev_value_hash.hexdigest(),
         dc_rev_value])
    raw_protocol += generate_redis_protocol(
        ["SADD",
         record_pred_key,
         "{}:{}".format(dc_rev_hash.hexdigest(),
                        dc_rev_value_hash.hexdigest())])
    raw_protocol += generate_redis_protocol(
```

```
                    ["SADD",
                     "{}:subj-obj".format(dc_rev_hash.hexdigest()),
                     "{}:{}".format(record_hash.hexdigest(),
                                  dc_rev_value_hash.hexdigest())])
        raw_protocol += generate_redis_protocol(
                    ["SADD",
                     "{}:subj-pred".format(dc_rev_value_hash.hexdigest()),
                     "{}:{}".format(record_hash.hexdigest(),
                                  dc_rev_hash.hexdigest())])
```

For the aggregation record's `sourceResource`, `provider`, and `originalRecord` predicates, the values are other RDF subjects that also need RESP output generated by the `dpla2resp.py` script. These three RESP generation functions are `sourceResource2resp`, `provider2resp`, and `originalRecord2resp`. For our sample record, we can examine each of the Python dictionaries and generate the SHA1 hash keys for the aggregation record properties, as seen here in our Python shell for the `sourceResource` property:

```
>>> source_resource_subject = record.get('sourceResource').get('@id')

>>> source_resource_subject_hash = hashlib.sha1(source_resource_subject.
encode())

>>> print(source_resource_subject, source_resource_subject_hash.
hexdigest())

http://dp.la/api/items/b85d182ccb7d800c8c13b65743ef9ac7#sourceResource
e777561816eb6ff634b310cbb3e19ad09cdd2a4c
```

In the actual `dpla2resp` function, the other functions of these subjects are expanded and the RESP is generated and added to the RESP stream that will be passed to the bulk upload process.

The Python code we have so far is too verbose and is in need of refactoring to simplify and generalize some common patterns that will be left up to the reader to explore on your own. The output RESP for the `aggregation2resp` function is displayed in the following graphic:

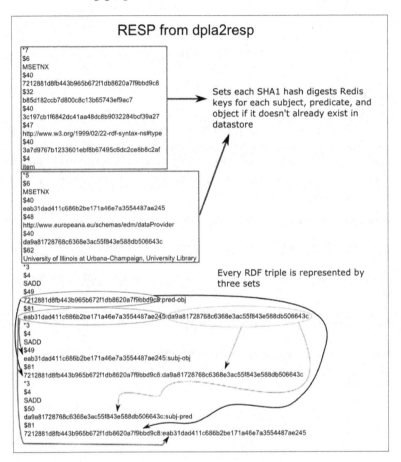

Security considerations when managing Redis

A criticism of Redis is its weak out-of-box security and the lack of safeguards. Prior to Redis 3.2, bringing up a Redis instance on a public server exposed the server to any traffic connecting to the default port of 6379. The main operational assumption with regards to security with Redis is that Redis runs in a secured network with trusted clients accessing the datastore. Applications that access Redis, such as a web server implementing a cache, would provide the necessary security to isolate Redis from direct interaction with untrusted input by the users of the application.

A general recommendation regarding security and Redis is to use other technology, which at a minimum should be a firewall, if running a public server, to provide access controls between the running Redis instance and the outside world. If your situation requires your client to connect over the public Internet to a Redis server, you should consider using an SSL proxy (one recommendation is using spiped at `http://www.tarsnap.com/spiped.html`) to encrypt the channel, as Redis itself does not offer encryption communication between the client and server.

Redis protected mode

Starting with Redis 3.2, a Redis instance will no longer be accessible from outside the environment it is being run in. This special operational mode, called Redis protected mode, occurs when two conditions exist:

- The server is not explicitly binding to one or more IP addresses using the `bind` directive in the `redis.conf` configuration file
- No password is set in the `redis.conf` configuration file with the `requirepass` directive

We can easily simulate this situation by running Redis 3.2 in a virtual machine and then attempting to connect to the instance with our Redis Python client from our host:

```
127.0.0.1:6379> dbsize
```

(error) DENIED Redis is running in protected mode because protected mode is enabled, no bind address was specified, no authentication password is requested to clients. In this mode connections are only accepted from the loopback interface.

If you want to connect from external computers to Redis you may adopt one of the

following solutions: 1) Just disable protected mode sending the command 'CONFIG

SET protected-mode no' from the loopback interface by connecting to Redis from the same host the server is running, however MAKE SURE Redis is not publicly accessible from internet if you do so. Use CONFIG REWRITE to make this change permanent.

2) Alternatively you can just disable the protected mode by editing the Redis configuration file, and setting the protected mode option to 'no', and then restarting the server.

3) If you started the server manually just for testing, restart it with the '--protected-mode no' option. 4) Setup a bind address or an authentication password. NOTE: You only need to do one of the above things in order for the server to start accepting connections from the outside.

As you can see from this error message, to disable Redis's protected mode requires connecting to a Redis server instance with a Redis client running in the same environment and running CONFIG SET command:

```
127.0.0.1:6379> CONFIG SET protected-mode no
```

Alternatively, you can either change the protected-mode directive in the redis. conf file to no, use the bind directive to restrict access to selected IP addresses and network interfaces, or use requirepass directive to set a password for clients to provide when connecting to the Redis instance.

> Passwords in Redis are stored and transmitted in plain text! If an attacker is able to snoop on the traffic between a client and a Redis server, the password is compromised. Likewise, if the attacker can access a Redis server's redis.conf configuration file, the password is stored in the file in plain text as well.

To see how setting a password works with Redis, we'll restart the Redis server running in a VM, and add a simple password, v3ryBadPassw0rd, to a Redis configuration file. Relaunching our Redis server instance, we'll connect with a Redis-cli client and issue a simple DBSIZE command:

```
127.0.0.1:6379> DBSIZE
(error) NOAUTH Authentication required.
```

The NOAUTH error message was received by the client because the password defined in the redis.conf configuration file was not sent to the Redis server using the AUTH command:

```
127.0.0.1:6379> AUTH v3ryBadPassw0rd
OK
127.0.0.1:6379> DBSIZE
(integer) 0
```

After a successful AUTH command with the correct password, subsequent calls by the client are processed normally by the Redis server. In master-slave replication, if the master Redis instance has a password set, slaves of that master need to set the masterauth configuration directive in its redis.conf file.

Command obfuscation

While Redis does not have the equivalent of access controls for specific commands in a mixed use environment where some clients may need to have reduced privileges, Redis does provides a method to disable or obfuscate Redis commands so that even if a client is compromised, certain commands, such as CONFIG SET, FLUSHALL, or any write commands, are unavailable or disguised for use by connecting clients.

To demonstrate command obfuscation with the rename-command command, we will open a copy of redis.conf and add the following lines:

```
rename-command CONFIG aReallyLongConfigtoGuess
rename-command FLUSHALL ""
rename-command DEL ""
```

Setting a Redis command to an empty string " " will disable the command. We'll test by starting a new Redis 3.2 server using this redis.conf and then with a Redis-cli session attempting the following:

```
127.0.0.1:6379> CONFIG GET maxmemory

(error) ERR unknown command 'CONFIG'

127.0.0.1:6379> aReallyLongConfigtoGuess GET maxmemory

1)  "maxmemory"

2)  "0"

127.0.0.1:6379> FLUSHALL

(error) ERR unknown command 'FLUSHALL'
```

When renaming Redis commands, be sure NOT to use a numeral as the first character in your command, otherwise Redis will go into an infinite loop on your client! Other Redis commands that you may want to rename include KEYS, PEXPIRE, DEL, SHUTDOWN, BGREWRITEAOF, BGSAVE, SAVE, SPOP, SREM, RENAME, and DEBUG.

Operational monitoring with a Redis web dashboard

Monitoring the state of multiple systems with a web-based operational dashboard is common enough that there are open source dashboards projects that allow real-time observation of running Redis instances, including any master-slave, or the complex topology of a Redis cluster. Commercial Redis hosting companies such as Redis Labs offer similar services for monitoring and responding to problems through a dashboard interface. In 2012 Nitin Kumar wrote a blog post, refer bullet point number 3 in *Appendix, Sources, Chapter 10: Measuring and Managing Information Streams*, announcing the release of RedisLive, a dashboard for monitoring Redis instances using, primarily, Redis INFO and MONITOR command.

RedisLive, available on GitHub at `https://github.com/nkrode/RedisLive`, offers a web-based dashboard for displaying the activity and current latency spikes of your monitored Redis instance. RedisLive requires at least one dedicated Redis instance to store statistics, although there is an option to use a SQLite database instead.

Besides web-based specific monitoring tools such as RedisLive for Redis, dedicated, native apps for Android and Apple's iOS for system monitoring also offer more general ways to monitor your system:

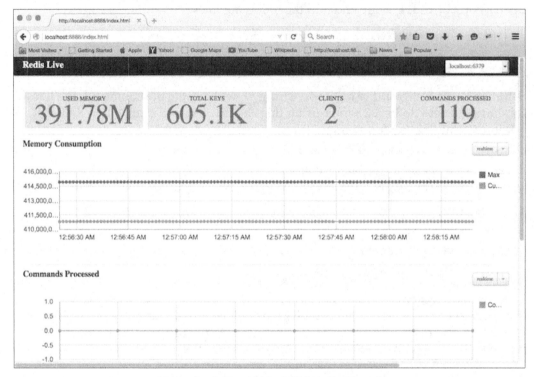

Monitoring Redis with the RedisLive Dashboard

Machine learning and Redis

While the hype cycle continues for what is generally called "Big Data", Redis offers numerous ways to actually accomplish some of what the advertising and media is promising to business users and leaders. Besides being a good choice for performing quick-and-dirty loading and manipulation of data, Redis also performs well as a staging platform for data in a transitional mode that is later manipulated towards a final state, depending on the application. Redis use as a datastore in machine learning techniques and approaches helps as an easily malleable store supporting a particular learning algorithm.

This section takes two supervised learning tasks, Näive Bayes and linear regression, to demonstrate different approaches to statistical analysis with Redis as a transitory datastore for intermediate results. For the first example, the dataset is a pre-existing set of 52 MARC21 records for Jane Austen's *Pride and Prejudice* and Herman Melville's *Moby Dick*. This dataset will be converted to BIBFRAME entities and then randomly divided into two datasets, one for training the algorithm and the other to test the testing Näive Bayes dataset. For the linear regression example, we will take three of publicly available datasets and combine them into a master dataset that we will then split into two random groups again, and like the Naïve Bayes, use one for testing the linear regression and one to test the results.

For the second example, a weather time series data will be used to calculate summary statistics, while storing the resulting computations like mean and variance to a Redis instance. Taking a similar approach as described by Sachin Joglekar in a 2015 blog post, refer bullet point 4 in *Appendix, Sources, Chapter 10: Measuring and Managing Information Streams, Efficient computation and storage of basic data statistics using Redis*, we'll keep the raw weather data as CSV files and using the numpy Python module, store the results of computing various linear regressions for specific questions in a Redis instance. This linear regression example uses a simplified approach to linear regression that only uses two variables, an independent variable x and a dependent variable y for illustration purposes. Although these types of models do not allow for multiple dependent variables that is typically the case for many problems, the simplified model is a surprisingly powerful tool, and once you are able to understand the specifics and approach, computing the regression for multi-variable models is an easy progression to make.

Naïve Bayes and work classification

Thomas Bayes, an 18th century English clergyman and amateur mathematician, first described how the probability of an event can be calculated or later altered based on other conditions that may be related to the event. Bayes' theorem can be succinctly stated as:

$$P(A|B) = \frac{P(B|A)P(A)}{P(B)}$$

Where the probability of an event *A* given that *B* has occurred is calculated as the product of the probability of *B* given *A* and the probability of *A* divided by the probability of event *B*, the *conditional probability* of an event is said to be dependent on the existence of prior events. Naïve Bayes is commonly used for such classification tasks as identifying spam in either e-mail or comments sections of a website:

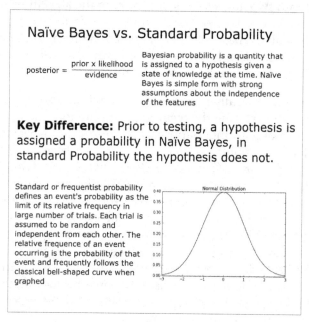

Naïve Bayes verses Standard Probability

In developing a usable catalog with the BIBFRAME 1.0 vocabulary from the Library of Congress, a challenge of classifying an unknown Work as either an existing Work in the catalog or as a new Work is not necessarily a simple or easy task. The BIBFRAME vocabulary has built into its resource specification a specific property called `authorizedAccessPoint` that is intended to provide a crude mechanism for de-duplicating entities, that is, if two Works share the same `authorizedAccessPoint` then the Works are assumed to be the same. This approach is acceptable for a quick analysis, but there are a number of problems with just relying on a character string for this task. First, even a slight difference in the original recording of a title means that the presence or absence of a punctuation mark or if a word is capitalized or not results in a strict classification where Works that should be classified as the same by humans are not considered to be the same Work by an automated process. Using just string comparisons of the `authorizedAccessPoint` for Works for classification results in a higher level of false negatives (Works are not being classified the same but should be) than most librarians or cataloguers are comfortable with in their catalogs, as well as introducing a source of confusion for patrons or end users that are attempting to search the catalog to find material.

A more forgiving approach would account for these minor variations in the `authorizedAccessPoint` while still being robust enough to minimize the chances of false positives when identifying potential Works as pre-existing Works in the catalog. Another complicating factor is that in late 2015, the Library of Congress released version 2.0 of BIBFRAME that removed the `authorizedAccessPoint` property from most of the classes, thereby making it even more critical to develop a strategy de-duplication or algorithmic that is more sophisticated in handling this important task. Fortunately, Näive Bayes can be used to train algorithms that use multiple inputs instead of just relying on the simplistic string matching used in just the depreciated `authorizedAccessPoint` element.

In the first iteration of a Näive Bayes approach to de-duplicating Works in BIBFRAME, we use two characteristics of Works that usually present, namely the Work's title and the Work's creator, to determine the likelihood that a new Work can be classified as a previous Work. Ideally, this approach accounts for minor spelling variations in both the Title and the Creator to minimize incorrect identifications, either by the algorithm incorrectly identifying a Work as a pre-existing Work, or the more likely scenario, where these minor variations cause two Works to be identified as separate when in fact they are the same Work. Another complicating factor in this Work identification is that there is no robust or agreed-upon definition of what constitutes a Work in bibliographic theory; in practice this delineation is usually more pragmatic and data-driven.

OCLC, one of the largest companies in the library services industry, outlines their approach and algorithms for clustering similar Works (defined within an influential bibliographic theory called FRBR) in a 2003 article, refer bullet point number 5 in *Appendix, Sources, Chapter 10: Measuring and Managing Information Streams*. In the article, Work clusters in WorldCat (the name of OCLC's flagship union catalog made up of hundreds of millions of items from library collections primarily in North America) are identified by matching the main entry – typically the author responsible for the work – and keywords extracted from the title. Similar approaches have been tried in the intervening years by OCLC with a 2014 announcement that all of their WorldCat records now provide Work identifiers based on schema. org's CreativeWork definition for all of their collections, along with an explanatory website at `http://www.oclc.org/developer/develop/linked-data/worldcat-entities/worldcat-work-entity.en.html`.

Creating training and testing datasets

Starting with two MARC21 `pride-and-prejudice.mrc` and `moby-dick.mrc` files, we will process and convert these records to BIBFRAME RDF graphs using the Library of Congress MARC2BIBFRAME Xquery project hosted on GitHub at `https://github.com/lcnetdev/marc2bibframe`. In this Library of Congress project, Works are identified and created based on MARC21 fields and records, but not de-duplicated either locally or remotely from a larger catalog. In our Python shell, we'll first import the `pymarc` Python module and create two lists of MARC21 records:

```
>>> import pymarc
>>> pride_and_prejudice_recs = [r for r in pymarc.MARCReader(open("pride-and-prejudice.mrc", "rb"), to_unicode=True)]
>>> moby_dick_recs = [r for r in pymarc.MARCReader(open("moby-dick.mrc", "rb"), to_unicode=True)]
>>> len(pride_and_prejudice_recs)
30
>>> len(moby_dick_recs)
22
```

Next we will import the Redis Python client, create a Redis instance, and then load our `add_get_triple` Lua script that we tested earlier:

```
>>> import redis
>>> bayes_datastore = redis.StrictRedis()
>>> bayes_datastore.dbsize()
0
>>> with open("linked-data-fragments/redis_lib/add_get_triple.lua") as lua_file:
    raw_lua = lua_file.read()

>>> add_get_triple_digest = bayes_datastore.script_load(raw_lua)
>>> add_get_triple_digest
b'6ac0387e16f9408cece6502a279a4d4c8971bf97'
```

Before continuing, we'll need to import the standard Python `socket` module along with the `rdflib` third-party module:

```
>>> import rdflib, socket
```

We now pass the MARC XML files to a socket server that we connect through an `xquery_socket` function and get back the RDF BIBFRAME graphs for the MARC record that we'll store in a second Python list, `all_graphs`:

```
>>> for recs in [pride_and_prejudice_recs, moby_dick_recs]:
  for marc_record in recs:
    all_graphs.append(xquery_socket(pymarc.record_to_xml(marc_record,
namespace=True)))
>>> len(all_graphs)
52
```

To assist with ingesting these graphs into our Linked Data Fragments server, we will create a `process_graph` function that calls the `add_get_triple` Lua script with each graph's subject, predicate, and object:

```
def process_graph(graph):
    for s,p,o in graph:
        bayes_datastore.evalsha(
            add_get_triple_digest,
            3,
            str(s),
            str(p),
            str(o))
```

Now with the BIBFRAME graphs, we will process individual graphs in the list by calling the `process_graph` function on each graph in the `all_graphs` list. At the end we check to see how large our Redis datastore is with the ingested RDF graphs:

```
>>> for graph in all_graphs:
  process_graph(graph)

>>> bayes_datastore.dbsize()
10433
```

We can retrieve and save all of the subject-predicates for BIBFRAME Work IRI `http://bibframe.org/vocab/Work` – in this case all of the predicates should all be the SHA1 hash digest `3c197cb1f6842dc41aa48dc8b9032284bcf39a27` for the RDF type IRI of `http://www.w3.org/1999/02/22-rdf-syntax-ns#type` – by executing a SMEMBERS command on the `5d1377f4476a1cbfb3caea106dc6b0a7d086410a:su bj-pred` keys and then retrieving the subjects with the Python string `split` method:

```
>>> bayes_datastore.scard(
'5d1377f4476a1cbfb3caea106dc6b0a7d086410a:subj-pred')
114
```

```
>>> work_digests = []
>>> for row in bayes_datastore.smembers(
'5d1377f4476a1cbfb3caea106dc6b0a7d086410a:subj-pred'):
  work_digests.append(row.decode().split(":")[0])
>>> len(work_digests)
114
```

With our 114 Work subject digests, we can now randomly divide the subjects into two Redis sets, `bf-training` and `bf-testing`, which we will store in the datastore:

```
>>> for subject in work_digests:
  if random.random() >= .5:
    bayes_datastore.sadd("bf-training", subject)
  else:
    bayes_datastore.sadd("bf-testing", subject)
```

Our `bf-training` and `bf-testing` sets are close in size and are what we would expect in a near 50/50 random sorting:

```
>>> bayes_datastore.scard("bf-training")
59
>>> bayes_datastore.scard("bf-testing")
55
```

Now that we have testing and training data sets, we will begin our exploration of using Naïve Bayes for BIBFRAME Work identification by using the open source Python module called `redisbayes` available on GitHub at `https://github.com/jart/redisbayes`. This `redisbayes` module requires a string of words, called tokens, that is extracted from the object we are interested in classifying as either a part of a Work or not.

Extracting word Tokens from BIBFRAME Works

As these records were converted using the BIBFRAME 1.0 converter, we could simplify our example by just using the `authorizedAccessPoint` for each work. Before depending on the Work's `authorizedAccessPoint` as the data point to test, we double-check with our Python shell for those Works in the datastore have an `authorizedAccessPoint` - using the SHA1 hash digest of `a548a25005963f85daa1215ad90f7f1a97fbe749` - available for testing or for training our Bayes application:

```
>>> total_missing_auth_pts = 0
>>> for i,digest in enumerate(work_digests):
```

```
result = bayes_datastore.sscan("{}:pred-obj".format(digest),
        match="a548a25005963f85daa1215ad90f7f1a97fbe749:*")
if len(result[1]) < 1:
  total_missing_auth_pts +=1
```

```
>>> total_missing_auth_pts
21
```

Based on this result of 21 missing `authorizedAccessPoint`, the `marc2bibframe` conversion program does not generate this property for all BIBFRAME Works in its conversion process. Instead, we'll check to confirm that all of the works have at least one of the following:

- **BIBFRAME title**: `http://bibframe.org/vocab/title` with a SHA1 hash digest of `e366a989e4becead9409ca4d44ddf307afc126b3`.

- **BIBFRAME workTitle**: `http://bibframe.org/vocab/workTitle` with a SHA1 hash digest of `f610f749c5c2eaf6718eb2bc24bf74559d14637d`. This typically is an IRI that resolves to another resource that is an instance of the `Title` BIBFRAME class.

In the `bayes_works.py` Python code file that accompanies this chapter, the `generate_work_tokens` function takes a Subject digest and the Linked Data Fragments Server Redis instance (defaulting to `http://localhost:6379`), and creates a `tokens` list a Work predicate-object Redis key called `work_pred_objs`, and retrieves and stores the size of the `work_pred_objs` with a Redis `SCARD` command into a `total_triples` variable:

```
def generate_work_tokens(
    work_digest,
    datastore=redis.StrictRedis()):
    tokens = []
    work_pred_objs = "{}:pred-obj".format(work_digest)
    total_triples = datastore.scard(work_pred_obj)
```

Given that every Work should have either a title or `workTitle`, the code next attempts to retrieve the BIBFRAME title with the value by using the glob-pattern matching with the `SSCAN` Redis command and explicitly setting the count to the `total_triples` variable. Finally, the internal function `extend_tokens` is called with the result:

```
    bf_title_result = datastore.sscan(work_pred_objs,
        match="e366a989e4becead9409ca4d44ddf307afc126b3:*",
```

```
        count=total_triples)
if len(bf_title_result[1]) > 0:
    extend_tokens(bf_title_result[1])
```

The `extends_tokens` function that takes the BIBFRAME title's value is retrieved from the datastore and split into word tokens that are lowercased before being appended to the `tokens` list:

```
def extend_tokens(result):
    for row in result:
        first_key, second_key = row.decode().split(":")
        value = datastore.get(second_key)
        tokens.extend([word.lower() for word in value.split()])
```

If the `bf_title_result` is an empty list, the code then tries to retrieve the SHA1 for the `workTitle` and if there is a result, retrieves the SHA1 of the `Title` class and then retrieves the BIBFRAME `titleValue` and calls the `extend_tokens` with the result:

```
else:
    bf_work_title_result = datastore.sscan(work_pred_objs,
        match="f610f749c5c2eaf6718eb2bc24bf74559d14637d:*",
        count=total_triples)
    if len(bf_work_title_result[1]) > 0:
        for row in bf_work_title_result[1]:
            rdf_title_key = row.decode().split(":")[1]
            rdf_title_value_result = datastore.sscan(
                "{}:pred-obj".format(rdf_title_key),
                "0859add153c1fcda5e32853e22ccfe8514702b2e:*")
            if len(rdf_title_value_result[1]) > 0:
                extend_tokens(bf_work_title_result[1])
```

The last section in the `generate_work_tokens` function attempts to retrieve all of the name information from all of the BIBFRAME creators (`http://bibframe.org/vocab/creator` with a SHA1 hash digest of `0f08c96e756a4fa720257bf3090efdf76b5d3acc`) and BIBFRAME contributors (`http://bibframe.org/vocab/contributor` with a SHA1 hash digest of `a20301af19937f3787275c059dae953eaff2cb5f`), before returning the complete tokens list for each creator's or contributor's label using the SHA1 hash for the BIBFRAME label:

```
for key_digest in ["0f08c96e756a4fa720257bf3090efdf76b5d3acc",
                   "a20301af19937f3787275c059dae953eaff2cb5f"]:
    bf_result = datastore.sscan(
        work_pred_objs,
        match="{}:*".format(key_digest),
        count=total_triples)
```

```
      if len(bf_result[1]) > 0:
          for row in bf_result[1]:
              agent_key = row.decode().split(":")[1]
              agent_scan_result = datastore.sscan(
                  "{}:pred-obj".format(agent_key),
              match="56375fdb9714268c237e4eb7e74f6f0544098935:*"
                  count=100)
              if len(agent_scan_result[1]) > 0:
                  extend_tokens(agent_scan_result[1])
    return tokens
```

Applying Naïve Bayes

Now that we have a function to generate word tokens, we turn to our training set,
bf-training; to test the Naïve Bayes formula. So, for example, the Bayes' theorem
equation for *Pride and Prejudice* would be as follows:

- $p(c|x,y)$ is the probability that a BIBFRAME Work is *Pride and Prejudice*, given
  a title of *Pride and Prejudice* and the author, Jane Austen

- $p(x,y|c)p(c)/p(x,y)$ is the probability that title is *Pride and Prejudice* and author
  is *Jane Austen* given that the Work is *Pride and Prejudice* multiplied by the
  probability of a BIBFRAME Work all divided by the probability that Work is
  Pride and Prejudice

To simplify the calculations of these probabilities, the assumption of feature
independence is a given. Under the feature independence assumption, each term
in the title and author are statistically independent from each other. While this
Naïve assumption is most likely not true (that is, the likelihood that the term *Pride* is
likely higher in the presence of *Prejudice* in the Work's title than by chance alone), in
practice this assumption works well for classification tasks.

Now, going back to the bayes_works.py module, the train function takes our
training set of Works, generates word token strings for each Work, and then prompts
the user to manually assign each of the Works as either **pp** if the Work is *Pride and
Prejudice*, **md** if the Work is *Moby Dick*, or **uk** if the Work is unknown. To illustrate,
we will start a Python 2.7 shell (the redisbayes module currently runs under
Python 2.7), import the required modules, and we'll start a second Redis instance
running on port 6380 for use by the redisbayes module, create a redisbayes object
with this Redis instance, and check the size of both Redis instances:

```
>>> import redis, redisbayes
>>> ldfs = redis.StrictRedis()
>>> bayes_datastore = redis.StrictRedis(port=6380)
```

```
>>> rb = redisbayes.RedisBayes(redis=bayes_datastore)
>>> print(ldfs.dbsize(), bayes_datastore.dbsize())
(10435L, 0L)
```

We'll import our `bayes_works.py` module into our Python shell and create a list of all the Work digest keys in the `bf-training` Redis set:

```
>>> import bayes_works
>>> training_works = list(ldfs.smembers('bf-training'))
>>> len(training_works)
59
```

For each BIBFRAME Work digest in the `training_works` list, the `generate_work_tokens` function will be called and the string of words will be classified and stored with a call to the `rb.train` method (a selection of these Works being classified is presented here instead of including all 59 Works in our training set):

```
>>> for digest in training_works:
...         tokens = bayes_works.generate_work_tokens(digest)
...         print(tokens)
...         classify = input("Classify pp, md, uk> ")
...         rb.train(classify, ' '.join(tokens))
['mansfield', 'park', 'austen,', 'jane,', '1775-1817.', 'wiltshire,',
'john.']
Classify pp, md, uk> "uk"
['short', 'stories.', 'selections.', 'hawthorne,', 'nathaniel,', '1804-
1864.']
Classify pp, md, uk> "uk"
['moby', 'dick.', 'melville,', 'herman,', '1819-1891.']
Classify pp, md, uk> "md"
['pride', 'and', 'prejudice', 'austen,', 'jane,', '1775-1817.']
Classify pp, md, uk> "pp"
```

After going through the training set and classifying all of the Works in one of these three categories, we'll now open a Redis-cli session to the Redis instance storing the intermediate data for the Naïve Bayes calculations used by the `redisbayes` module:

```
127.0.0.1:6380> dbsize
(integer) 4
127.0.0.1:6380> keys *
1) "bayes:md"
```

```
2)  "bayes:pp"
3)  "bayes:uk"
3)  "bayes:categories"
```

The `bayes:md`, `bayes:uk`, and `bayes:pp` are Redis hashes with each word token as a field, and the field's value is an integer containing the number of times the term was present during the training session. The `bayes:categories` is a set containing all of the different classifications, in this case **md**, **uk**, and **pp**. With the training completed for the Naïve Bayes implementation, we'll now take three random Work digest keys from our `bf-testing` set and see which of three options the `redisbayes` instance classifies the random Work from our Python 2.7 shell as:

```
>>> test_work_1 = ldfs.srandmember("bf-testing")
>>> test_work_1
'bffd57ebcad72b7f5a98a8cc3e7eac178815dbbb'
>>> test_work_2_tokens = bayes_works.generate_work_tokens(test_work_1)
>>> test_work_2_tokens
['pride', 'and', 'prejudice.', 'austen,', 'jane,', '1775-1817.']
>>> rb.classify(' '.join(test_work_2_tokens))
'pp'
>>> test_work_2 = ldfs.srandmember("bf-testing")
>>> test_work_2
'448910eeaa3908bab9213cff291074667872adfa'
>>> test_work_2_tokens = bayes_works.generate_work_tokens(test_work_2)
>>> test_work_2_tokens
['moby', 'dick,', 'or,', 'the', 'whale', 'melville,', 'herman,', '1819-
1891.']
>>> rb.classify(' '.join(test_work_2_tokens))
'md'
```

The Naïve Bayes classifier performance is as we would expect for this small sample. Clearly, to expand this approach to all of the Works in even a small library would require additional modification and expansion of the tokenization and processing code. Hopefully, this example will help you in the design of your own Redis application that may need a method for classifying incoming data streams using a simple Naïve Bayes machine learning approach.

Linear regression with Redis

Linear regression, a fundamental statistical technique in many fields, including medicine, economics, psychology, and general data analytics, attempts to predict target values that come from a continuous data source. In general, with linear regression it is easy to interpret the results (that is, a *dependent* variable is the result of adding or subtracting one or more *independent* variables modified by *regression weights*) and is computationally light compared to other machine learning techniques. The downside to linear regression is poor performance and inaccurate results when applied to non-linear data.

Crafting and programming a linear regression solution starts with collecting the data and preparing the data. Linear regression requires numeric values and any discrete, non-numeric data to be mapped to binary values. For our testing and examples, we will assume a simple linear relationship between a scalar dependent variable y and one or more explanatory independent variables. For our regression model, we will use the ordinary least squares fitting solution which tries to minimize the sum of the squares of the errors made in the results of all the equations in the linear regression model. A general outline of the ordinary least squares model is as follows:

$$y = \alpha + \beta x$$

Where the data consists of *n* observations with a scalar response *y(i)* and where is the parameters of the model with missing alpha character being the intercept and the missing beta character being the slope coefficients.

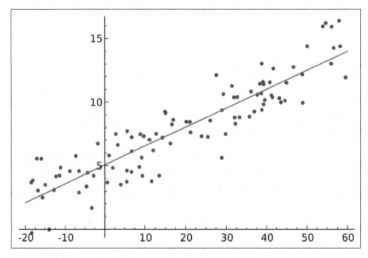

Simple Linear Regression Model from
https://en.wikipedia.org/wiki/Simple_linear_regression#/media/File:Linear_regression.svg

To illustrate using simple linear regression, we will use time-series datasets for the calendar year 2014 for the weather from three different cities – Denver, Tokyo, and Cape Town – available from the Weather Underground website at `http://www.wunderground.com/`. These datasets are in comma-separated-value format with columns for date, temperature, dew point, humidity, barometric pressure, wind speed, precipitation, and cloud cover. Each of these files, `denver-2014.csv`, `tokyo-2014.csv`, and `nairobi-2014.csv`, can be downloaded from the *Mastering Redis* website or the book's GitHub repository. We'll begin our analysis of the weather by selectively storing certain variables such as `date`, `Mean TemperatureC` (in Celsius), `Dew PointC` (in Celsius), `Mean Humidity`, `Mean Sea Level Pressure hPa` (Pascal unit), and `Precipitation mm` (in millimeters).

To load these fields into our Redis instance, we will create a Python function `extract_load` that uses the standard CSV module to read in a CSV file, extracts the fields we want to store in Redis, creates five hashes for each city, one for each variable, and then adds the variable as a hash value with the field name being the date string:

```python
def extract_load(datastore=redis.StrictRedis()):
    for filename in ['cape-town-2014.csv',
                     'denver-2014.csv',
                     'tokyo-2014.csv']:

        weather_csv = csv.reader(open(os.path.join(
            CURRENT_DIR,
            filename)))
        field_names = next(weather_csv)
        city_date = filename.split(".")[0]
        temp_key = "{}-temp-mean".format(city_date)
        dew_point_key = "{}-dew-point-mean".format(city_date)
        humidity_key = "{}-humidity-mean".format(city_date)
        pressure_key = "{}-pressure-mean".format(city_date)
        precipitation_key = "{}-precipitation".format(city_date)
        for row in weather_csv:
            if len(row) < 8:
                continue
            pipeline = datastore.pipeline(transaction=True)
            date_field = row[0]
            pipeline.hsetnx(temp_key, date_field, row[2])
```

```
        pipeline.hsetnx(dew_point_key, date_field, row[4])
        pipeline.hsetnx(humidity_key, date_field, row[8])
        pipeline.hsetnx(pressure_key, date_field, row[11])
        pipeline.hsetnx(precipitation_key, date_field, row[19])
        pipeline.execute()
    print("Finished {}".format(city_date))
```

After all the 2014 data is loaded into our regression Redis instance, we'll do a quick sanity check to confirm that the data meets our expectations:

```
127.0.0.1:6379> HLEN cape-town-2014-temp-mean
(integer) 365
127.0.0.1:6379> HLEN denver-2014-temp-mean
(integer) 365
127.0.0.1:6379> HLEN tokyo-2014-temp-mean
(integer) 365
```

Because by definition dew point is dependent on temperature, we would expect a positive relationship, as shown in the following graph:

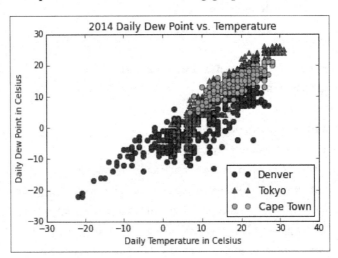

Using a pure Python implementation of a simple linear regression available at
`https://code.activestate.com/recipes/578914-simple-linear-regression-with-pure-python/`, that uses the Pearson product-moment correlation coefficient to calculate the regression, results in the following table for each of the cities:

City	(Y-intercept)	(Slope)	
Cape Town	3.0738312142044553	0.6096462268894843	0.8380281574300148
Denver	-5.110855159000105	0.7013438731440127	0.8441417541071602
Tokyo	-5.261920573865529	1.1013535521237958	0.946832088113318
All	-4.482081471645017	0.9542228667781014	0.880891021556839

Interpreting the results of a linear regression in our dew point as the dependent y variable and the independent variable x as the temperature, our regression models show strong correlation coefficients with the overall simple linear regression model correlation coefficient of .88.

We will now examine it to see if there is a relationship between the barometric pressure as a dependent variable and temperature as an independent variable, by first graphing the two as follows:

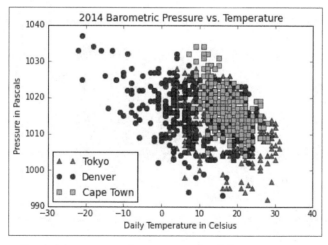

Barometric pressure and temperature simple linear regressions

The relationship between the barometric pressure and the temperature seems to be generally negative, with the following table displaying the results of simple linear regression for each city and all of the cities combined:

City	(Y-intercept)	(Slope)	r
Cape Town	1029.483421	-0.730263	-0.580355
Denver	1018.148958	-0.266547	-0.3866715
Tokyo	1019.549379	-0.410279	-0.450956
All	890.079774	-14.4720573	-0.254273

For average barometric pressure, temperature is loosely correlated for all of the cities at -0.25, meaning that for our simple linear regression model, temperature is not a statistically explanatory variable for barometric pressure.

If relative humidity, defined as the ratio of air-water mixture relative to maximum or highest point that is possible for water vapor at a particular temperature, as the dependent variable and the temperature as the independent variable; our hypothesis that a higher relative humidity should mean a greater chance for precipitation is visually graphed as follows:

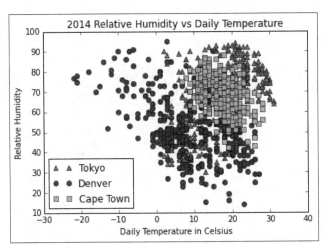

2014 Daily average relative humidity versus temperature for Denver, Cape Town, and Tokyo

Like the previous two simple linear regression examples, we will calculate the regressions for this example in the following table:

City	(Y-intercept)	(Slope)	r
Cape Town	85.525525	-0.954431	-0.453038
Denver	59.200518	-0.663125	-0.433978
Tokyo	46.291846	1.232326	0.578158
All	58.190660	0.303417	0.162543

As seen from the results, the simple linear regression model is a poor explanation for the relationship between higher temperatures and higher relative humidity, at least for Cape Town, Denver, and Tokyo in 2014. The correlation coefficient for the combined dataset of all three cities was a poor 0.162543, with a lot of the variation in the data being unexplained by a linear model.

Summary

This chapter's focus comes full circle to the reasons for using Redis in the first chapter of Master Redis. Redis's role as a "glue" technology is well-suited for connecting various data sources to end targets for many extract-transform-load workloads. We saw a simple example of loading a DP.LA dataset that contains the metadata for a collection of images and other content from the University of Illinois. The speed difference was orders of magnitude faster using the bulk loading options in Redis, where you create Redis protocol (RESP) directly from the incoming data source (the extract and transform steps) to finally being loaded with either Netcat or a special mode in the Redis-cli program. We touched upon minimum security strategies for protecting your Redis instance. We then finished up this chapter by examining two common machine learning techniques – Naïve Bayes and simple linear regression – and showed how Redis can be used for turning raw data streams into information and knowledge in your enterprise.

Writing *Mastering Redis* challenged and humbled this academic librarian's technical skills and knowledge of Redis, but reinforced the impression that Redis's value is in its scope, speed, and flexibility in solving the everyday problems people encounter in our technology-heavy society, even in supposedly "low tech" fields like libraries! Starting from his early forays in developing a website cache, Salvatore Sanfilippo's real brilliance is his opinionated and passionate leadership and real programming skill into the sophisticated tool that has become what we know as Redis.

Because of Sanfilippo's vision and active development of Redis, new functionality and bug fixes are constant, with an active code base which, if you want to maintain your new Redis mastery, requires continual monitoring and learning as Redis evolves and changes over time. Even with the high delta of Redis, most of the existing features and commands have not significantly changed once they are incorporated into the main Redis branches for production use. In most fields of endeavor, a "Master" never stops learning, so my hope is that you now have not only a broader and deeper knowledge of Redis, but that you also have new skills for continuing learning and experimenting on your journey to mastering a fast – in all meanings of the word – technology as rich in possibilities as Redis.

Sources

Chapter 1: Why Redis?

1. *How to take advantage of Redis just adding it to your stack,* from *antirez weblog* by Salvatore Sanfilippo at `http://oldblog.antirez.com/post/take-advantage-of-redis-adding-it-to-your-stack.html`.

Chapter 2: Advanced Key Management and Data Structures

1. *An introduction to Redis data types and abstractions,* retrieved from `http://redis.io/topics/data-types-intro`.

2. Christopher Stover, "Big-O Notation". From *Mathworld--A Wolfram Web Resource,* created by Eric W. Weisstein at `http://mathworld.wolfram.com/Big-ONotation.html`.

3. *,What are the differences between memcached and redis?* by Animesh Dash from Quora `https://www.quora.com/What-are-the-differences-between-memcached-and-redis/answer/Animesh-Dash?srid=Kgp`.

4. *Redis Bitmaps – Fast, Easy, Realtime Metrics* retrieved from `http://blog.getspool.com/2011/11/29/fast-easy-realtime-metrics-using-redis-bitmaps/`.

Chapter 3: Managing RAM – Tips and Techniques for Redis Memory Management

1. *Using Redis as an LRU cache* by Salvatore Sanfilippo retrieved from `http://redis.io/topics/lru-cache`.

2. Redis source code file, `redis-cli.c`, retrieved from `http://download.redis.io/redis-stable/src/redis-cli.c`.

3. *Using hashes to abstract a very memory efficient plain key-value store on top of Redis* by Salvatore Sanfilippo retrieved from `http://redis.io/topics/memory-optimization`.

4. *Raspberry Pi and Redis*, blog posting by Stefan Parvu retrieved from `http://kronometrix.blogspot.com/2014/10/raspberry-pi-and-redis.html`.

5. *Redis Android NDK port*, blog posting by Riccardo Cecolin retrieved from `http://rikiji.it/2012/08/21/Redis-Android-NDK-port.html`.

Chapter 6: Scaling with Redis Cluster and Sentinel

1. *Redis Presharding* by Salvatore Sanfilippo from antirez weblog. `http://oldblog.antirez.com/post/redis-presharding.html`.

2. *Redis data sharding – part 2 – hash-based keys* from blog by Marius Przydatek at `http://mariuszprzydatek.com/2013/08/23/redis-data-sharding-part-2-hash-based-keys/`.

3. *Redis Cluster tutorial* retrieved from `http://redis.io/topics/cluster-tutorial`.

4. *Twemproxy, a Redis proxy from Twitter* by Salvatore Sanfilippo from `http://antirez.com/news/44`.

5. List-serv archive retrieved from `https://groups.google.com/forum/#!msg/redis-db/eTtCNAosiiU/h7ifK2K3FA0J`.

Chapter 7: Redis and Complementary NoSQL Technologies

1. *DB-Engines Ranking* retrieved from `http://db-engines.com/en/ranking`.

2. *The Beautiful Marriage of MongoDB and Redis* blog posting by Cody Powell retrieved from `https://dzone.com/articles/beautiful-marriage-mongodb-and`.

3. *Redis, MongoDB & the Power of Incremency* blog posting by DJ Walker-Morgan retrieved from `https://www.compose.io/articles/redis-mongodb-and-the-power-of-incremency/`.

4. *Why (and how to) Redis with your MongoDB* blog posting by DJ Walker-Morgan retrieved from `https://www.compose.io/articles/why-and-how-to-redis-with-your-mongodb/`.

5. *Linked Data* article by Tim Berners-Lee, retrieved from `https://www.w3.org/DesignIssues/LinkedData.html`.

Chapter 10: Measuring and Managing Information Streams

1. *Redis Mass Insertion* retrieved from `http://redis.io/topics/mass-insert`.

2. DPLA Bulk data downloads retrieved from `http://dp.la/info/developers/download/`.

3. Kumar, Nitin. "Real time dashboard for redis". Published 8/5/2012. Retrieved from http://www.nkrode.com/article/real-time-dashboard-for-redis.

4. *Efficient computation and storage of basic data statistics using Redis* by Sachin Joglekar published on 3/7/2015, retrieved from `https://codesachin.wordpress.com/2015/07/03/efficient-computation-and-storage-of-basic-data-statistics-using-redis/`.

5. *The Concept of a Work in WorldCat: An Application of FRBR*, published in 2003 by Bennett, Rick. Lavoie, Brain, O'Neill, Edward retrieved from `http://www.oclc.org/content/dam/research/publications/library/2003/lavoie_frbr.pdf`.

Index

Symbol

A

B

C

S

Schema.org
  reference link 136
security, considerations
  about 308, 309
  command obfuscation 311
  operational monitoring, with Redis web
       dashboard 311, 312
  passwords 310
  passwords, setting 310
  protected mode 309
service-oriented architecture (SOA) 231
sets 38, 39
Software as a Service (SaaS) 231
Software Development 150
sorted sets
  about 39-42
  advanced operations 42
**SPARQL Protocol and the RDF Query
       Language 196**
strings 35

T

task management
  adding, with RestMQ 290-292
  with Redis and Celery 283-287

Technology Operations 150
time complexity, Redis data structures
  about 34
  hashes 36
  lists 37, 38
  sets 38, 39
  strings 35
time to live (TTL) 66
Todo list application
  public access 115
  replication 115
  updating, with Node.js 113-115
  updating, with Redis 113-115
Twemproxy
  about 163
  Redis, clustering with 163
  testing, with Linked Data
       Fragments server 164-170

U

unit test
  URL 21
usage patterns 10-12

W

World Web Consortium (W3C) 220

CPSIA information can be obtained
at www.ICGtesting.com
Printed in the USA
FSOW04n1627310117
30233FS